THEOLOGY AND
THE GOSPEL OF CHRIST

By the same author

He Who Is (Darton, Longman & Todd)
Christ, the Christian and the Church (Longmans)
Existence and Analogy (Darton, Longman & Todd)
Corpus Christi (Longmans)
Christian Theology and Natural Science (Longmans)
Via Media (Longmans)
Words and Images (Longmans)
The Recovery of Unity (Longmans)
The Importance of Being Human (Columbia University Press)
Theology and History (Faith Press)
Up and Down in Adria (Faith Press)
The Secularisation of Christianity (Darton, Longman & Todd)
The Christian Universe (Darton, Longman & Todd)
Theology and the Future (Darton, Longman & Todd)
The Openness of Being (Darton, Longman & Todd)
Grace and Glory (SPCK)

THEOLOGY AND
THE GOSPEL OF CHRIST
An Essay in Reorientation

E. L. MASCALL

LONDON
SPCK

First published 1977
SPCK
Holy Trinity Church
Marylebone Road
London NW1 4DU

Printed in Great Britain by
The Camelot Press Ltd, Southampton

ISBN 0 281 03584 9

TO THE CLERGY AND LAITY OF
THE DIOCESE OF TRURO
AN OFFERING FROM THEIR
CANON THEOLOGIAN

De longinquo te saluto . . .

CONTENTS

Contents

ACKNOWLEDGEMENTS

Thanks are due to the following for permission to quote from copyright sources:

The Athlone Press: *New Testament Interpretation in an Historical Age* by D. E. Nineham

Canon J. A. Baker and the Editor of *Christian*: 'The Golden Handshake?' by J. A. Baker in *Christian* (Easter 1973)

Basil Blackwell (Publisher) and Fortress Press: *Sacra Doctrina: Reason and Revelation in Aquinas* by P. E. Persson

Cambridge University Press: *Christ, Faith and History* edited by S. W. Sykes and J. P. Clayton; *The Humanity and Divinity of Christ* by J. Knox; and a review by H. P. Owen in *Religious Studies* VI (1970)

The Church Literature Association: *Faith and Society* by A. M. Ramsey, and *Reforming the Bishop* by J. Livingstone

William Collins Sons & Co. Ltd: *The Church and the Reality of Christ* by J. Knox; *A Historical Introduction to the New Testament* by R. M. Grant; and *Christology* by D. Bonhoeffer

Darton, Longman & Todd Ltd: *Theological Investigations* by K. Rahner and *Method in Theology* by B. Lonergan (US publisher: The Seabury Press); *Theology and the Future* by E. L. Mascall (US publisher: Morehouse-Barlow Inc.); *The Secularisation of Christianity* by E. L. Mascall (US publisher: Holt, Rinehart & Winston CBS Inc.)

Denholm House Press, Nutfield, Surrey: 'The Worth of Arguments' by J. L. Houlden in *Women Priests? Yes—Now!*, edited by Harold Wilson

The Editor, *Downside Review*: Article by E. I. Watkin in *Downside Review* XC (1972)

Editions Aubier-Montaigne SA: *The Decomposition of Catholicism* by L. Bouyer

Editions Lethielleux: *La Personne du Christ*, *La conscience de Jésus*, and *Vers une nouvelle christologie*, all by J. Galot

Editions du Seuil: *Introduction à la théologie chrétienne* by C. Tresmontant

Eyre & Spottiswoode Ltd: *Summa Theologiae*, by St Thomas Aquinas, edited by T. Gilby, L. Walsh, and R. Potter (vol. 1, *Christian Theology*; vol. 49, *The Grace of Christ*; and vol. 52, *The Childhood of Christ*)

The Editor, *Faith*: 'This Our Common Crisis' by O. Cullmann in *Faith* IV (1972)

Acknowledgements

The Editor, *The Heythrop Journal*: 'Christology in Historical Perspective' by R. C. Ware in *The Heythrop Journal* XV (1974)

Hodder & Stoughton Ltd: *Ring of Truth: A Translator's Testimony* by J. B. Phillips

Industrial Christian Fellowship Quarterly: 'On the Authority of the Bible' by C. F. Evans in *Industrial Christian Fellowship Quarterly* (Spring 1973)

Liber Grafiska AB: *Memory and Manuscript* by B. Gerhardsson

Macmillan, London and Basingstoke: *The Logic of Gospel Criticism* by H. Palmer

New Blackfriars: review by J. Redford in *New Blackfriars* LVI (1975)

James Nisbet & Co. Ltd: 'Christology at the Crossroads' by J. Hick in *Prospect for Theology* edited by F. G. Healey

Oxford University Press: *Theological Science* and *God and Rationality* both by T. F. Torrance; and *Roman Society and Roman Law in the New Testament* by A. N. Sherwin-White

SCM Press Ltd: *The Remaking of Christian Doctrine* and an article in *Working Papers in Doctrine* both by M. F. Wiles; *The Kingdom of Christ* by F. D. Maurice; *The Historian and the Believer* by V. A. Harvey, copyright © 1966 by Van A. Harvey (US publisher: Macmillan Publishing Company); *The New Testament in Current Study* by R. H. Fuller (US publisher: Charles Scribner's Sons)

Search Press Ltd: *Theology of Revelation* by G. Moran and *On Heresy* by K. Rahner (US publisher: The Seabury Press); *Structures of the Church* by H. Küng, copyright © 1964 by Thomas Nelson & Sons Inc. (US publisher: Thomas Nelson Inc.); and *Holy Writ or Holy Church?* by G. Tavard

The Society for Promoting Christian Knowledge: *Kerygma and Myth: A Theological Debate* edited by H. W. Bartsch; and a review by K. Grayston in *Theology* LXXII (1969)

William B. Eerdmans Publishing Company: *Christian Reflections* by C. S. Lewis, edited by W. Hooper. Used by permission. (UK publisher: Geoffrey Bles)

Our Sunday Visitor: *Le Fils Eternel* by L. Bouyer

Random House Inc: *The Christian Philosophy of St Thomas Aquinas* by E. Gilson, translated by L. K. Shook

The Westminster Press: *Philosophy of God and Theology* and *A Second Collection* by B. Lonergan, and *The Openness of Being* by E. L. Mascall (UK publisher: Darton, Longman & Todd Ltd); *Redating the New Testament* and *The Human Face of God* by J. A. T. Robinson (UK publisher: SCM Press); *Truth and Dialogue*, edited by J. Hick (UK publisher: Sheldon Press)

Trahison des Clercs

The four chapters of which this book is composed have more in common than may appear on the surface. They are the outcome of a conviction, reached with reluctance and distress and after long and anxious thought, that the theological activity of the Anglican Churches is in a condition of extreme, though strangely complacent, confusion and that this is having a disastrously demoralizing effect upon the life and thought of the Church as a whole and of the pastoral clergy in particular. Faced as these brave men are with problems of abnormal stress and difficulty in the spiritual, intellectual and practical realms alike, they look in vain for enlightenment from their brethren in the academic world, and such echoes as percolate to them are for the most part unhelpful and disquieting. The gulf between the academic theologians and the parish clergy has by now become notorious, and if the few attempts that have been made to bridge it have met with little success I do not think that the chief reason is that the parish clergy are in general intellectually lazy or timid, being content either to shuffle on in a purely pragmatic way or to take refuge from thought in a narrow fundamentalism. I think that the blame lies overwhelmingly on the academic side and that, with luminous and honourable exceptions, we professional theologians have grossly misunderstood the nature of our task and have in consequence performed it uncritically and inefficiently. We have been so anxious to be accepted as intellectually respectable in our modern secularized universities – an ambition which, if kept in due proportion and pursued with moderation and prudence, is, of course, not in itself reprehensible – that we have taken for granted the desupernaturalization of Jesus and have substituted the study of early Christian psychology for the study of divine revelation. And as a result we have frequently produced naturalistic explanations of the primordial Christian events which, purely as arguments, are less coherent and plausible than the traditional supernatural ones. This is, clearly, a sweeping statement, and it can be justified only by taking the individual cases into account. It is, however, significant that scholars in other disciplines, when they contemplate the theological field, do not appear to discern any obvious correlation between the degree of antisupernaturalism of a theologian's outlook and his general intellectual competence. If there has been – as I believe there has – a real *trahison des clercs* on the part of theologians, I do not think it has been forced on them by sheer pressure of facts, but rather by something more insidious, namely pressure of fashion. I am not, however, concerned to assess degrees of individual responsibility and it would be improper for me to do so; a man may err and be in good faith.

The fundamental weakness in the contemporary theological situation in this country was pointed out with great discernment by John M. Redford in a review of a recent symposium on the New Testament:[1] The work in question, *What about the New Testament? Essays in honour of Christopher Evans*,[2] is accurately described by the reviewer as a 'wide-ranging series of articles, by contributors from various fields of vocation, most of whom had been students of Professor Evans at some time during their past life, and who wish[ed] to register their thanks in printed form'. The title itself is perhaps significant, and I myself was not being altogether frivolous when my immediate reaction was to suggest that it might have been more interesting to have a symposium entitled *What about Christopher Evans? Essays in honour of the New Testament*. In the reviewer's words, the title

> indicat[es] what we may call the 'Scriptural crisis' which has been a commonplace for some time in the Anglican and Protestant communions, and is already beginning to afflict Roman Catholic theology now we are recovering from post-Vatican II scriptural euphoria, and realising some of the problems involved. This crisis is nothing other than that of the 'credibility' of the Bible granted the modern approach to scripture study. Thus we have here a timely work on an equally relevant subject.

Nevertheless, in spite of these welcoming remarks, Dr Redford immediately put the question 'Where, then, do these offerings to Professor Evans so obviously fall short?', and he answered:

> The primary and most important defect to my mind is that no evidence is given from the articles that any of the questions at issue have been adequately thought through *at the theological level* by the majority of the contributors. This would be excusable if the subject of the essays were simply popular exegesis; but, in this symposium, the main preoccupation is precisely that of hermeneutics, questions ranging through the whole field of the principles of form criticism, the relationship between Jesus and the primitive community in the

formation of the Gospel tradition, primitive christology, biblical inspiration, and canonicity. In this area, the Scripture scholar must do his theological and philosophical homework.

And this defect is what makes so many of the essays deeply dissatisfying.

Dr.Redford was not blind to the useful points that were made by some of the symposiasts; he instanced Mrs Clare Drury and Dr Graham Stanton. I would add in particular Dr Morna Hooker.[3] But he pointed out that 'no contributor to this book has tried in any sense systematically to deal with the criteria of authenticity, so basic both to form and redaction criticism', and he gave his general verdict in terms that are important in that their reference is far wider than to one particular book.

Perhaps [he wrote] my complaint boils down to criticism of a common tendency in Anglo-Saxon biblical scholarship in general, namely doctrinal empiricism, a *Weltanschauung* which has its uses when dealing with grammatical and philological questions, but which shows up severe limitations when grappling with more speculative issues. For this, German thoroughness, Latin logic, and French profundity are often more useful virtues.

Thus, while also commending Dr Eduard Lohse, Dr Redford wrote:

To my mind, the contribution which came fully to the point was the last, by Dr Ellen Fleeseman-van Leer ('Dear Christopher') who threw out a direct challenge to her former professor in the form of a letter rather than of an article since she considers herself a non-specialist.

For her, the problem was a very plain one.

Dear Christopher [she wrote], I asked you once in one of our discussions why you were devoting so much of your time to studying the New Testament when you considered it neither authoritative or normative, nor a primary source of faith-truth.[4]

The only answer which she received was that the Church should have the Bible at its elbow and that therefore it was necessary that biblical scholarship should go on. This, however, did not satisfy her; it seemed to be élitist and to assign the study of the Bible to a few academics, and therefore to widen rather than narrow the gap between scholars and ordinary believers. I sympathize with her whole-heartedly, though her own suggested remedy – that the Bible should be taught to adults, if not to children in school, 'in such a way that the question of its authority is for the time being left on one side and that modern biblical scholarship is taken into account at every step'[5] – seems a trifle vague. At least one of the needs, in my opinion, is a drastic analysis and critique of the methods of 'modern Biblical scholarship', whatever that somewhat elastic term in fact connotes. I fully agree with Dr Redford that it was unfortunate that this question was left to the end and therefore was virtually ignored.

This attitude of doctrinal empiricism, to use Dr Redford's term, or doctrinal positivism, as it might also be named, is typified by two examples to which I have referred in the text of this book,[6] namely Mr J. L. Houlden's contention that, since both Scripture and tradition have lost their authority, all decisions in Church matters must be made simply in the light of 'appropriateness' and 'expediency', and Dr D. E. Nineham's proposal that, philosophy having ceased to function as a partner for theology, a new partner – and, it becomes pretty clear, it is to be the senior partner – should be found in the guise of sociology and, in particular, of the sociology of knowledge.

Consciousness of the prevalence of this attitude, but also a healthy refusal to be intimidated by it, was shown by the Bishop of Chichester during the debate in the General Synod of the Church of England in July 1975 on the subject of the ordination of women to the priesthood. After referring to the Gospel records of the words and actions of Jesus himself, Dr Kemp went on to say:

> There are two aspects of contemporary theology which create difficulties for us here. The first is that we have, and have had for some years now, a strong sceptical school, deriving from Form Criticism, and teaching that we can have little certainty about what our Lord said, did, or intended. This seems to me to lead either to a kind of Catholic modernism which says that Christianity rests upon its value in experience but has no historical base, or to a view that our only teacher and guide is the Church, unchecked by any scripture and free to make what adaptations it thinks right to the circumstances of the day. In common with some others trained as historians, I do not share this excessively sceptical approach to historical evidence, but I also find when I look at the writings of New Testament scholars outside this country that this scepticism which has come to dominate our scene and the American, is by no means universal.[7] The most profound and fresh studies of the ministry in the New Testament that I have seen in recent years come from France, where the lack of vocations, much

more serious than ours, creates immense pressure to reconsider traditional practice, but where there is a much less sceptical attitude to the Scriptures. . . .

The other aspect of contemporary theology which seems to me to create difficulties is the issue of Christology, which affects the authority that we ascribe to our Lord's words and deeds, and which was raised, to give one example, in some perhaps not very well chosen words in the recent Open Letter on Exorcism. Here also there is a diversity of views among theologians. Some, even within our own church, appear to suggest that the belief in Jesus as true God and true Man as hitherto held by the Church is mistaken, and some of the issues about the person of Christ which divided Christendom in the fourth and fifth centuries are being reopened. The existence of such confusion in a vital area of belief affecting the authority of the Lord adds to the difficulty of reaching a conclusion about the significance of the Gospel evidence on what Jesus said and did.

There are two particular areas in which theological disintegration has led to disastrous weakness in practice, namely those of Christian social concern and ecumenism. From the time of Frederick Denison Maurice onwards it has been one of the glories of Anglicanism to have inspired a body of social teaching and activity that rested not simply upon goodwill and compassion, striking as those have often been, but upon clearly grasped Christian doctrine expressed in disciplined and penetrating theological thinking.[8] After Maurice, the outstanding names in this context are of course those of Charles Gore and William Temple, but hardly less important, though less widely known, are those of P. E. T. Widdrington, Maurice B. Reckitt and V. A. Demant, by all of whom Christian sociology was envisaged as a necessary part not merely of Christian sentiment and moral endeavour but specifically of Christian theology. In the period before the Second World War the movement received a remarkable accession of younger men, most of whom, though widely scattered, are still alive. It was the basic conviction of this group – the 'Christendom Group', as it was known, from the periodical in which most of its writing was published – that, unless a proper order of priorities and subordination was achieved between the different levels of human activity – familial, social, political, economic and financial – enthusiastic and conscientious operation of the system would lead not to human happiness, but to frustration and misery. It is true that a great deal of the Group's thinking was concerned with the structure and operation of national and international finance, but the notion that it was committed to Major Douglas's 'Social Credit' was baseless. What it was convinced was that, if a system is constructed to achieve the wrong ends, then the more efficiently and devotedly it is operated the worse the results are likely to be; and it saw the contemporary economic and financial system as constructed for the achievement of ends that were inconsistent with the nature and condition of man as the Christian religion understands those to be. Ridicule was often directed at the phrase 'Christian sociology' on the alleged ground that sociology was a purely rational science and that you could no more have a Christian sociology than a Christian mathematics or a Christian chemistry, but the Christendom Group insisted that sociology should be concerned not only with what society is as an observable phenomenon but, because it is made up of human beings, with what society is meant to be. Christian ethics is derivative from Christian dogma, and this is as true of social ethics as of individual. There has been nothing like this creative theological social thinking since the War, in spite of the outstanding work on certain specific problems that has been done by Dr G. R. Dunstan in the chair of Moral and Social Theology founded in Maurice's memory at his own King's College in London.[9] This decline was remarked upon and diagnosed by Dr A. M. Ramsey over twenty years ago in an address given by the future Archbishop in 1955 to the Church Union Summer School of Sociology,[10] and it will, I think be instructive even now to see what he then had to say.

Paradoxically, he saw part of the reason to lie in two features of the British social climate which might on the surface seem to cancel each other out. On the one hand, the advent of the Welfare State, providing for the people so many of the benefits for which socially conscious churchmen had campaigned in the past, might seem to make it the Church's duty to bring home to them the truth that politics is not everything and that they should think about eternal life, the worth of the soul and the worship of God for his own sake. On the other hand,

> the security of the Welfare State is crossed by the radical insecurity of a world that might suddenly be blown to bits. . . . So it is that one realm of our existence gives us so much security that we are driven to emphasize the other-worldly elements in our religion, and the other realm of our existence keeps us so near to a precipice that our theology is 'on the edge of things'. Not security, we say, but God the creator and judge of human souls.

Nevertheless, Dr Ramsey continued, there might still be possibilities for theology if we were still preaching a gospel which demanded and enabled the response of man *in the totality of his being*. 'But the disturbing fact is that in recent years *the preaching of the Gospel has gone awry*.' In reaction from a pragmatist apologetic which commended religion for the this-worldly benefits which it was alleged to bring with it, indeed 'rightly reacting from this perversion of the Gospel we are now eager to say that God is to be proclaimed for God's own sake and his glory, without much mention of the sort of *society* which reflects God's glory'. Rather strangely, Dr Ramsey did not appear to see this as in any way connected with the revival of extreme theological revelationism by Karl Barth, in spite of the tremendous impact which this had had and was still having on English theology. He placed all the blame on biblical fundamentalism, for which 'the moral will is separated from its context, because the appeal is made to less than the whole man as a reasoning being and a social being. So it is that Billy Graham, the Intervarsity Fellowship and Moral Rearmament all help to destroy the ground of a Christian sociology.' And he drew the conclusion: 'For all these reasons the tradition of Christian social thinking, the tradition of Maurice, Westcott, Holland and Gore is at a discount: its disciples are discouraged, and some of them adopt a rôle of *laudatores temporis acti*.' He had no doubt that the collapse was basically a theological one, and that its reversal must be theological too. But he saw the collapse as conditioned by the social and cultural environment, and there was more than a suggestion that the theology, as distinct from the revelation which was its ultimate court of appeal, had been environmentally conditioned itself. 'The Incarnational theology which produced the sociology of the period from 1890 until almost 1940 was framed in the idiom of an evolutionary and progressive world which no longer exists, and its idiom no longer suffices.' Dr Ramsey concluded his lecture by adumbrating an answer to the question what the theology would be which could restore to Christian social thinking and prophetic witness its sanctions and its impetus.

His answer was that, while it was right to start from the doctrine of the Church as the redeemed community and the new creation, standing over against the world, three special insights needed to be accepted and their consequences developed. First, the world itself must be seen as God's creation. Secondly, the world, and not only the Church, must be seen as having been redeemed. And, thirdly, the Church's own members must be seen as having a double existence: 'they belong to the new age of the regenerate; they also belong to a race which is created and creaturely, illuminated by conscience and subject to natural law.'

> Such [Dr Ramsey maintained] is the outline of a theology which can make Christian sociology to be a real possibility, indeed a necessity. This theology, when stated, seems familiar enough and orthodox enough; but it has become far to seek as an effective doctrine in the Church today, especially the truth that the supernatural status of the Christian enhances his grasp of the natural. We have had much theology, both in Protestant and in Catholic circles, which does not take the natural order with due seriousness. And we have theology which takes the natural order seriously enough, but levels the supernatural down to it.

He gave two instances of the latter outlook. The first was provided by the Gifford Lectures of Charles Raven, entitled *Natural Religion and Christian Theology*, delivered at Edinburgh in 1951;[11] the second, by the Report on the Doctrine of Man of the Lambeth Conference of 1948, in which 'the distinction between the natural and the supernatural slips out of sight, and the inference seems to be that it is replaced by the most misleading antithesis of 'spiritual' and 'material'. So the fog continues.'

In the twenty years since Dr Ramsey delivered his lecture the fog can hardly be said to have been dispersed. The hope which he then expressed that 'sociology [would] find renewal from a theology in which the concepts of the supernatural and the natural are held distinct and yet in relation, and in which the glory of the former is seen in a power to descend to accept the meaning of the latter . . ., a theology which goes hand in hand with a spirituality, with a vocation of other-worldly sanctity', has certainly not been fulfilled. What we have had is the secularized theologies, exemplified in a comparatively mild form by various writings of Dr John A. T. Robinson[12] and more drastically by Dr Paul van Buren's *Secular Meaning of the Gospel*, for which God does not exist and Jesus did not survive death, reaching their culmination in the 'Death of God' school of Gabriel Vahanian, William Hamilton and Thomas J. J. Altizer. It is noteworthy that secularized theology, while theologically revolutionary, tends to be socially and culturally conformist; more than one critic remarked that Dr Harvey Cox's book *The Secular City*, published in 1965, really amounted to a religious glorification of the American Way of Life at the very time when the latter was causing serious qualms in the minds of thoughtful American citizens.[13] There has, of course, been the German Catholic 'Political

Theology' of J. B. Metz, which provoked vigorous criticism from Karl Rahner, Josef Ratzinger and others,[14] but it presupposed such a specialized transcendentalist metaphysic and was conducted in such a sophisticated Teutonic idiom that it received little attention outside its land of origin. There has also been the mass of writing typified by the phrases 'Theology of Revolution', 'Theology of Liberation' and even 'Black Theology',[15] which was stimulated by the awaking social restlessness of the unprivileged in Africa, Asia, and Latin America, but it has drawn its inspiration rather from the contemporary human predicament than from the classical sources of Christian thought. There have also been, in the Roman Communion, the impressive social encyclicals *Mater et Magistra* (1961) and *Pacem in Terris* (1963) of Pope John XXIII and *Populorum Progressio* (1967) of Pope Paul VI, while *Gaudium et Spes*, the Pastoral Constitution on the Church in the Modern World, is by far the longest of all the documents promulgated by the Second Vatican Council. But the degree of interest taken in any of these by professional academic English-speaking theologians has been quite abysmally minimal, and the effect of this is well shown in the theological poverty of many of the discussions and utterances of the World Council of Churches. A gleam of hope has appeared at the time of writing in the formation within the Church of England of the 'Jubilee Group', which aspires to produce the same kind of Catholic social critique as was the concern of the Christendom Group before the Second World War; and it is significant that it has emerged from the ranks of the parish clergy and not from those of the professional theologians.

So much for the sphere of the Church's sociological thinking. I can refer more briefly to the other theologically neglected sphere which I mentioned earlier, namely that of ecumenism. An ecumenism which was adequately grounded and motivated theologically would be one in which the members of the different churches were led, through their common study and mutual conversation, to a deeper understanding of both their own and one another's traditions, so that previously unrecognized presuppositions and prejudices could be brought to light, deficiencies mutually supplied and distortions mutually corrected, and, without any of the parties abandoning the special insights, both in thought and in practice, which under the providence of God it had been privileged to achieve, there would be a real sharing and an enrichment of life from which both parts and whole would benefit. I attempted to make some contribution of material for such a dialogue nearly twenty years ago in a book entitled *The Recovery of Unity: A Theological*

9

Approach,[16] and, although much of its content has become superseded since Vatican II, I venture to believe that its approach is methodologically sound. Dialogue of this kind has indeed to some extent already taken place. The two volumes *Modern Eucharistic Agreement* (1973) and *Modern Ecumenical Documents on the Ministry* (1975)[17] show the surprising advances in understanding that can be made in previously intransigent matters when the governing motive is that of theological exploration and understanding rather than of negotiation or of polemics. Only too often, however, ecumenism is taken as implying not an obligation to engage in hard and demanding thinking but rather as an excuse for abandoning it. Frequently some decision or action is announced as a 'great ecumenical breakthrough' when it is the outcome of a weary and despairing consent to treat a recalcitrant problem as if it did not really exist. This, however, is not in fact a breakthrough, but merely a lie-down. A genuine breakthrough – if that somewhat unhappy military metaphor is to be used at all – will involve, among other things, persistent, perceptive, and penetrating thinking on the *theological* plane.[18]

I believe that, if academic theology is once again to be of use to the Church in its tremendous pastoral and evangelistic task – and I emphasize that this does not imply the abandonment of intellectual integrity or the conversion of theological faculties into propaganda-organizations or advertising agencies – nothing less is needed than a radical reorientation of our attitude to our task. This will involve a deliberate reconsideration of the nature of that task itself; this is the subject of my first chapter. Then, because Christian theology is concerned above all else with Jesus Christ, I have devoted the central part of this book to two chapters dealing respectively with the Gospels and with Christology; and I would remark that these are precisely the two topics which the Bishop of Chichester, in his address to the General Synod, picked out as being in the most unsatisfactory theological condition at the present time.

That many of the conclusions to which I have come would be described by many as conservative I have no wish to conceal, though I would myself prefer the adjective 'orthodox'. I would, however, make three points. First, the positions are argued and not merely asserted; and the material adduced shows the falsity of the common assumption that all respectable modern scholarship is anti-supernaturalistic.

Secondly, orthodoxy, so far from being static and rigid, is flexible and dynamic; while I am firmly convinced that the Christology of Chalcedon is true, and that therefore positions inconsistent with it are false, I do not believe that, as it stands, it provides a ready-made answer to every possible Christological question, especially to those questions which had not arisen when it was formulated. As I hope will be seen, its strength is that it offers far more possibilities for development and new applications than do the self-consciously up-to-date 'new approaches', which have already run into a sheer dead-end. Thirdly, I am very much aware of the unfinished character of my own discussions. So far from wishing to bring theology to a halt, the most I can hope to have done is to indicate the lines on which I believe it can most usefully proceed.

The final chapter is, frankly, speculative and is offered as such. Its justification, if it needs any, is simply that it occurred to me that the notion of *relation*, which St Augustine used so impressively in his doctrine of the Trinity and which Père Galot has fruitfully extended into the realm of Christology, might have other applications as well; and on trying it out I was surprised to discover how wide its range appeared to be. In view of its links with the previous chapter, it seemed worth while to include it, but, in spite of the importance of some of the topics involved, it is logically much more peripheral and is suggestive rather than conclusive. It may have the additional value of providing a concrete illustration of the point made above, that orthodoxy encourages and does not inhibit fruitful speculation.

ONE

The Nature and Task of Theology

1 THE CONTEMPORARY CRISIS

No sensitive observer will deny that at the present day both Christian theology and the Christian Church are in a condition of crisis and indeed of confusion. This is true not just of one but of all Christian denominations, though it has affected the Eastern Orthdox churches less than most. The two crises – the theological and the ecclesiastical – are not independent of each other; this is only to be expected, and in itself a close connection between the thought of the Church and its life is no bad thing. It can keep theologians from getting airborne in a cloudcuckooland of theoretical abstractions and it can keep the Church from capitulating to emotional urges and the pressures of a secularist environment. In the great formative period of Christian dogma in the fourth and fifth centuries, it was their adequacy as accounts of Christ's work of salvation and as directives of Christian worship and living that, equally with their faithfulness to the apostolic tradition, provided the criteria for assessing doctrinal proposals as orthodox or heretical. No doubt the writings which have come down to us derive from the intellectually more sophisticated circles of the Church, and there may be much truth in the suggestion that the present-day Ethiopian church, sheltered as it has been in the past from external cultural and economic pressures and not over-equipped with professional intellectuals, gives a more adequate picture of the religion of the ordinary Christian men and women in an average congregation of the fourth century than we receive if we assume that they were all Gregories, Athanasiuses or Hilaries. Nevertheless, most of the theological writers of those early centuries were bishops with pastoral responsibilities, deeply concerned with the spiritual welfare of their flocks; they were not, like so many of the later Western medieval theologians, members of a professional intellectual corporation, by whom the nature and purpose of the wood could easily be forgotten in the cultivation by each of his individual tree. There can of course be a breakdown of communication between the clergy and the laity, that 'gulf which too often separates the pulpit from the pew' which it was the avowed ambition of the Library of Constructive Theology to do something to bridge in the days before the Second World War. It should, however, also be remembered that the academic community can easily become more isolated than the parish clergy from the interests and needs of the human community as a whole. This is extremely serious at a time such as the present, when most of the clergy who are concerned with what is now called theology have withdrawn from the pastoral to the academic field and when the gulf, not between the pulpit and the pew but between the theologian and the parish priest, has become notorious, if not indeed scandalous. Canon Charles Smyth has trenchantly affirmed that,

> with a few significant exceptions, our professional theologians nowadays tend to give (however unjustly) the impression of being a sheltered academic *coterie* or debating-society, conducting animated discussions among themselves about textual criticism or philosophy, while in the parishes – the front-line trenches, where most of the real battle for the faith is being fought – the Church, amid much discouragement, heroically combats the materialism and indifference of our day and age.[1]

And the root cause of this, as I hope to make clear, is that, in spite of the variety of academic pursuits that nestle together under the blanket-label of 'theology', theology in the proper sense of that term – the study of God and of God's creatures in their relation to him – has become progressively rarer in our modern academic and scholastic institutions and is now in imminent danger of becoming virtually extinct. As long ago as 1963 Mr Harry Blamires, with the prophetic perceptiveness which characterizes the really sensitive and intelligent layman, wrote a book entitled *The Christian Mind*, from which I quote the opening paragraphs:

> There is no longer a Christian mind.
>
> It is a commonplace that the mind of modern man has been secularised. For instance, it has been deprived of any orientation towards the supernatural. Tragic as this fact is, it would not be so desperately tragic had the Christian mind held out against the secular drift. But unfortunately the Christian mind has succumbed to the secular drift with a degree of weakness and nervelessness unmatched in Christian history. It is difficult to do justice in words to the complete loss of intellectual morale in the twentieth-century Church. One cannot characterise it without having recourse to language which will sound hysterical and melodramatic.
>
> There is no longer a Christian mind. There is still, of course, a Christian ethic, a Christian practice, a Christian spirituality. As a moral being, the modern Christian subscribes to a code other than that of the non-Christian. As a member of the Church, he undertakes obligations and observations ignored by the non-Christian. As a

spiritual being, in prayer and meditation, he strives to cultivate a dimension of life unexplored by the non-Christian. But as a *thinking* being, the modern Christian has succumbed to secularisation. He accepts religion – its morality, its worship, its spiritual culture; but he rejects the religious view of life, the view which sets all earthly values within the context of the eternal, the view which relates all human problems – social, political, cultural – to the doctrinal foundations of the Christian Faith, the view which sees all things here below in terms of God's supremacy and earth's transitoriness, in terms of Heaven and Hell.[2]

Had he been writing ten years later I suspect that Mr Blamires might have detected an erosion of Christian ethics, practice, and spirituality, as well as of Christian thinking, but, be that as it may, he is certainly right about the evanescence of the Christian mind. One of its most striking manifestations is in the book entitled *The Remaking of Christian Doctrine*[3] by the Regius Professor of Divinity in the University of Oxford, Dr Maurice Wiles, a work in which the erosion of a specifically Christian standpoint is most disquietingly indicated by an apparently complete unconsciousness of the fact that it has occurred; I shall discuss it at greater length later on. The frequent insensitiveness of theological academics to the real needs and problems of the pastoral clergy was painfully exemplified in 1975 by the fact that the only contribution which a group of no less than sixty-five of them felt itself able to make towards a solution of the pressing and complex questions connected with the use of exorcism was to petition the bishops and the General Synod of the Church of England to disallow the practice altogether.

The deliquescence of theology in this country is no sudden or unheralded phenomenon. In an essay which is now almost entirely forgotten but which is even more relevant today than it was when he wrote it in 1933, the late Norman Powell Williams, then Lady Margaret Professor at Oxford, drew a dramatic contrast between theology as it had been understood in its grand period and as it was already coming to be in his own time.

'Theology' [he wrote] should mean 'the science of God'; and, accordingly, its contents should consist in the cardinal ideas of the Christian religion, ideas of which the objective truth would be taken for granted by the student, and which human reason would *ex hypothesi* be unable to vary or modify, its task being confined to (*a*) the elucidation of these ideas by means of the most accurate categories available, (*b*) the exhibition of their mutual interdependence and impressive coherence into a single indiscerptible body of truth, and (*c*) their integration with the assured deliverance of scientific observation and metaphysical thought as to the nature of the world and of man. . . .

At the present day, however, the term 'theology' is more commonly used to denote the *historical* and *genetic* study of the leading ideas of Christianity, a discipline which does not assume or even investigate the truth of these ideas, but is solely interested in discovering the steps of evolutionary process whereby they have come to be what they are. 'Historical theology', in this sense, does not differ, in respect of method, from the science of 'comparative religion', of which, indeed, it might be described as the specifically 'Christian' branch. . . . This is the 'theology' which is taught in the now undenominationalised faculties of modern Universities, though indeed it is not so much the 'science of God' as the 'science of men's thoughts about God'; and 'theology', interpreted in that classical and 'systematic' significance which in olden days won for her the proud title of 'the Queen of Sciences', must be content to find a home in seminaries and other specifically ecclesiastical institutions.[4]

I am not so sure at the present time even about the seminaries, but I am sure that the kind of training to which most of our future clergy are subjected in our universities, dominated as it is by the writings of the more sceptical New Testament scholars, tends to paralyse their prayer and deviscerate their preaching. It is not surprising, even if it is regrettable, that for many the only way out appears to be into an anti-intellectual biblical literalism, which, for all its narrowness and insensitiveness, has at least a firm grasp of the authority of Christ and of the uniquely revealed character of the Christian religion. And it must be admitted that, in spite of their attitude of academic objectivity and disinterestedness, theological faculties have not on the whole impressed the other sections of their universities with their relevance to human life as a whole. Very few are the universities in which the theological faculties or departments give the impression that their members have, or even believe or would wish themselves to have, as a consequence of the faith which they teach and study, any contribution of importance to offer to the solution of the problems, personal, intellectual, cultural, or political, which face men and women in the world today.

Not only has the assumption grown that, in modern universities, theology must be the science of men's thoughts about God rather than the science of God, but also, as Williams foresaw, a pressure has emerged in many places, largely because of the general climate of scepticism about Christianity in general, to transform or absorb faculties of Christian theology into departments of Comparative Religious Studies. Many theologians have shown themselves ready to accept this development, with attitudes ranging according to the depth of their own convictions from passive acquiescence to enthusiastic support. For some it seems to be the only way in which, under increased economic stringency and increased dependence upon state assistance in a secularized society, theology can achieve some manner and degree of survival. For some it seems to offer a wider scope for the claim of theology to be an academically respectable discipline. For some, in whom theological deliquescence has reached an advanced condition, it reflects their own loss of conviction that Christianity is in any important sense unique. Thus Mr Don Cupitt has described Christianity as simply 'a family of monotheistic faiths which in various ways find in Jesus a key to the relation of man with God' and 'a form of monotheism guided by Jesus seen as Christ', and has suggested that 'if this were more generally understood relations between Christians and members of so-called "other faiths" would be easier.'[5] Professor John Hick envisages a future in which the future developments of the great world religions may be on 'gradually converging courses'. 'The future I am thinking of', he writes, 'is accordingly one in which what we now call different religions will constitute the past history of different emphases and variations within something that it need not be too misleading to call a single world religion.'[6] And, as regards the 'seminaries and specifically ecclesiastical institutions' which even forty years ago Williams saw as the only surviving refuge for the Queen of the Sciences, it is doubtful whether, under the economic conditions of the future, they will continue to exist at all, unless our ecclesiastical leaders and the Church as a whole become more conscious than they appear to be at present of the inadequacy of academic theology as now understood to produce either a properly equipped pastoral clergy or a theologically educated body of Christian lay intellectuals, who can help the Church to speak intelligibly and creatively to the confused and misled men and women of the contemporary world.

Now there is clearly nothing disreputable or illegitimate about studying men's thoughts about God or about dealing, in Williams's words, with texts and manuscripts, with monumental inscriptions, ostraka, and papyri, with documentary sources and the processes of their compilation and redaction, with the reconstruction of historical events, the disentangling of developments of religious thought and feeling, the tracing of the influence of non-Christian cultus and philosophy upon the faith and practice of the Christian Church.[7]

From the point of view of theology itself, these, like other intellectual pursuits and disciplines, must be reckoned as praiseworthy studies in their own right, as well as being valuable ancillary aids to theology. In St Thomas Aquinas' language, they are parts of that 'philosophy' for which he expressed so much respect when he wrote that 'there is nothing to stop the same things from being treated by the philosophical disciplines in so far as they are knowable by the light of natural reason and by another science in so far as they are known by the light of divine revelation.'[8] It is, however, deeply regrettable that so many Christian academics are involved in these ancillary disciplines and so few are involved in theology proper. It is instructive to note that, when Dr E. J. Burge analysed the subjects of Ph.D. theses accepted by theological faculties and departments in British universities from 1950 to 1962 inclusive, he found that, out of a total of 611, 128 were biographical studies (a notoriously easy option and the largest group), 120 were on Church History, 90 were on the Old or the New Testament, and only 89 fell under the description of Theological Thought.[9] (It should be remembered that many, probably most, of the Old and New Testament theses would have been textual and historical, rather than strictly theological studies.) I doubt whether subsequent years would show very much difference in· proportion. Whatever the significance of these figures may be, they certainly do not give the impression that the majority of students embarking upon research in theological faculties have acquired from their previous studies a burning conviction of the need of the contemporary world for the Christian religion and of their obligation to place their minds at God's disposal for the satisfaction of that need on the intellectual plane. And this is not surprising if we consider what has been understood by 'theology' in the syllabuses for the first degree in theology in Anglophone universities.

Details have, of course, varied from time to time and from place to place and at present a good deal of revision is taking place, though it seems to be more in the direction of 'religious studies' than of theology in the strict sense. A fair example is provided by the syllabus of the

University of London, as it was when I retired from my chair in 1973; it was itself the result of a fairly conservative revision a few years before. There were six compulsory papers, three of which were in Biblical Studies, one in Christian Doctrine, one in a selected period of Church History and the sixth in the Philosophy of Religion. Two further papers had to be taken in one of these subjects or in Christian Ethics, Liturgical Studies, or the Comparative Study of Religions. One more paper had to be taken in one of the subjects already mentioned, with certain restrictions. In consequence, out of a total of nine papers, the candidate would have taken three, four, or five on the Bible, and one, two, or three on Christian Doctrine. At first sight this might seem to accord with even St Thomas' understanding of Christian Theology, since it gave more space to the Bible – *sacra scriptura* – than to any other subject, and Christian Doctrine seems well, if mainly optionally, provided for. These appearances are, however, misleading. The Biblical studies were almost entirely critical and historical, and tended to leave any but the most independently minded student with the impression that the Scriptures, especially those of the New Testament, are unreliable or irrelevant or both; while, apart from a valuable compulsory introduction to the Christian understanding of God, the world, and man (itself a recent introduction), the most readily available doctrinal option took the student to the Council of Chalcedon in A.D. 451 and left him there. Liturgical studies consisted, not of a study of the theological principles and implications of the Church's liturgical life – matters on which Jungmann, Dix, and Bouyer have written so inspiringly and fruitfully – but were almost entirely historical and textual. The Comparative Study of Religions contained no *explicit* reference in its syllabus to Christianity at all. Only in Christian Ethics was there any indication of the relevance of Christianity to the contemporary life and witness of the Church. It should, however, in fairness be remarked that London, alone or almost alone among British universities, insisted upon the candidate for the theological degree receiving at least a minimal training in the discipline of philosophical thought.

It would ill become me to speak churlishly of a faculty in which for more than a decade I received continual kindness from my colleagues and in whose failings I was as deeply involved as anyone else. I am nevertheless more convinced than some that British academic theology is in a profoundly unsatisfactory condition and I do not believe that the cure can be achieved by its absorption into the comparative study of the great world religions. Salvation will not be achieved by suicide. It may, however, clear the air for a more constructive approach to our problem if we look at the causes which lie behind the strange structure of British theological syllabuses.

As a matter of history, these have been influenced by two chief considerations. The first was the need to prevent denominational squabbles. All denominations, it was felt, would agree upon the importance of the Bible, and if it was studied from a critical and historical angle theological embarrassments could be minimized. Doctrinal studies could hardly be eliminated altogether, but they could be defused by treating them historically and keeping them firmly located in the past; these are the beliefs that Christians persecuted one another for when they took them seriously, but how much more tolerant and broad-minded we are today! The other consideration was the need to make theology appear to be intellectually respectable in the context of a virtually secularized university; it therefore had to be represented as a purely rational study, with no appeal to revelation. And the result has been, as Williams pointed out, that, for good or ill, theology, in the strict and proper sense, as the study of God and of his revelation of himself to man in Jesus Christ, has been overshadowed, and indeed effectively superseded, by the various disciplines which in the past were held to be ancillary to it. And this has had two unanticipated and lamentable consequences.

The first is a primarily academic one. Theology, having lost its overriding unifying factor – its formal principle, its *lumen sub quo* –, has fallen apart into a number of disparate activities having little in common as regards either aim or method. In contrast with other subjects, in which the candidate for an honours degree is given a systematic and disciplined training in a particular intellectual expertise, the unfortunate theological aspirant is taught a little philosophy, a little historical method, a little literary criticism, a little philology and so on, in a way that would be more appropriate to a pass degree. Anyone who has taught in a theological faculty knows the desperate struggle that is waged to keep the standard of such a diversity of subjects up to the level of an honours degree without making impossible demands on the candidate. And even when the more resilient student moves into an area of specialized research, he only too often finds himself at a disadvantage in comparison with his more adequately trained colleagues in cognate disciplines in secular faculties. I will only mention here the judgements passed upon the dominant assumptions and methods of New Testament scholars from the historical and logical standpoints by Mr Sherwin-White and Dr

Humphrey Palmer respectively,[10] and Dr James Barr's devastating philological attacks upon some of the most widely and portentously propagated views about the theological implications of Biblical vocabulary.[11] Having myself had no academic training in any of these disciplines, I am obviously not in a position to express a professional verdict on the matter, but even a Philistine can tell a hawk from a handsaw and, having come to theology from a scientific background and from the Cambridge Mathematical Tripos — an intellectual training which I venture to think is not less exacting than that of the Oxford Greats School — , I have often been astonished at the way in which theologians, especially in the field of New Testament study, frequently set forth interesting though highly speculative hypotheses which only a few pages later become the assured results of modern scholarship. However, I have devoted a long chapter to this subject elsewhere in this book and I shall say no more about it now.

The second, and from the point of view of the Church and its mission the far more serious, consequence of this morcellation of theology and the loss of any unifying principle is that gulf between academic theology and the pastoral and evangelistic work of the Church to which I drew attention at the beginning of this essay. I will emphasize again that, in deploring the way in which theology has been swamped by what I have described as ancillary studies, I am in no way advocating their abolition or suppression. Nor is any derogation implied in describing them as ancillary; the greatest of God's creatures owes her exalted status to her readiness to declare herself to be *ancilla Domini*. Indeed in their own spheres they are not ancillary at all. New Testament philology is as respectable a study as classical Greek philology, early church history as the history of the United States of America, the authorship of the Pauline epistles as the authorship of the Platonic dialogues. What is in danger of abolition and suppression, and has indeed already largely been suppressed and abolished, is theology itself, in the strict and traditional sense of the term. Now the central characteristic of theology in this strict and traditional sense is that, in spite of the occasional tendency of its practitioners to indulge in abstractions and complications for their own sake, as a delightful but self-indulgent kind of intellectual gymnastics, it is fundamentally concerned with the same theme as the Church's pastoral ministry, namely the redemption and glorification of man by God his creator through the passion, death, and resurrection of Jesus Christ, the incarnate Son. This is the central and dominant theme of the Gospels and Epistles of the New Testament, it was the dynamic of the primordial explosion of the Church into the Gentile world which is recorded in the Acts of the Apostles, it produced the condemnation of Arianism at Nicaea and the definition that the Son is consubstantial with the Father, it produced as surely the condemnation of Nestorianism and Eutychianism at Chalcedon and the definition that in Christ two whole and perfect natures, of Godhead and manhood, are united without confusion in the one person of the eternal Son. It is this pastoral concern with God's dealing with man in Christ that lies behind Athanasius' repeated assertion that the Word was hominized in order that man might be deified, and behind Gregory Nazianzen's pithy apophthegm that anything not assumed by the Word was not healed. And it is this that is conspicuously absent from the academic attitude which finds it interesting to investigate why men thought as they did about God but is unconcerned whether what they thought about him is true or false.

In stressing the pastoral concern by which theology should be penetrated I am in no way pleading for the kind of philistinism which would reduce theology to homiletics and would repudiate any interest in scholarly questions as 'wisdom according to the flesh'. There will always be a place for the kind of material that fills the pages of the *Journal of Theological Studies*, though one might perhaps wish that properly theological studies were more often to be found in those pages. The relevance of a piece of research to the work of man's salvation may be remote and yet real. Furthermore, just as one of the purest branches of 'pure' mathematics may at any moment become 'applied' (one thinks, for example, of the way in which tensor-calculus and matrix-algebra suddenly found their application in general relativity and quantum-theory respectively), so it can happen in theology; the Qumran scrolls may provide an instance. What is involved is proportion, direction and emphasis, and I suggest that two questions need urgently to be asked. What are the faculties and departments of theology in our universities constructed and organized to *do*? And how do professional theologians envisage their vocation? And, since the majority of holders of theological appointments in this country, and a sizeable minority elsewhere, appear still to be Anglican priests, it may be relevant to remind them that, at their ordination, they were solemnly charged 'to give [themselves] wholly to this office [that is, to the priesthood]', to 'apply [themselves] wholly to this one thing, and draw all [their] cares and studies this way'. With the tremendous proliferation of what I have described as 'ancillary studies' it is vital that these should be co-ordinated with one another and integrated with theology in the strict sense of the term. The only recent writers, as far as I know, who have attempted to do this in a full and systematic way are the Presbyterian Dr T. F. Torrance, in his book *Theological Science*[12] and the Roman Catholic Fr Bernard Lonergan, SJ, in his book *Method in Theology*[13] I shall discuss these in some detail. So far I have simply tried to depict, as I see it, the present condition of the Anglophone, and in particular the Anglican, theological scene. However, before proceeding to my central and more constructive task, which is concerned with the nature, sources, and methods of Christian theology, there is one further preliminary matter which needs attention.

It is impossible today to discuss any topic of Christian faith, ecclesiastical policy or religious practice without finding oneself allocated, if not by oneself then by one's audience, into one of two sharply opposed camps. On the one side are those variously described as left-wing, courageous, liberal, radical, progressive, and democratic; on the other are those described as right-wing, cautious, conservative, traditional, reactionary and authoritarian. This dichotomy, of course, largely derives from the situation that has developed in the Roman Catholic communion since Vatican II, but it has overspilt into other Christian communions as well, and its consequences have been regrettable. It would be generally agreed that, in spite of such magnificent and spectacular achievements as the missionary work of the counter-reformation religious orders, the Roman communion has suffered, from Trent to Vatican II, from excessive regimentation and repression. Now that the pressure has been considerably released it is not surprising that in some quarters the reaction has gone to extremes of individualism and irresponsibility, which have understandably provoked in certain other quarters a somewhat helpless counter-reaction of frustrated authoritarianism. What is quite ridiculous is that in the Anglican churches, which have not within living memory manifested any noticeable tendency to theological conformism, the contemporary antinomianism within the Roman communion is frequently urged as an appropriate example for Anglicans to emulate, in doctrine and practice alike. But in any case this terminological polarization is both inaccurate and mischievous.

Its vocabulary is largely drawn not from Christian or any other religious sources but from secular politics, and it carries emotional charges which inhibit rather than promote rational discussion. Furthermore, it obscures the fact that a man may quite reasonably and consistently be conservative on one issue and radical on another, and that on a particular issue his views may be conservative when judged from one standpoint and radical when judged from another. Thus, to take an example from Dr Hans Küng's controversial book *Infallible? An Enquiry*,[14] the position there put forward in 1971 regarding the infallibility of the Church, and in particular of the Pope, was certainly radical from the pen of a Roman Catholic but would be traditional from the pen of an Anglican, having been stated in its general outlines by so respectable an Anglican as the future Archbishop of Canterbury Dr A. M. Ramsey[15] in *The Gospel and the Catholic Church*[16] in 1936. In contrast another thesis maintained by Dr Küng in the same work, that any doctrinal or ecclesial development that goes beyond the explicit evidence of the New Testament is at best unimportant, is radical from the standpoint of Roman Catholicism, Eastern Orthodoxy and Anglicanism alike, though no doubt traditional from the standpoint of most Protestant bodies.[17] Finally, even to the limited extent to which the two constellations of epithets specify identifiable positions, they are very extreme positions, to either of which only a relatively small proportion of persons belong. There is a whole spectrum connecting the two, and to insist that everyone must be labelled as either a 'radical' or a 'reactionary' is grossly to distort the facts, to encourage conflict and bitterness where there should be dialogue and sympathy, and to commit the serious academic crime of substituting polemics for the conscientious pursuit of truth.

It is because of their perception of the highly complex character of the present religious situation, and not because of the proverbial reluctance of the elderly and middle-aged to contemplate any but the mildest forms of change, that some of the theologians who in the days before Vatican II had acquired the reputation of dangerous questioners of the *status quo* have shown themselves as highly critical of the more extreme tendencies of post-conciliar radicalism. The official recognition accorded at Vatican II to such men as Henri de Lubac, Jean Daniélou, Yves Congar, M. D. Chenu and Louis Bouyer was not purchased by any recantation on their part, but they were far too clear-headed not to distinguish between the necessary questioning of the medieval and Tridentine crystallization of Western Catholicism and the virtually total abandonment of the supernatural and revealed character of the Christian religion demanded by the more anarchistic radicals as the true implementation of Vatican II. And, however much one may be irritated by the excessive tortuosity and incessant self-qualification of the literary style of Fr Karl Rahner, it is only fair to recognize that it is the outcome of an almost morbid determination to carry through this same task of deliberate discrimination.

Fr Bouyer's small book *The Decomposition of Catholicism*,[18] written in 1968 with the theological and liturgical predicament of the French church specially in mind, is radical indeed in its demands, but his radicalism is one that plants its roots more, not less, deeply in the living soil of Christian thought and worship. While he insists on the need that adequate information about the humane sciences should be informed by an intelligent Christian reflection – this, he says, 'is one of the primary tasks of the Christian philosophers, aided by the theologians'[19] –, he adds:

> However, a properly Christian culture, and its capacity to open itself to human culture in general, does not rely solely on scholarly research, however important that may be. It presupposes a substructure, or rather a fertile soil, into which everyone, the most cultivated Christians as well as the most ignorant, must plant their roots; it is itself the basic ground for this culture. This substructure, this soil, can be constituted for us only by the liturgical life in all its human and sacral fulness, with the living interpretation of the Word of God that it alone can procure for us.
>
> Once again, at this point, we must speak plainly: there is practically no liturgy worthy of the name today in the Catholic Church. Yesterday's liturgy was hardly more than an embalmed cadaver. What people call liturgy today is little more than this same cadaver decomposed.[20]

These remarks might be profitably pondered by some Anglican liturgical specialists!

It is not only on the Catholic side that these voices of alarm have been raised. Dr Oscar Cullmann is one of the leading continental New Testament scholars, has been actively engaged in ecumenism, and was an invited Lutheran observer at Vatican II. Early during the Council, on 23 November 1962, he emphasized the large areas of agreement on many issues between Catholic, Orthodox, and Protestant thought.[21] Nine years later, however, on 6 November 1971, addressing the Colloquy of Catholic Intellectuals of Europe at Strasbourg, while he rejoiced in the development of the ecumenical movement during the previous twenty-five years, he felt bound to condemn a certain fashionable type of ecumenism as false to the very nature of the Christian faith.[22]

I see not only true ecumenism menaced by a false ecumenism, but the very Christian Faith itself so threatened, and I certainly do not think that in order to save the fundamentals of the Gospel, one has to retreat to the inner cloisters of the Church to which one belongs. On the contrary, it is absolutely necessary for us to unite our forces to work for the preservation of the Christian Faith from the compromising which threatens to destroy it. . . . It is in deepening our faith together that we will find ourselves converging on a common centre, in unity, by that very fact. . . .

I do not consider this to be a fall into a sinful conservatism.

These labels, besides, are becoming meaningless. A Progressivism which lacks the Faith is corrupt, and a Conservatism without the Faith is corrupt. I am happy to find myself, in this message, at one with Catholic friends who far from being obscurantists are known for their openness of mind and heart, but who are concerned that the sort of evolution we are actually witnessing in theology, and throughout the Christian Churches, compromises the essence of unity itself.

As symptoms of this crisis, Cullmann pointed to the visible facts of the drying up of vocations, the falling off in numbers, defections from the Church and the indifference of the world to the churches. But he saw the essence of the sickness as located in the realm of Faith itself and as manifested especially in the devaluation of prayer and in the disorientation of theology. 'Today', he said,

> theology is so often transformed purely and simply into one of the natural sciences, say psychology, or sociology. As a result theologians end up by saying less well what other intellectuals say much better. This is hardly the way to get the world to listen to theology.

Thus, Cullmann argued, 'theology is in process of losing its proper object.' And he saw, as proof of this,

> the interminable list of 'theologies of the genitive' which burgeon around us. Theology *of* the death of God, theology *of* revolution, theology *of* sex, and so on, when the only legitimate genitive for theology is that contained in its very name as *theo-logy*: the knowledge *of God*. It is a platitude to say that theology must concern itself seriously with all these other domains, of course it must, but precisely as these are focused through that first object of theology, which is the Revelation of God, and in so far as they remake us in the likeness of God through faith, and through that Holy Spirit which is poured out within us by the Faith.

For Cullmann, then, the present crisis of Christianity is above all else a crisis of faith. While there are legitimate and necessary adaptations to the circumstances of the times that the Church has to make in the manner of her preaching of the gospel, 'whenever, in the course of history, conformity to the world has been pushed too far, involving in the "aggiornamento" the very essence of the Christian Faith, the consequences have always been disastrous for Christianity.' In his view, both the Protestant reformers of the sixteenth century and the fathers of Vatican II were trying to eliminate the consequences of certain excesses of compromise which past generations had made with the world. But, in fact, certain post-conciliar Catholics, like certain self-styled 'modern' Protestants, have borrowed their very norms of Christian thought and action from the world rather than from the gospel. While asserting that many of the structures of the Church, which have become hardened, need to be revivified by the Holy Spirit, Cullmann declares that 'it is not the Holy Spirit who is at work, but spirits of quite another kind, when without discernment of spirits we abolish radically and without reverence all that has been handed down to us.'

The primary remedy for this crisis, as Cullmann sees it, is therefore simply a recovery of faith: 'Christians must regain both the courage and the joy to preach what is "folly" to the world – faith in what has been accomplished by another, by Jesus the Christ.' He denies that this is 'immobilism': 'there must be reforms within, and a willingness to go to the world outside. But, prayer and meditation must be the mainspring of our activity.' Nor is he an isolationist:

> Certainly, we must collaborate for certain tasks with 'secular' non-Christian groups of men, among whom we trust to find an ideal near to the gospel, and we ought to be glad at heart if we find some of them not far from the Kingdom of God, nearer indeed than some who call themselves Christians. . . .

But he insists,

> We will do such friends no service if we content ourselves with repeating nothing more than they say themselves. We owe it to them to say something different when necessary, and we must have the courage, in their interest, to oppose them with a categorical 'no' when the ends they pursue or the means they urge run counter to the Gospel of Christ.

Finally, in raising the question what is the most urgent task at present before ecumenism, Cullmann gives a serious and timely warning:

The present crisis of faith risks engendering a facile sort of ecumenism, in which Christians of different denominations find their common ground on the basis of a critique of their Churches always negative and never constructive; moreover, and more gravely, on a basis of capitulation to the world. In this way Ecumenism risks uprooting itself from the Faith itself. The uniformity to which this sort of Ecumenical movement opens out has nothing at all in common with the unity spoken of in the New Testament, which is founded on the diversity of gifts confided by the One Spirit.

So Cullmann proposes, as the most urgent task for ecumenism, 'that Christians of all the Confessions, who are concerned with the situation which faces us, should unite to put the individual charisms of their own Churches at the service of the common defence of the Gospel of Christ.'

And finally he rebuts any suggestion that he is a pessimist:

The Faith is faith in the victory of Jesus Christ. Our faith in the Faith carries also a certainty that the crisis we are going through, all of us together, has some special sense and meaning in the divine plan of the history of salvation. But what falls to hand for each one of us now, is to accomplish together the duty which God has given us, in the place and time in which we find ourselves put by him. There is the task before Ecumenism today.

This is an invigorating appeal and it merits much more attention than it has received, for no one could write Dr Cullmann off as either an unscholarly fundamentalist or a tool of the establishment. Genuine ecumenism is intellectually highly demanding, for it requires sympathetic, persistent, and discriminating examination of all our inherited positions. Too often, however, ecumenism is made the excuse for a type of theological laziness which, on the ground that differences must ultimately be reconciled, persuades itself that they are reconciled already. Neither Bouyer nor Cullmann would tolerate this.

2 WHAT IS CHRISTIAN THEOLOGY?

St Thomas Aquinas at least had no doubts about the nature of Christian theology, for he tells us about it in the very first question of the *Summa*.[23] And, although I do not think he has said the last word on the subject, we might do worse than let him have the first. Christian theology – or, as he calls it, *Sacra Doctrina* – is necessary, since God has revealed to us truths which could not be discovered by the normal activities of the natural human reason and which therefore are outside the scope of what he calls 'philosophy' and of what we usually call 'science' today. It is nevertheless a *science*, in the sense of a kind of knowing, since it is based upon God's own knowledge, which he shares with the blessed in heaven and communicates in various ways and degrees to us. It is a single science, and not, like the 'theology' which we have seen to be practised in our modern universities, a collection of fragments of various other sciences, though it has an overarching and unifying character with respect to them all and is able to make use of them in carrying out its own tasks. It is speculative rather than practical, though it has its practical aspects too. (We must remember that for St Thomas 'speculative' does not mean conjectural, but concerned with thought rather than with action.) It is 'worthier' (*dignior*) than the other sciences, because of its certitude and of the supreme 'worth' of its subject, and because it directs men to eternal happiness. It is therefore not only a science but is also the highest kind of 'wisdom'. Its primary subject is God himself, though it deals also with other beings in their relation to him. It is also argumentative, and its most appropriate argument is the argument from authority, both the authority of God himself and that of those to whom revelation has been made, but it also uses rational argumentation, both to resolve arguments against the Faith and to make its implications manifest. Finally – and here under the name of 'Holy Scripture' – it often makes use of symbolic or metaphorical language, in such a way that one passage of scripture can have several meanings.

This is clear enough but it raises a number of questions. There is first of all the Angelic Doctor's quiet identification of Sacred Doctrine with Sacred Scripture. Plainly he did not understand by Sacred Scripture the simple text of the Bible divorced from its place in the tradition of the Church, though he is as firm as any counter-reformation Roman Catholic that revelation, in the strict sense, was complete by the death of the last apostle and that therefore the apostolic witness is embodied in

Scripture in a final manner, neither needing nor allowing any supplementation. Dr Per Erik Persson has pointed to the fact that in St Thomas's day the doctor of divinity was the *magister in sacra pagina*, the teacher of Holy Scripture, and that in the teaching of the faculty of theology the exposition of Sacred Scripture held a predominant position.[24] Fr George Tavard has argued forcefully that the notion of Scripture and Tradition as two distinct and virtually unconnected sources of doctrine emerges only in the fourteenth century. 'The greatest centuries of the Middle Ages – twelfth and thirteenth – ', he writes, 'were thus faithful to the patristic conception of "Scripture alone".'[25] And, although he sees the beginnings of a different view as early as Henry of Ghent, he describes the situation as follows:

> The Fathers and the great medieval schoolmen assumed that Church and Scripture coinhere. The fourteenth century introduced a cleavage between them. The former view still prevailed in many minds. Yet there were from the beginning of the century patent omens of disruption. Once cut off from each other in theory, Holy Writ and Holy Church are likely to drift apart in practice. For the reading of the word of God is then severed from the listening to the Church's voice. And the voice of the Church is superadded to, rather than growing with, the contents of Scripture.[26]

We may notice, incidentally, here how the dichotomy Scripture/Tradition has become the dichotomy Scripture/Church. As the title of Fr Tavard's book indicates, Holy Writ is set over against Holy Church. And the reason is plain. It is that Scripture, something written in ink on parchment or paper, has become virtually dead. What still lives is Tradition, and it lives in the living body of the Church.

This, however, is taking us far from St Thomas, whose position is well summed up in this longish passage from Dr Persson:

> In the writings of Thomas we find that the concept of *traditio* has a certain lack of preciseness. This is explained by the fact that tradition cannot be discussed in isolation from the exegesis of scripture. We do not therefore find in Thomas any explanation of tradition, which he regards as something as natural and necessary as the church itself. . . . Formally, even the biblical writings themselves represent one element in this tradition, but materially this *traditio*, which is transmitted within the church, is the continuing exposition throughout the ages of the truth given in scripture. In Thomas tradition is not *complementary* but

interpretative. Thus the scriptural principle does not mean that scripture is in any way opposed to the interpretation of the church, the tradition of the fathers, and the pronouncements of the *magisterium.* These three elements constitute a unity – and even as early as this we can see the development in theology which gradually led to the dogma of infallibility – but this unity means that the teaching of the church, *doctrina ecclesiae,* is to be understood essentially as the *interpretation of scripture.*[27]

Again, Fr Thomas Gilby has written with his usual lightness of touch:

To appreciate the place of Scripture in theology – or more justly the place of theology in Scripture – according to St Thomas two extremes are to be avoided; on one side, of treating the Bible as the sole rule of faith, or as its systematic statement, or as a catalogue of the truths necessary for salvation, or as the title-deeds or charter of incorporation for the Christian Church giving chapter and verse for every item of its teaching, sacraments, and government; on the other side, of separating the sources of Christian teaching into two, namely Scripture and Tradition, even though their streams, like the Mississipi and Missouri, commingle. Both contain a truth, the first that objective revelation was completed with the Scriptures in the Apostolic Age, the second, that the Scriptures are silent about some necessary religious truths, for instance, about what in fact are the canonical books.

Fr Gilby adds that 'what are the precise relations between Scripture and Tradition is still an open question for discussion'[28]; I must leave it here, only stressing that, for St Thomas, Scripture, the Fathers and the contemporary teaching of the Church are not three mutually isolated organs but are three aspects and elements of the reception and progressive understanding of the revelation given by God in Christ. Of the development of doctrine, as we have come to understand it today, I do not think that St Thomas was conscious. After all, as Dr Owen Chadwick has remarked, Newman's exposition of the notion had a very mixed reception in Rome itself – and, in America, as with Orestes Brownson.[29] What St Thomas would have made of the post-Reformation controversies and of the homogeneous evolution of Catholic dogma, as envisaged for example by F. Marín-Sola, I cannot guess. I think he would have both sympathized and quietly smiled at the misadventures of Fr Gaspar Hurtado, who denied that it was *de fide* that Clement VIII was the successor of St Peter, on the grounds that, while it was *de fide* that a validly elected pope was the successor of St Peter, it was only a matter of natural moral certainty that Ippolito Aldobrandini had been validly elected pope.[30] But what I think St Thomas was sure of was that theology, while it makes use of human reason in various ways, must be conducted within the atmosphere of the believing Church and therefore presupposes in the theologian the virtue of faith. In Fr Gilby's words:

> Faith itself is based on nothing else but God's own truth. Christian theology, however, is not naked faith, but faith invested by grace with reason and imagination, and its direct and immediate authority is God's revelation as embodied in the living Scriptures, that is to say, the living Church.[31]

So much, then, for St Thomas's view of theological method, but what of his view of the subject-matter of theology? M. Gilson describes it simply as 'the revealed', the *revelatum*, and he defines this very carefully. 'According to St Thomas, the *revelatum* embraces solely that whose very essence it is to be revealed, because we can only come to know it by way of revelation.'[32] God may have, and St Thomas asserts that he has, for very good reasons, revealed in addition some truths that are in principle discoverable by the human reason, and so the notion of the 'revealed' needs to be supplemented by the notion of the 'revealable', the *revelabile*. And this is why, in his professedly theological work, the Angelic Doctor makes so much use of philosophical considerations which, as such, do not depend on revelation. 'Taken in itself', writes Gilson, 'this "revealable" is philosophical, but it is drawn, so to speak, into the orbit of theology as included in revelation which assumes it in view of its own end.'[33] But, he also tells us,

> Taken in itself, revelation is an act which, like every act, has a certain end in view. This end, for revelation, is to make possible man's salvation. For man, salvation consists in attaining his end. He cannot attain it unless he knows it. Now this end is God, who is infinitely beyond the limits of man's knowledge. If man was to attain his salvation, God had to reveal to him knowledge beyond the limits of reason. The whole body of this knowledge is called sacred teaching, *sacra doctrina*, *sacra scientia*.[34]

This, then, is St Thomas's notion of theology. Neither in content nor in method does it closely resemble what is commonly understood by 'theology' in the universities of the English-speaking world. And there can be no question of simply going back to the thirteenth century, or, for that matter, to the second or the fifth or even the nineteenth. Nevertheless, I believe that St Thomas, like all the great Christian thinkers of the past, had an understanding of the nature of theology and of the theologian that we have almost entirely lost and that we desperately need to recover. It is the understanding of theology as an ecclesial activity concerned with the revelation given by God to man through Christ in his Church. The theologian, as I see him, is concerned with the revelation which God has delivered to the Church in Christ and only secondarily with the truth that he can discover by his natural powers. He is operating within the great tradition of thought and life into which he was incorporated by his baptism, and the dynamic process which is the enterprise of theology down the ages takes place within the People of God, the Body of Christ. The theologian is right in desiring objectivity, but objectivity is not to be achieved by pursuing it as an ultimate ideal, with frequent glances out of the corner of the eye for the approbation of the secular scholar. He needs, of course, certain gifts of intellect and a technical training, otherwise he would not be a theologian at all but just that excellent person the simple believer, but far more than these and antecedently to them he needs an intense conviction of the truth and vitality of the Christian religion, a confidence in the relevance of theology to matters outside the academic sphere, and a combination of humility with intellectual integrity. But most of all he needs that feel of the truth, that 'knowledge by connaturality', which comes from living as a member of Christ in the Church which is Christ's body. *Pectus facit theologum*, and the really great theologian will also be a saint. For, while revelation can and must be *expressed* in concepts, images and words, it has been *given* supremely in a person, Jesus Christ, the incarnate Word of God. I should like in this connection to recall an outstanding book which appeared in 1967 but which appears to have been almost entirely forgotten, even, alas, by its author; this is Brother Gabriel Moran's *Theology of Revelation*.[35] His basic theme was that revelation is essentially human, personal and social, and that the key to a personal revelation lies in the arrival of a human consciousness which is entirely receptive to God the revealer, that is to say the human consciousness of the incarnate pre-existent Word. Although books and institutions have an organic and indispensable function in its preservation and communication, the primary enduring locus of revelation is the consciousness of the ascended and glorified Christ. 'The risen and glorified Lord', Moran wrote, 'is the one place where revelation continues to happen in fulness.'[36]

This raises, but also illuminates, a host of problems, but they are problems which arise in any case: The limitations and the development of Christ's human knowledge (Moran deals with this in much the same way as Karl Rahner,[37] Louis Bouyer,[38] and Wolfhart Pannenburg);[39] the special status of the Apostles as primary witnesses and of Scripture as revelation's literary precipitate; the finality of revelation in Christ and, together with this, its proliferation in the developing doctrinal tradition of the Church (Moran tells us that the Church is the prolongation not of the historical but of the heavenly Christ);[40] the inevitable limitations of all verbal formulae, however august and solemn they may be, and yet together with this the overshadowing and indwelling guidance of the Spirit; the place within revelation of the non-Christian religions and of human aspirations in general; and finally the consummation of revelation in heaven. On this last point it is emphasized that the beatific vision is a communion with Christ and so is fully achieved only with and through other men who are united with Christ and with one another in Christ and at the resurrection of the body: 'The perfection of revelation is found at that point where, bodily and socially sharing life with his brothers in Christ, *man* lives in communion with the Trinity.'[41] Behind this whole discussion there lies the fundamental assumption, though it is not expressed in these terms, that grace (of which revelation is an aspect) neither ignores nor suppresses nature, but needs and perfects and transforms it. I shall be following Moran's line of thought if I describe the development of Christian doctrine as a progressive translation, into the conceptual and linguistic frameworks of our earthly modes of knowing and speaking, of successive and interrelated aspects of the truth which is contained in the mind of the glorified Christ, who is himself the Truth and the Word of the Father. In this work of translation the theologian has a very special part to play, while it is one of the functions of the Christian bishop to ensure that new formulations do not distort the primordial deliverances of the gospel and the essential content of the tradition.

Christian theology, to sum up, is an ecclesial activity, a function of the Church. Its subject-matter is the revelation which God has given to the Church in Christ, though it is also concerned with the world in which, and for the salvation of which, God has given it and within which the Church itself lives. The theologian himself is a member of the Church, baptized into Christ and living by the sacraments. Since grace perfects nature and does not destroy it, whatever natural gifts he has of intelligence and judgement will find ample scope for their operation, but within the climate of faith, hope, and charity and as renewed and strengthened by it. And because the world is God's world, created and renewed by him, theology will have much to say about the world and the way in which man should handle it as God's vice-gerent. God forbid that theology should be secularized, but there must be a theology of the secular.

I should perhaps make it plain at this point, in order to avoid any misunderstanding, that this ecclesial understanding of the theological enterprise has very little in common with the view for which Dr John Knox has argued in his book *The Church and the Reality of Christ*.[42] I have discussed that work at length in my own book *The Secularisation of Christianity*;[43] here I will only repeat my conclusion that Knox reduces all theology to ecclesiastical psychology and I will simply add that to make a psychological study of the Church's thinking is very different from thinking theologically within the life of the Church. The straits to which a theologian can be reduced when he abandons a genuinely theological and ecclesial stance is well illustrated by the way in which the Principal of Ripon College, the Revd J. L. Houlden, finds himself left with nothing but the canon of 'appropriateness'. The matter with which he was specially concerned was the ordination of women to the priesthood and he showed himself ready to abandon not only Christian tradition but any specific difference between Christian and secular criteria of judgement in order to justify it. At least he was frank about what he was doing. 'If the theological and ecclesiastical present is to be determined by the theological and ecclesiastical past,' he wrote, 'then the ordination of women must fight hard for a hearing.'[44] 'Pure theology', he asserted, 'concerns God. The rest is comment, extrapolation, application.' Well and good, but how are these three functions to be performed? 'Can we for a moment suppose', he asked, 'that [God] wants us to do anything other than use our common sense?' Well, 'common sense' is an ambiguous and question-begging term; who would admit that he was deficient in it? Here is what it means to Mr Houlden:

> If social institutions point that way, if there is need, if there is desire, let not 'theology' be falsely involved. It has no bearing on the matter, at least not in the way of solemn, elaborate argument. It is a matter of expediency for the Church, no more, no less; that is the level at which judgement must be made.[45]

And the only theological method to be accepted is 'symbolic' – another ambiguous and question-begging term. And here, as illustration, is its application to the matter in question:

> How can we be in the way for 'doing theology'? The method is symbolic, and the glory of symbolism is appropriateness. In this language, Jesus is what he is for us because he is the superbly appropriate symbol of God. Not (let us add hastily) by his maleness, but by his teaching, by the nature of his death and his new life, by all that has flowed from him. The priest of the Church too is a symbolic figure and it is best if the symbol is as complete as possible – many-sided and appropriate.[46]

Is it not clear that appropriateness is so protean a symbol that it can be adapted to whatever end is desired? For Mr Houlden it means adapting the Church's faith, practice, and structures to those of contemporary social institutions and, as he says quite explicitly, making the Church's judgements on the level of expediency. In this situation it is perhaps not surprising to find the Warden of Keble, Dr D. E. Nineham, pleading that the proper partner for theology today is sociology, and in particular the sociology of knowledge.[47]

Here I would gladly leave the matter, having done my best to show how theology, if it is rightly conceived, is intimately and organically related to the evangelistic and pastoral concern of the Church. There has, however, appeared from the pen of the Regius Professor of Divinity in the University of Oxford, who has also held the prestigious office of Chairman of the Doctrine Commission of the General Synod of the Church of England, a work which conceives the nature and function of theology in so radically different a manner from that which I have expounded that I feel unable to ignore it. It is not, I hope unfair, to say that Dr M. F. Wiles is determined at all costs to bring Christian theology into line with what he takes to be the intellectual outlook of the present day. Echoing the title of an earlier work, *The Making of Christian Doctrine*,[48] which was concerned with the development of Christian thought in the early centuries, he has entitled his later book *The Remaking of Christian Doctrine*.[49] Both he and his publishers admit that to many of his readers his handling of Christian doctrine will seem to be an unmaking, rather than a remaking, of it; this is undoubtedly true, and I think their judgement will be correct. He himself admits that two reviewers of the earlier book accused him of having set out to write about the development of doctrine but of having in fact abolished the notion altogether without realizing that he had done so. His reply is that there are various ways of understanding development and that for him it is most usefully thought of as 'change through alteration of perspective';[50] more specifically, he appeals to the objectives of 'coherence' and 'economy'.[51] He does indeed make frequent reference to Scripture and doctrinal tradition, but he makes it clear that his ultimate appeal is to the cultural outlook of the present day, though he recognizes that that outlook is itself relative and transitory and that his own re-making of Christian doctrine will have no permanence. It is true that he claims to 'have drawn throughout on the witness of Scripture and on the history of the Christian tradition', while admitting that he has 'seldom quoted explicit texts of Scripture or specific conciliar decisions'.[52] but I do not think that he ever brings any Christian judgement to bear on the assumptions and prejudices of the contemporary world. It is not that he holds the traditional understanding to be demonstrably false; in various places he admits its possibility. But he holds it to be quite unimportant and, to him, very uncongenial. His radicalism as regards the Church's tradition goes hand in hand with a complete conformism as regards the beliefs and values of the secularized industrialized culture in which he lives. On only one point is he lacking in conformity; in a way that is reminiscent of some of the earlier Gifford lecturers, he professes a somewhat vague and pietistic theism, though with the stipulation that, whatever the appearances might suggest, God must never be taken as acting differently in any one being or event from the way in which he acts in any other. In this he shows himself to be remarkably akin to the deists of the seventeenth and eighteenth centuries. Both in his discussion of God and in his Christology, he rejects any kind of supernaturalism and any real uniqueness of persons or events. He writes:

> Talk of God's activity is, then, to be understood as a way of speaking about those events within the natural order or within human history in which God's purpose finds clear expression or special opportunity. Such a view is not deistic in the most strongly pejorative sense, in that it allows for a continuing relationship of God to the world as source of existence and giver of purpose to the whole. It is deistic in so far as it refrains from claiming any effective causation on the part of God in relation to particular occurrences.[53]

And this, Wiles admits, leads to a non-incarnational view of the person and the work of Christ. He is clearly in a dilemma here. 'That the transforming impact of Jesus, of his death and resurrection in particular, is enormous goes without saying', he tells us.[54] And so he writes:

> The issue is one of the greatest complexity and difficulty. I can only here declare my own tentative judgement. The move from concentration on the figure of Jesus alone to concern with the whole Christ-event strengthens the case for giving some special evaluation to that series of events as a whole; it does not seem to me to show that this can only be done adequately by giving a special evaluation to Jesus himself of the unique kind that Christian orthodoxy has in fact given. It certainly does not show that evaluation to be false. The fundamental question that it raises is whether our evidence is sufficient to make possible, let alone to require, such a judgement.[55]

Thus it appears that belief in Jesus as God incarnate is tolerable, although it goes against the basic tenet of Wiles's particular form of deism. But it is not necessary and it is, in Wiles's opinion, improbable. This must be the first form of Christianity in which the deity of Jesus is looked upon as optional; in less sophisticated ages it was either the ultimate truth that gave meaning to life or else downright idolatrous blasphemy. As for grace and the Holy Spirit, in Wiles's remade Christian doctrine they become simply names for certain aspects of religious experience which, while they may be more conspicuous and impressive in certain events and occasions than in others, are not in fact any more present in those events and occasions than in the events and occasions of life as a whole.

In his final chapter, Dr Wiles revealingly lists the chief features which he sees to be characteristic of human knowledge and understanding today: they are a more empirical approach to knowledge, a changed attitude to authority, and a changed understanding of the accessibility of the past. He accepts all these obediently and without criticism. All that concerns him is whether he has applied them correctly, and his disrespect for authority does not extend to the authority of the contemporary outlook. He admits that his presentation of Christianity lacks the force of a more robust and confident faith. 'Christian belief . . .', he writes, 'can either be stated in a strong form, in which it is interesting but almost sure to be false. Or it can be stated in a weak form, in which it has some chance of being true but ceases to be interesting.'[56] All that he can say in defence of this theological neurasthenia is that interest is often of a superficial kind and that the truth is often dull, but I do not think that this justifies the detached and non-committed stance which he takes up towards Jesus Christ. 'I have been arguing', he writes, 'that that particular doctrine [sc., the doctrine of the unique incarnation of God in Jesus Christ] is not required for the whole pattern of belief to be true, or indeed for our having good grounds for believing it to be true.'[57] The trouble is that what Wiles describes by the phrase 'the whole pattern of belief' is, by his own account, so vague, both *de facto* and *de jure*, that it is difficult to see that it requires any definite doctrine at all. What is fundamentally lacking in Wiles's conception of the subject-matter of theology is anything that can be described as a gospel, any recognition of the present living activity of the incarnate Son of God in the lives of his followers and his body the Church; there is, significantly, little mention of the Church and no mention of the sacraments. In his last two paragraphs he admits that 'we speak of God's unique, incarnate presence in the life of Jesus',[58] but he has already discarded the notion of incarnation, and he tolerates such a variety of understandings of this admission that it is left totally unclear whether Jesus still exists and whether what saves us is our belief in Jesus, or our views about Jesus, or Jesus himself. The devastating criticism which Dr Wiles's book has received from Dr Colin Gunton, who is a minister of the United Reformed Church and a lecturer in the philosophy of religion at King's College, London,[59] shows that a conviction of its inadequacies is found in more than one ecclesiastical quarter. Gunton insists that gibes about 'mere orthodoxy' should not be made an excuse for evading the question of saving belief. 'If the Church as the body of believing Christians', he writes, 'ceases to occupy itself with that, then it will cease to be the Church, and simply become another ethical community and not the vehicle of a liberating word of God.' He admits that Wiles has recognized the danger that his theology might become merely intellectual in interest. 'But', he adds, 'his defence against this charge will not hold, for I do not believe that his theology, deprived as it is of a firm centre in the saving historical activity of the crucifying and crucified God, can speak to man's condition'.[60] This is, I believe, entirely true. Dr Wiles's desupernaturalized version of Christianity, in which nothing ever happens that is essentially different from anything else, would seem to leave us with neither a faith by which a man could live nor one for which he might die, and to substitute for a living saviour the most, shadowy, fluid, and subjective of abstractions. We have moved a long way from the triumphant proclamations of the Epistle to the Ephesians and from the uncompromising profession of Bishop Polycarp in the stadium at Smyrna: 'I have been his servant for eighty-six years and he has never done me any wrong. How then can I blaspheme my king who saved me?'[61]

On anyone whose theological memory goes back to the nineteen-twenties, Dr Wiles's writing leaves an odd impression of *déja vu*: for me at least, this is where I came in. The hands are the hands of Wiles, but the voice is the voice of Bethune Baker. (Incidentally, Professor S. W. Sykes has detected this same reincarnation in Dr J. A. T. Robinson.)[62] There is the same assumption that the theologian must fall into line with the intellectual climate of his day, though rather less confidence that the climate will be permanent. Writing such as that of Dr Wiles confronts us directly with the question whether the theologian is to function from within the Church or from outside it, and on the answer to this will depend the relation which the theologian will have to the life of the Church and in particular to its pastoral office. To say that theology must be a function of the Church in no way implies a negative or hostile attitude to secular thought and action, unless we hold – as I emphatically do not – that grace destroys nature and does not heal or perfect it. But, under the economic pressures of the present day, the Church is strongly tempted to abandon its theological function, while salving its conscience with the reflection that, after all, there will be plenty of state-supported departments of Religious Studies in the universities. The position is already compromised by the fact that for many years many professed theologians have been content to view their function in a purely academic light. And this, I believe, is the chief cause of the gulf between the theologian and the pastor which is so glaringly visible and unbridged today.

Something, however brief, needs to be said at this point about the much canvassed question of pluralism in theology. Fr Karl Rahner, in a lecture delivered in 1969,[63] stressed the deep impact which the notion had made upon the life of the Roman Catholic Church and the problem which it had raised about unity of belief. 'How', he enquired, 'can [unity of creed] be set apart and preserved from a pluralistic interpretation of the creed itself, while allowing for a legitimate pluralism in theology?[64] He insisted that this was a new problem, quite different from that of the existence of various theological schools in the Church. The latter, he said, were partly geographical and frequently they were not really reflected upon, or else 'the opposing theses were set against one another as "yes" and "no", and the controversy over them took place within a common intellectual ambience constituted by principles, ideas and ways of approaching questions which were common to all the parties involved.'[65] (The only exceptions were when there were basic differences of which the parties were totally unconscious.) 'It was possible to proceed from the basic principle that one could know the position of one's opponent', but 'today all this is in a real sense essentially different.'[66] Rahner saw this situation as due partly to the fact that today there is no single philosophical system to provide a common frame of argument, and partly to the fact that the modern sciences, historical, natural and social, by which our culture is dominated, have emancipated themselves from philosophy altogether. In consequence,

> when we speak of a pluralism in theology the decisive factor in this is not that the theologies involved contradict one another. . . . The pluralism of which we are speaking here, rather, consists precisely in the fact that it is quite impossible to reduce the theologies and their representative theses to a simple logical alternative in this manner, in the fact that they exist side by side with one another as disparate and mutually incommensurable.[67]

In this situation Rahner pointed to the difficulty of knowing whether theological statements made by different thinkers in their own conceptual frameworks are compatible or not. He instanced Karl Barth's teaching on justification, the teaching of Dutch theologians about the Eucharist, and the views of Catholic intellectuals who were untrained in scholastic theology. (An even better example, in my opinion, would be provided by the Thomist and Palamite confrontation on the question of essence and energies in God.)[68] Towards a solution, Rahner emphasized the dynamic character of the pluralistic situation, the abiding fact of the Church's teaching authority and the inevitably historically conditioned nature of all doctrinal statements, even the most august. While disclaiming a premature answer, he remarked that 'today the Church and her teaching authority are forced, to a notably greater extent than formerly, to leave to the individual theologies the responsibility for seeing that they genuinely do maintain themselves in agreement with the Church's creed.'[69] For, he added, 'today it must surely be recognized that even the Church's teaching authority is confronted with this situation and the consequences arising from it.'[70] Elsewhere, in a monograph on the subject of Heresy, Rahner has remarked on the special difficulty which doctrinal authorities have today from the fact that heresy has taken on a new pattern and tends to exist in latent or 'cryptogamic' forms:

The characteristically Christian attitude of anxiety, vigilance and sensitivity towards heresy should chiefly be directed at the present time against this cryptogamic heresy. This is particularly difficult because this heresy is found in members of the Church and it is very difficult to distinguish it from legitimate trends, a genuine contemporary style and so on.[71]

Rahner does not conclude, however, that this latent heresy needs to be combated by a vast increase of condemnatory utterances and doctrinal directives on the part of authority; he suggests in fact that such activity in the Roman Church in the early part of this century largely defeated its own purpose, first by discouraging legitimate and orthodox theological developments and scholarly research and secondly by failing to get to grips with the real enemy.

The Church's magisterium can do very little, with the means employed until now, against the danger of latent heresy. . . .

At all events the danger is inevitably greater today than before that if theological theses and opinions which are over-hastily considered to look dubious or insufficiently mature, are officially suppressed, heresy is not destroyed but only assumes its new form and so really becomes unaffected by measures taken by the Church's magisterium.[72]

What, then, is the answer, if the official magisterium is largely impotent in this situation? Rahner is quite clear: 'The battle against this implicit heresy of attitude is therefore chiefly a task incumbent on the conscience of the individual.'[73] And this, he stresses, concerns not just the individual in isolation but calls for 'the formation of a charismatically inspired "public opinion"'.[74] He shows an all-too-rare combination of respect for the human conscience and firm conviction of the importance of orthodox belief. Thus he writes: 'It is never possible to say with absolute certainty whether the heretic despite his heresy is in the truth by reason of the Christian truths to which he adheres, or whether despite these truths he is really in error because of the heretical doctrines which he holds.'[75]

Speaking as an Anglican, I can only endorse this last judgement of Fr Rahner, for in the Anglican Communion we have suffered and are suffering most grievously from the irresponsible way in which many religious spokesmen have blazoned forth novel, controversial, and destructive interpretations of the Church's gospel, not just as tentative hypotheses for critical assessment by those competent to make it, but as the only possible positions for acceptance by contemporary man. To take into account the effect which his pronouncements may have upon members of the Church at large who, whether simple or sophisticated, are not for the most part trained academic specialists, is, as I see it, one of the most imperative duties of the professional theologian. And it is often most scandalously neglected. Freedom to express one's views without becoming the victim of physical, economic, or social sanctions does not carry with it the right to hold and to propagate whatever views one finds congenial, but rather the moral obligation to bring one's views under the most exacting scrutiny to find out whether they are true or false. But, to return to Rahner's main point, I would suggest that mutual understanding between different theological systems in a situation of theological pluralism, though difficult, ought not to be ultimately impossible, since between the different theologies and antecedent to them all there is, if they are legitimate at all, the common revealed truth which it is the purpose of all of them to express. I do not think that a plurality of theologies is in fact an ideal situation, for if there is genuine mutual respect and understanding it is to be hoped that they will ultimately find a home together as different elements in an enlarged and enriched theology of the future. Furthermore, some may turn out to be useless and some to be downright false. Only time will show. And, however much any theology will bear the imprint of its environment, it must be remembered that, when it is really living and sensitive, Christian theology does not only submit to the cultural and conceptual framework of its time and place, but also regenerates and reforms it, sometimes very dramatically. See, for example, what St Thomas did to Aristotelianism, or St Augustine and St Gregory Palamas to Platonism! A quarter of a century ago Fr Lionel Thornton made it the theme of his great but neglected book *Revelation and the Modern World* that 'Revelation *masters* its environment, because God identifies himself with human history in order to transform it.'[76] I do not think one could find a better statement of the conviction with which the Christian theologian should approach his task.

3 TWO CONSTRUCTIVE APPROACHES

One of the very few British theologians of recent years who have seriously enquired into the nature of the discipline to which they are committed is the Presbyterian scholar Dr Thomas F. Torrance, who occupies the chair of Christian Dogmatics in the University of Edinburgh. At the conference with the title 'The Future of the Church' held in Brussels in September 1970 by the review *Concilium*,[77] he caused a mild sensation by denouncing some of the more radical Roman Catholics for introducing into the Roman communion the worst features of nineteenth-century Liberal Protestantism. In 1969, in his book *Theological Science*,[78] he undertook to investigate the nature of theology and, in doing this, to justify its existence as a respectable academic pursuit. As we might expect from a convinced and enlightened Calvinist, theology for Dr Torrance does not mean the literary and historical criticism of the Bible or the historical study of Christian beliefs and ecclesiastical events, though he is in fact a very erudite textual and critical scholar;[79] it means the science whose object is God himself. While discussing repeatedly and at length the relation between the objective and subjective elements in human knowledge, both theological and non-theological, Torrance made it plain in his book that he had no use for the reduction of theology to the study of the psychology of believers, and he faulted Schleiermacher on this very issue. In the contemporary setting he took firmly the side of Barth against Bultmann, while he defended Barth against the charge of extreme anti-rationalism which was, at any rate in his early days, commonly brought against him.

Torrance opened his discussion by vindicating the claim of theology to be, as the title of his book implied, a science in the strict sense of the word. It conforms, he maintained, to the general pattern of sciences *en masse*, while having, as they all have, certain special characteristics determined by the nature of its object. That object – God himself – is, of course, a very special object indeed, and in consequence theology has some very special, and indeed quite unique, characteristics; this fact, however, does not deprive it of its status as a science. Torrance did not attempt in this book to demonstrate the existence of the special object of theology; he was not writing a work of apologetics, and there were fairly clear indications that anything like the traditional natural theology would be, to say the least, uncongenial to him. He nevertheless held that the question of natural theology *solvitur ambulando*. Theology, he affirmed,

> presupposes, of course, as [the special sciences] all do, that its object is intelligible and therefore open to rational investigation along certain lines, and it assumes the existence of its object without stopping to justify its undertaking for these are questions that will be resolved in the actual process of examination and construction.[80]

I have said that for Torrance the special object of theology is God himself, but this needs to be amplified, for, as a good Calvinist, he insisted that this means God as revealed in Jesus Christ and apprehended by faith. This clearly raises a number of issues for discussion. Again as a good Calvinist, Torrance maintained that this apprehension is mediated through the Scriptures. He repudiated the Bultmannian thesis that little or nothing can be known of the words and deeds of Jesus as historical facts and that the proclamation of the gospel – the *kerygma* – which leads to faith and justification is unconcerned with factuality. I think, however, that he gave less than adequate discussion of the nature of Scripture and of its relation to the tradition of the Church. Again, I think that he might well have given attention to Brother Gabriel Moran's thesis that the human mind of the ascended Christ is the locus in which all revelation is now and for ever situated.[81] Furthermore, I am not convinced that the undoubted truth that the object of *Christian* theology is God-as-revealed-in-Christ necessarily renders natural theology either perverse or otiose; does the fact that Jesus is the incarnate personal Son of a transcendent personal Father make it impossible to derive *any* knowledge of God from the general character of the world that he has made and preserves? I should have welcomed, too, some reference to the non-Christian religions; does the perfect revelation of God in human form in Jesus exclude *any* revelation of himself elsewhere, and, if it does not, how is that revelation to be explained and understood? Some cognate problems – though not, alas, these, are discussed by Dr Torrance in a small work entitled *Space, Time and Incarnation*[82] and others in the volume *God and Rationality*.[83] In this last he shows himself highly critical of the 'new theology' of such writers as Dr J. A. T. Robinson, and he is insistent that, whatever else it may be, it is certainly not coherent with the mental outlook of modern science. It is important to notice that, in claiming for theology the status of a science, Torrance is not adopting the position that religious dogmas, like scientific hypotheses, are tentative suggestions which are to be confirmed or discarded by empirical testing of their logical consequences; his basic gravamen against the 'new theologians' is that they lay such stress upon the subjective element in human experience as in effect to deprive our knowledge of any genuine objectivity. Thus he writes, in a passage which must be quoted at length:

> This is the problem with Gogarten who interprets history as a form of self-encounter, for history is what we men create; and this is the problem with Bultmann who argues that when we speak about God the only content our statements can have is the determination of our existence by the impact of His "Word" upon us, and so he reduces the content of revelation to our own "self-understanding". But is this not also a basic problem with John Robinson, that he is a theological solipsist, who cannot see finally outside of himself or identify a God "out there" in distinction from the ground of his own being, and who makes matters much worse by insisting on thinking of God only "in pictorial images" for then he is unable even to conceive of a theism except in the obsolete forms of a Ptolemaic cosmology? Is it not Dr Robinson himself who requires, as it were, to be demythologised? But we are concerned here with a far deeper problem than that of a few notorious thinkers out on the flanks of historic Christianity: it is the problem of an ingrowing subjectivity, a sort of stuck-adolescence, that has come to effect [*sic, qu.* affect] multitudes of modern people, who are unable to break out of the teenage mentality in which they are engrossed with their own self-fulfilment, and are unable to reach the maturity of those who love their neighbours objectively for their own sakes, because they cannot love God objectively for his sake. Their relations with God and with their neighbour are inverted upon themselves. Scientifically speaking, this is the loss of objectivity, a failure to understand things out of themselves in accordance with their natures. That is why we have to regard not a little of the "new theology" as an irrational flight from the exact thinking of science.[84]

This is hard-hitting stuff, but Dr Torrance argues his thesis forcibly and consistently. As a good Calvinist (and he is more conscious of the contrast between Calvinism and Lutheranism than are most Catholic scholars), he insists upon the objectivity of reformed doctrine. So he writes again:

> Theological statements do not carry their truth in themselves, but are true in so far as they direct us away from themselves to the one Truth

of God. That is why justification remains the most powerful statement of objectivity in theology, for it throws us at every point upon the Reality of God and what he has done for us in Christ, and will never let us rest upon our own efforts. It is therefore from this ground that we must direct our challenge to those "new theologians" who deliberately make self-understanding the criterion of their interpretation of the Gospel, or who insist upon an anthropocentric starting-point for theological enquiry. If modern science has learned anything from Christianity, it has learned just this, that in any sphere of investigation we understand things out of themselves and according to their natures, and not out of our own preconceived ideas, yet it is this basic principle of science and theology that they sin against so badly.[85]

Dr Torrance is admittedly a controversial figure in the theological field; this is largely because he insists on bringing out into the light of day many issues that others are content to brush under the carpet. One of his aims he describes as 'to draw out the implications for the human subject of the fact that he is addressed by God and summoned to faithful and disciplined exercise of his reason in response to God's Word and therefore to call a halt to the romantic irrationality and bloated subjectivity with which so much present-day theology is saturated.'[86] I am doubtful about some of his views and I have indicated some of the questions which I think he fails to answer adequately. Nevertheless, his fundamental orientation is, in my view, sound and important. Perhaps the greatest weakness of theological writing today arises from the fact that so many of its practitioners never stop to enquire what they are supposed to be doing or how it ought to be done. Even when they do not brush the dust under the carpet they are happy just to pull down the blinds. It is of course possible for a scientific discipline to become smothered by methodology, but theology today is in danger of dying of inanition through its absence. Dr Torrance has done his best to make us face the issue. So has Fr Bernard Lonergan, to whom I now turn.

In deploring the virtual suffocation of theology proper by the proliferation of what I have described as ancillary disciplines, I made it plain that there can be no question of suppressing or abolishing the latter and that no derogation is implied in speaking of them as ancillary. What is important is that they should be co-ordinated with one another and integrated with theology itself; this is what Fr Bernard Lonergan has set out to do in his remarkable work *Method in Theology*.[87] Much of the difficulty which some readers have found in it lies in the fact that it presupposes the massive structure of cognitional theory and metaphysics built up in the earlier work *Insight: A Study of Human Understanding*,[88] though it does not demand an intimate acquaintance with all the details of that formidable and monumental volume. Lonergan's basic theme is that the human mind, simply as mind, as spirit and not inanimate matter or sub-intelligent sensitivity, has a virtually unrestricted desire to know, a desire which is radically motivated by love, and that, in knowing, the mind enters into a vital union with its object in the depth of that object's being. Knowledge is literally *in*sight, seeing into, getting into, not just taking a casual superficial glance or, in the phrase Lonergan often uses, not just 'taking a look'. He is totally opposed to those modern views which envisage perception as analogous to the elastic impact of solid bodies and the operations of thought as analogous to the functioning of an electronic computer. Mental activity, for Longeran, is essentially dynamic and – in the technical sense of the word – *intentional*. Therefore, except when it is a matter of producing the same result over and over again, 'as in the assembly line or "The New Method Laundry"', method is not to be conceived as 'a set of rules that, even when followed blindly by anyone, none the less yield satisfactory results'.[89] I have given some discussion of Lonergan's general philosophical position and its implications for Christian theism in the chapters on 'Transcendental Thomism' in my Gifford Lectures *The Openness of Being*.[90] Here I am concerned with it only as it affects his view of the nature and method of theology. He sees theological thinking as requiring a threefold conversion on the part of the thinker, in the intellectual, moral, and religious realms respectively, and he sees the basic requirement of the theologian as being a burning love of God. Indeed, he goes so far as to assert that, while the maxim *Nihil amatum nisi praecognitum*, 'Nothing can be loved unless it is previously known', is generally true, it ceases to hold when God is the object, for God cannot be known unless he is first of all loved. Lonergan is thus far from the position of those who would hold that an unbeliever can be a perfectly sound theologian, and indeed perhaps the soundest type, since he is free from the believer's bias.

Nevertheless, Lonergan insists that theology must conform to the requirements of a sound philosophy, and for him this involves the 'transcendental method' which he has expounded and defended in *Insight* and elsewhere. And it is the basic contention of the transcendental method that theory of knowledge must precede metaphysics. Thus he writes:

The introduction of transcendental method abrogates the old metaphor that describes philosophy as the handmaid of theology and replaces it by a very precise fact. Transcendental method is not the intrusion into theology of alien matter from an alien source. Its function is to advert to the fact that theologies are produced by theologians, that theologians have minds and use them, that their doing so should not be passed over but explicitly acknowledged in itself and in its implications. Again, transcendental method is coincident with a notable part of what has been considered philosophy, but it is not any philosophy or all philosophy. Very precisely, it is a heightening of consciousness that brings to light our conscious and intentional operations and thereby leads to the answers to three basic questions. What am I doing when I am knowing? Why is doing that knowing? What do I know when I do it? The first answer is a cognitional theory. The second is an epistemology. The third is a metaphysics where, however, the metaphysics is transcendental, an integration of heuristic structures, and not some categorial speculation that reveals that all is water, or matter, or spirit, or process, or what have you.

Lonergan is, however, clear that theology is more than just one among many academic disciplines, and he immediately adds:

It remains, however, that transcendental method is only a part of theological method. It supplies the basic anthropological component. It does not supply the specifically religious component. Accordingly, to advance from transcendental to theological method, it is necessary to add a consideration of religion. And before we can speak of religion, we must first say something about the human good and about human meaning.[91]

These three topics – the Human Good, Meaning, and Religion – occupy nearly a hundred very tightly packed pages; no brief summary can do them justice. An indication of their scope may be given by simply saying that under the first heading Lonergan discusses skills, feelings, values, beliefs, co-operation, progress and decline; under the second he deals with the development of human intersubjectivity from early language and the world of common sense to the more sophisticated 'differentiations of consciousness' of philosophy, science, and literature; under the third he insists upon the 'transcendental tendency of the human spirit that questions, that questions without restriction, that questions the significance of its own questioning, and so comes to the question of God.'[92] Thus he writes:

> The question of God, then, lies within man's horizon. Man's transcendental subjectivity is mutilated or abolished, unless he is stretching forth towards the intelligible, the unconditioned, the good of value. The reach, not of his attainment, but of his intending is unrestricted. There lies within his horizon a region for the divine, a shrine for ultimate holiness. It cannot be ignored. The atheist may pronounce it empty. The agnostic may urge that he finds his investigation has been inconclusive. The contemporary humanist will refuse to allow the question to arise. But their negations presuppose the spark in our clod, our native orientation to the divine.[93]

For 'man achieves authenticity in self-transcendence', and, 'as the question of God is implicit in all our questioning, so being in love with God is the basic fulfilment of our conscious intentionality.'[94] And at this point loving God becomes explicit:

> To speak of the dynamic state of being in love with God pertains to the stage of meaning when the world of interiority has been made the explicit ground of the worlds of theory and of common sense. It follows that in this stage of meaning the gift of God's love first is described as an experience and only consequently is objectified in theoretical categories.[95]

And this is no merely natural human achievement. It is 'the gift of God's love'; 'the gift we have been describing really is sanctifying grace but notionally different from it.'[96]

Before we examine Lonergan's detailed exposition of theological method we must take a step back and familiarize ourselves with his theory of the basic operational constitution of the human mind. This has been both developed and, in some respects, simplified since he produced the monumental study *Insight* in 1957. In 1972 he summarized it as follows:

> Different levels of consciousness and intentionality have to be distinguished. In our dream states consciousness and intentionality commonly are fragmentary and incoherent. When we awake, they take on a different hue to expand on four successive, related, but

qualitatively different levels. There is the *empirical* level on which we sense, perceive, imagine, feel, speak, move. There is an *intellectual* level on which we inquire, come to understand, express what we have understood, work out the presuppositions and implications of our expression. There is the *rational* level on which we reflect, marshal the evidence, pass judgement on the truth or falsity, certainty or probability, of a statement. There is the *reasonable* level on which we are concerned with our selves, our own operations, our goals, and so deliberate about possible courses of action, evaluate them, decide, and carry out our decisions. . . .

Intentionality and consciousness differ from level to level, and within each level the many operations involve further differences. . . . On all four levels, we are aware of ourselves but, as we mount from level to level, it is a fuller self of which we are aware and the awareness itself is different.[97]

In accordance with this scheme, Lonergan lays down the four precepts: 'Be attentive', 'Be intelligent', 'Be reasonable', 'Be responsible'; and he stresses that if one's theologizing is to be a really human enterprise they cannot be carried out simply automatically.

Method [he writes] can be thought of as a set of recipes that can be observed by a blockhead yet lead infallibly to astounding discoveries. Such a notion of method I consider sheer illusion. The function of method is to spell out for each discipline the implication of the transcendental precepts, Be attentive, Be intelligent, Be reasonable, Be responsible. Nor does the explicitness of method make the occurrence of discoveries infallible. The most it can achieve is to make discoveries more probable.[98]

The four precepts are correlated with the four levels of intentionality, namely the empirical, the intellectual, the rational, and the responsible, and with the four kinds of act that respectively go with them, experience, understanding, reflection, and decision. These in turn seem to correspond, at least schematically, to the fundamental structural operations of the human soul as found in Thomist Aristotelianism, though Lonergan is clearly not anxious to draw very much attention to this. Experience corresponds to sensation; understanding and reflection to the intellectual operations of conception and judgement respectively; and all three are types of cognition. In contrast, decision is an operation of appetition or volition. The correspondence is, however, not altogether exact; there is a great deal of overlapping and interpenetration, which is fully accounted for by the fact that Lonergan's system is radically dynamic, while Aristotelianism is rejected by him as basically static. Nevertheless, his exposition of theological method closely follows this fourfold scheme, though, since like the famous Duke of York he first climbs up to the top of the hill and then climbs down again, the ultimate shape is not fourfold but eightfold. First the four precepts are successively manifested in 'mediating theology', in the four disciplines of Research, Interpretation, History, and Dialectic, in which the content of the truth is being elucidated and assimilated; then the reverse process of 'mediated theology', through which the truth is imparted to the world, is maintained and developed in the four disciplines of Foundations, Doctrines, Systematics, and Communications. On this eightfold path an absolutely necessary part is played by the three 'conversions', an intellectual conversion, which takes place between Interpretation and History in the transition from conceptualization to judgement, and moral and religious conversion, which are chiefly involved on the higher levels of History, Dialectic, and Foundations and specially at the peak where mediating theology passes over into mediated theology.

It is impossible here to give a detailed account and critique of Lonergan's eight 'functional specialties', as he calls them, and of their place in his whole system and theory of theological method. More than half of his book *Method in Theology* is devoted to their detailed exposition and to the problems which they raise individually and collectively. Clearly one of the main concerns by which he has been motivated in constructing this massive and complex system has been the desire to welcome into the ambit of theology the ancillary disciplines which have proliferated in recent years and at the same time to bring them into a coherent and co-ordinated relationship in which their rightful functions are respected while theology itself is not stifled by them. One of the most striking general impressions which he leaves is that of a total refusal to accept the fashionable polarization of conservative and radical which has done so much harm in the Church in recent years. He holds firmly to the permanence of the meaning of Christian dogmas, while arguing that a genuine theological pluralism is fully consistent with the unity of the faith. In a passage of remarkable penetration he writes:

The real menace to unity of faith does not lie either in the many brands of common sense or the many differentiations of human consciousness.

It lies in the absence of intellectual or moral or religious conversion. The pluralism that results from lack of conversion is particularly perilous in three manners. First, when the absence of conversion occurs in those that govern the church or teach in its name. Secondly, when, as at present, there is going forward in the church a movement out of classicist and into modern culture. Thirdly, when persons with partially differentiated consciousness not only do not understand one another but also so extol system or method or scholarship or interiority or slightly advanced prayer as to set aside achievement and block development in the other four.[99]

Theologically, Lonergan will appear to many to be, if not radical in the popular sense of violent or destructive, at any rate radical in the proper sense of getting to the roots of the matter. *Doctrinally*, he is by his own confession 'a Roman Catholic with quite conservative views on religious and church doctrines', but, he adds,

I have written a chapter on doctrines without subscribing to any but the doctrine about doctrine set forth in the first Vatican Council. I have done so deliberately, and my purpose has been ecumenical. I desire it to be as simple as possible for theologians of different allegiance to adapt my method to their uses. Even though theologians start from different church confessions, even though their methods are analogous rather than similar, still that analogy will help all to discover how much they have in common and it will tend to bring to light how greater agreement might be achieved.[100]

Clearly Fr Lonergan is far from holding that differences about doctrine are of a purely relative or secondary nature, but he has tried, and believes he has succeeded, in finding a common methodological basis on which they might be discussed. In the very last chapter of his book he suggests that it is in the practical realm that ecumenical action can chiefly lie, while the intellectual dialogue is going on:

While the existence of division and the slowness in recovering unity are deeply to be lamented, it is not to be forgotten that division resides mainly in the cognitive meaning of the Christian message. The constitutive meaning and the effective meaning are matters on which most Christians very largely agree. Such agreement, however, needs expression and, while we await common cognitive agreement, the possible expression is collaboration in fulfilling the redemptive and constructive roles of the Christian church in human society.[101]

It is, however, with his views of the nature of theology as an intellectual enterprise that we are concerned here and his special importance is that he appears to be the only modern theologian who has attempted to present in detail a comprehensive system which will include what I have described as the ancillary disciplines, will recognize their very diverse individual characteristics, and will set them in a coherent relationship with one another and with the whole overarching revelation given by God in Christ. It is not really surprising that so ambitious an undertaking has raised problems and doubts in some quarters. A chapter-by-chapter critique of his book would be extremely valuable but it cannot be undertaken here. Only some general points can be made.

If we had only the earlier work *Insight* to refer to, the accusation of an excessive intellectualism might seem to be justified; God might seem to be sought simply in order to satisfy man's curiosity. However, in his later work, as we have seen, Lonergan has given a more and more dominant place to love – both God's love for man and man's love for God, and in his latest work, the three lectures *Philosophy of God, and Theology*, he emphasizes that in human development the 'I' of the child emerges from the 'we' of the family, so that the primordial genetic fact of consciousness is not the individual but the community. (We may note that Père Galot, in his discussion of Christology, stresses the fact that the characteristic of a *person* is not so much incommunicability in an isolationist sense as relatability and communicability.)[102] Again, it might appear that, when he argues in the same work for a unification of natural theology and systematic theology, he does not sufficiently demarcate the two realms of reason and revelation. Again, in his welcome stress on the importance of religious conversion as essential for the theologian, he might seem to understress the uniqueness of Christianity, though he does in fact repudiate this accusation, while he claims to give a better solution to the problem of the salvation of the unbeliever than has usually been given.[103] Again, in his desire to communicate with the modern world, he seems to accept too uncritically the modern climate of thought or, as he would call it, the 'scientific differentiation of consciousness'.[104] Again, in his anxiety to integrate the ancillary disciplines with theology, he would appear, in his explicit expositions – for I have no doubt whatever about his personal religious orientation – , to give insufficient emphasis to the fact on which I have laid so much stress throughout the present chapter, that the theologian is, or at any rate should be, operating within the great tradition of thought and life into which he was incorporated at baptism, and that the dynamic process which is Christian theology takes place within the Body of Christ. If it be replied that this is implicit in Lonergan's insistence upon religious conversion, I fully agree, but it needs to be made explicit at the crucial points and its consequences need to be developed. Finally, we are left with the question whether Lonergan's doctrine of method stands over and above all philosophical systems as the criterion to which they must all conform, or whether it stands beside them, as one among others, itself under judgement and needing justification. That is to say, is it the ultimate metamethodology, appealing to no more ultimate principles and demonstrated solely by the fact that all counter-positions turn out to be self-destructive, or not? In Fr Lonergan's judgement, it clearly is. Like the soul of the youthful Tennyson in 'The Palace of Art', it sits as God, holding no form of creed, but contemplating all. This would imply, however, that the cognitional theory and metaphysics upon which it is based are also ultimate; and this, I think, some will wish to dispute.[105]

These are very inadequate comments upon the work of a thinker who, as Dr Hugo Meynell has suggested, may have provided the new paradigm which Christian theology urgently needs today and who may have reduced the contemporary theological chaos to order in a way parallel to the achievements of Copernicus, Newton, and Lavoisier in the physical sciences.[106] Even if that estimate should turn out to be over-favourable, Lonergan will certainly stand out as one of the most important thinkers of our time in the realm where theology and the human sciences meet. That he leaves so many questions still to be answered is a sign of his greatness.

4 CONCLUSION

In heading this section 'Conclusion', I am fully conscious that, in one very important sense, it is not, and ought not to be, conclusive at all. For it has been my whole purpose to argue that theology, properly understood, is a function of the Church which is Christ's Body, and it must therefore be expected to grow and develop in accordance with the growth and development of the Body itself. Quite apart from periods of stagnation and periods of unco-ordinated hypertrophy, which are equally morbid and deleterious, there will be periods of relative stability and consolidation and periods of rapid expansion and development. But all this should take place within the conscious ambit of the Church's tradition as an ecclesial enterprise and service. At their most perceptive, theologians have known that this is true.

Dr M. F. Wiles, an an essay first published in 1957 but republished without comment in 1976 and therefore presumably still bearing his approval,[107] took the late Leonard Hodgson to task for holding that 'the doctrine of the Trinity is the product of rational reflection on those particular manifestations of the divine activity which centre in the birth, ministry, crucifixion, resurrection and ascension of Jesus Christ and the gift of the Holy Spirit to the Church', events which 'drove human reason to see that they required a trinitarian God for their cause.'[108] (Some more radical writers, we may remark in passing, have seen Christian doctrines as a rationalization not of God's acts in Christ but simply of the religious experience of early Christians.) Wiles clearly sympathizes with Hodgson's rejection of the view that divine revelation was given directly in the form of propositions, but he plausibly argues that the patristic material, in which he is an acknowledged expert, does not support the theory that the doctrine was formulated in order to rationalize the primary revelational acts.

> We are . . . [he writes] bound to conclude that the ante-Nicene Fathers did not adopt a trinitarian scheme of thought about God because they found themselves compelled to do so as the only rational means of explanation of their experience of God in Christ. Rather they came to accept a trinitarian form, because it was the already accepted pattern of expression, even though they often found it difficult to interpret their experience of God in this particular threefold way.[109]

He adds that 'by the fourth century . . . the threefold pattern was fully and firmly established.'[110] And having rejected Hodgson's theory, he sees three possible explanations to choose between:

1 the revelation is given in a set of propositions;
2 God's acts have a threefold structure, so we have to think of him in trinitarian terms;
3 the trinitarian doctrine is an arbitrary analysis of God's activity, perhaps valuable but not of essential significance.

The first two of these he sees as much more in accordance with Christian tradition than the third. But, with Hodgson, he rejects the first, as inconsistent with the attitude to revelation to which Biblical criticism has led us; and he rejects the second as lacking in cogency and as an improvisation to take the place of the first. Thus he somewhat tentatively espouses the third view, which, he remarks, would provide 'a signal warning of the need for caution in the making of dogmatic statements about the inner life of God.'[111]

It is not my purpose here to discuss Dr Wiles's theology in detail, but only to use this particular example to show how an extremely erudite patristic scholar can miss the point of his argument through failure to understand the ecclesial nature of Christian theology. For, having very plausibly argued that the doctrine of the Trinity is neither a logical deduction from revealed premises nor an inductive hypothesis to explain Christian experience, he is quite unable to account for the central and basic place which it has come to hold in Christian thought, worship, and devotion and reduces it to the level of an arbitrary, unimportant, and dispensable speculation. There is no suggestion that, through the conflicts and agonizings of the pre-Nicene years, the Church was being led by the indwelling Spirit to a deeper understanding of him in whom it lived and moved and had its being. But in fact in the volume of essays from which I have quoted mention of the Spirit is almost entirely absent, almost the only reference being in the significant assertion that 'our conviction that the Holy Spirit has guided and does guide the church cannot be used to rule out in advance the propriety of questioning and, if judged necessary, abandoning any specific belief or practice of the early church.'[112] How this judgement of necessity is to be made is obviously the vital question, but Dr Wiles gives us very little help in answering it. It is, however, clear from our earlier discussion of his *Remaking of Christian Doctrine* that he attributes very little authority to the Christian tradition but a very great deal to the cultural climate of the contemporary democratic world.

The strong point of the anti-traditionalists is of course the fact that, as a matter of history, many beliefs that had long been taken as firmly embedded elements of the tradition have ultimately been abandoned or modified. Wiles has singled out for special mention the problem of scriptural inspiration. 'More recently', he tells us, 'the church has had to . . . repudiat[e] in practice the early church's understanding of Scripture at the behest of a modern approach to knowledge.'[113] Other cases which he does not mention can easily be found, in which, in one part of the Church or another, a position which seemed to be settled for good and all has yielded to fresh questioning to the great benefit of Christendom as a whole. To take some examples from the Roman communion, in which both the iron hand of the magisterium in the past and the readiness to question it in the present are particularly striking, we might instance the following topics: the view of Scripture and tradition as two independent sources of doctrine, which became universal from the fourteenth century onwards;[114] in Eucharistic theology, the simple identification of sacrifice with immolation,[115] and the medieval doctrine that Christ is not the principal offerer of the mass;[116] in the theology of grace, the 'pure nature' theory, first questioned in our day by Fr de Lubac;[117] in ecclesiology, the assumption, now openly brought under fire, that all the authority now exercised by the Pope over the Church inheres in him intrinsically as the successor of Peter and none by implicit concession from the Church itself.[118] Respect for tradition certainly need not imply that tradition itself may not at times suffer from loss of direction or of vitality or that ecclesiastical officials may not be short-sighted, timid, or tyrannical. Nor should there be any hesitation to make the best use possible of the achievements of the secular disciplines, especially those of history, archaeology, and textual criticism, as long as full account is taken of the necessarily provisional nature of the conclusions to which the researches of their practitioners point. What I hold is essential for the theologian is that his theologizing should be an aspect of his life as a member of the Body of Christ; he needs to be under not only an academic but also a spiritual ascesis, as indeed all the Church's greatest theologians have been. And the two need not just to exist side by side but to be integrated at every level. There is, of course, no automatic way of producing theology; as Fr Lonergan emphasized, the theologian needs insight and he needs conversion, neither of which are simply the routine application of rules. And, while the guidance of the indwelling Spirit in the Church involves, as I see it, more than the fluid 'kind of family likeness' which Dr Wiles believes Christian belief and practice to retain,[119] it certainly does not give us access to an oracle. What it does is to enable us to live confidently as members of the Church, although we do not know the answers to all our problems. For we know that the answers are in the mind of the ascended Christ, even if our own understanding of them, and indeed the Church's understanding of them, is, as far as its explicit formulation is concerned, very obscure and partial.

The promise of the Lord to his Church, that the Spirit of truth would lead it into all truth is not incompatible with continual vacillations from the strait and narrow way; this should not surprise us if we remember that the grace of God respects and does not annihilate the freedom he has given us. I would suggest that the guidance of the Spirit within the Church may be conceived as analogous to the cybernetic or 'negative feed-back' controls which have become so familiar to us today, and which, while they do not prevent the behaviour of an organism or a machine from diverging from the central and balanced condition of progress and development, correct the divergences and restore the norm, so that there is never a complete collapse into chaos and the purpose of the organism or machine is maintained. If so mechanical an analogy seems inappropriate, we may remember that our bodies were full of cybernetic controls long before we recognized their existence or applied the principle to machines! It is also important to notice that the purpose of the control is, more often than not, not simply to restore a *status quo ante* but to assist a further stage of motion or development towards the attainment of the organism's goal; the stability in question is a dynamic, not a simply static one. Often there has been a period of violent turbulence and oscillation before equilibrium could be restored; obvious periods of this kind in the early Church are those that led up to the Councils of Nicaea and Chalcedon. The fact that the equilibrium is dynamic does not in any way lessen the victory which the Spirit there achieved through the often mixed motives and imperfect intentions of sinful men; nor does it mean that there were no ambiguities to be resolved and obscurities to be clarified or that there were no further problems to be faced. Fr Karl Rahner has well observed that, 'even in theology, to settle one question, even correctly, raises three new questions that remain to be settled.'[120] But, when Dr Wiles asserts that the Church 'in repudiating in practice the early church's understanding of Scripture at the behest of a modern approach to knowledge . . . has survived the element of discontinuity involved in so doing, not without difficulty but certainly without the disasters foreseen by some',[121] I can only reflect that this perhaps depends on what you consider to be a disaster. I shall deal in detail in the next chapter with the question of New Testament criticism; here I shall merely suggest that, in view of the extraordinary lack of agreement that has been achieved on even the most basic matters after a century of critical research conducted by many hundreds of highly trained and experienced scholars, one may be excused for doubting whether even now an adequate methodological technique for the study of Christian origins has been devised. Rather than repudiate the early Church's understanding of Scripture, it might seem wiser to hold the whole matter in suspense in the hope of a future, but not a premature, reconciliation. Certainly I do not think we can afford to reject totally and without more ado the notions of inspiration and canonicity. But on the wider issues of the attitude of the theologian in general, I would conclude by repeating some words that I have written elsewhere:

> The Church's tradition is a great living inheritance of thought and life, most of whose content has hitherto been undiscerned and most of whose potentialities have hitherto been unactualised. It is by bringing this great living inheritance into impact upon the world in which we live that our task towards that world will be achieved.[122]

Note

This chapter was written before the publication of Dr Wiles's lucid and informative book *What is Theology?*, which is based on introductory lectures given to students in London, Southwark, and Oxford. I have received from it valuable confirmation of the views which I have here expressed.

TWO

History and the Gospels

What is the lesson that we are to learn from this story? Surely, this: that, as in that ancient legend, Abraham was willing to destroy his dearest possession, his only son Isaac, in obedience to what he mistakenly believed to be the command of God, so we must be ready to sacrifice our most cherished convictions on the altar of Biblical criticism.

> Sermon by the Regius Professor of Hebrew in Ely Cathedral, handed down by oral tradition.

'What's the evidence?' I asked him about some new theory which he was advancing. He answered very gravely: 'It rests on something better than evidence.' I opened my eyes; and he went on as gravely: 'Conjectural emendation.'

> T. R. Glover, *Cambridge Retrospect* (1943), 73.

An oddity of the contemporary theological situation, which has been pointed out by several authors, is that theologians often seem to be far more sceptical about the historical validity of the Gospels than secular historians without any theological axe to grind.

> Hugo Meynell, *The New Theology and Modern Theologians* (1967), 133.

It is impossible to prophesy how this debate will continue; it must seem to all who contemplate it to have reached a profoundly unsatisfactory stage.

> A. R. C. Leaney, *The Pelican Guide to Modern Theology* (1970), III, 263.

I suspect . . . that the real problems with the empty tomb are theological, not historical. Unless these theological problems are allowed to come into the open, I feel like an elephant fighting a whale, unable to make effective contact with my opponents.

> Gerald O'Collins, SJ, *The Easter Jesus* (1973), 91.

1 THE POVERTY OF HISTORICAL SCEPTICISM

One of the most refreshing of recent theological works, though its significance does not seem to have been very widely recognized, is the volume entitled *Christ, Faith and History: Cambridge Studies in Christology*, which appeared under the editorship of S. W. Sykes and J. P. Clayton.[1] While the editors suggested, possibly with their tongues slightly in their cheeks, that it might be considered as in some respects a successor to the earlier Cambridge *Soundings*,[2] which appeared just ten years earlier in 1962, the contrast between the two works could hardly have been more marked. For, while they rightly said that, like the editor of *Soundings*, they were 'unable to report on anything resembling a common mind', many of the essays in the new book showed a combination of confidence and penetration which was largely lacking in the earlier work. It is true that Dr Wiles posed the question 'Does Christology rest on a mistake?' and, appealing in a rather old-fashioned way to evolution, gave the answer Yes; but he received a very effective reply from Professor Peter Baelz. It is also true that Dr J. A. T. Robinson raised the question 'Need Jesus have been perfect?' and gave the answer No; but he too was answered cogently by Mr S. W. Sykes, who remarked that the question was asked by the late J. F. Bethune-Baker as long ago as 1921. And one of the most striking features of the book is the very independent line taken by the younger contributors, who showed much more respect for traditional orthodoxy than either was shown by their elders for traditional orthodoxy or was shown by them for the views of their elders. And among their essays special importance attaches to that entitled 'The Poverty of Historical Scepticism', by Dr Peter Carnley.

Carnley opened his attack with the following words:

> One of the recurring characteristics of much twentieth-century theology is its historical scepticism. It is my thesis that this scepticism is based on poor and inadequate philosophical reasoning, that it is therefore an unjustified scepticism, and that theologies which have been conditioned by it are in need of revision.[3]

He found the roots of this kind of scepticism in the turning of the tide at the beginning of this century against the earlier preoccupation with the 'Jesus of History'. Nineteenth-century liberal Protestantism had held that it was possible, by applying the methods of scientific historical criticism, to get back behind the supernatural figure of the 'Christ of faith' to a purely human Jesus, whose total concern was with the fatherhood of God and the brotherhood of man. In reaction against this,

> Martin Kähler and Wilhelm Herrmann argued that it was a fatal error to attempt to establish the basis of faith by means of historical investigation because faith, as a complete and final commitment and not a mere tentative acceptance, must necessarily be based on something fixed and secure. Historical research was disqualified because it was 'constantly constructing afresh' and modifying the results obtained from the records.[4]

Ernst Troeltsch was called in support with his contentions

> (a) that the everpresent possibility of a future discovery of new evidence prevents us from achieving certainty in the present, and (b) that relativity in historiography is unavoidable since the historian's judgments are always conditioned by his world view.[5]

Carnley found this same assumption in the writings of Rudolf Bultmann and Paul Tillich, the latter of whom 'rejoiced in the fact that the consequent emancipation of faith from historical research constituted the "greatest contribution of historical research to systematic theology"'.[6] It is also, he pointed out, to be found, surprisingly, in protagonists of the post-Bultmannian 'new quest of the historical Jesus' and he quoted the contemporary American writer Dr John Knox as giving one of its clearest statements:

> Since even the best attested fact of the history of the past can possess no more than a very high degree of probability and since, by definition, Christian and indeed all religious faith must from the believer's point of view be absolutely certain and secure, can faith ever be said to depend upon a historical fact, no matter how well established? Faith must *know* its object in a way we cannot know a historical fact.[7]

Before following Carnley's argument further, it will be pertinent to remark on the strange way in which many of the scholars who hold to historical relativism deduce from it the strange consequence that historical scholarship makes it impossible for us to hold the traditional doctrine of the Christ of faith and leaves us with a purely human and unsupernatural Jesus. Thus, for example, Bultmann, when writing on the Gospels, rules out any supernatural event or interpretation on allegedly critical grounds, and Knox will describe Jesus as divine only with the stipulation that divinity is to be re-defined as 'a transformed, a redeemed and redemptive, *humanity*.'[8] It is, however, clear that, if historical relativism is true, historical arguments are altogether irrelevant to questions about the life of Jesus. They cannot be used to prove that Jesus was what traditional orthodoxy has held him to be, but they cannot be used to prove that he was *not* what traditional orthodoxy has held him to be either. Historical relativism is, of course, incompatible with the view that the Jesus of history can be recovered by critical historical research. It is therefore incompatible with liberal Protestantism. It would also be incompatible with any Catholic Christology which claimed to be based solely on historical research, though I doubt whether this has ever existed. But, as I pointed out in an earlier work,

> it is perfectly possible, and intellectually respectable, to hold, on grounds of faith, that, while conclusive evidence for some particular historical event would destroy one's faith, such evidence will never, in fact, be forthcoming and that, if at any time it appears to have been produced, there must be further evidence, not yet at hand, which will point to a different conclusion.[9]

The late Austin Farrer put the positive aspect of this argument when he wrote:

> What Christians find in Christ through faith inclines them at certain points to accept with regard to him testimony about matter of fact which would be inconclusive if offered with regard to any other man. The Christian who refused to take that step would in my opinion be pedantic and irrational, like a man who required the same guarantees for trusting a friend which he would require for trusting a stranger. Thus it is possible through faith and evidence together, and through neither alone to believe that Christ really and corporeally rose from the dead, not merely that his death on the cross had a supernatural silver lining significant for our salvation.[10]

And Mr S. W. Sykes, from a slightly different angle, makes substantially the same point when he writes: 'I am inclined to think that the consequences of a doctrinal argument could well be applicable to history.'[11]

Now, in view of the tremendous influence which Bultmann has exercised on students of the New Testament through his programme of 'demythologizing', it is essential to recognize that his rejection as inauthentic of every supernatural element in the recorded words and acts of Jesus rests in the last resort not upon Biblical scholarship at all, but upon a preconceived and consistently applied dogma about the impossibility of the supernatural. He has made this perfectly plain in a well-known essay on 'New Testament and Mythology', which initiates the symposium *Kerygma and Myth*. 'It is impossible', he writes, 'to use electric light and the wireless and to avail ourselves of modern medical and surgical discoveries, and at the same time to believe in the New Testament world of daemons and spirits.'[12] And it is important to notice that what is conclusive for him is not that the outlook of the New Testament has been shown to be false – he nowhere attempts to prove that – but that it is incompatible with the outlook of secularized twentieth-century urbanized man.

> What matters [he writes] is the world view which men imbibe from their environment, and it is science which determines that view of the world through the school, the press, the wireless, the cinema, and all the other fruits of technical progress.[13]

It would, however, be wrong to suppose that Bultmann's sole reason for rejecting the supernatural from the Gospels is his subservience to what he supposes to be the psychological conditioning of men and women by a scientifically and technologically dominated cultural environment. Two other influences have been equally, if not more, strong upon his thinking. The first of these, as Dr R. P. C. Hanson has pointed out, derives from Lutheran theology. 'Strongest of all the motives for historical scepticism in the minds of New Testament scholars', he writes, 'has been the Lutheran distrust of the search for an objective basis of faith. It should be remembered that the vast majority of early Form Critics were Lutherans.'[14] The other great influence is that of Heideggerian existentialist philosophy. This is perfectly clear from any of the three leading discussions of Bultmann's thought as a whole, those of Owen, Schmithals, and Malet.[15] The common view that Bultmann's scepticism is the result of unprejudiced literary and historical criticism is simply due to the fact that most British New Testament scholars are not interested in Lutheran theology or existentialist philosophy. The fact is, however, that Bultmann is committed theologically and philosophically to the view that the purpose of the Gospels is not to convey to us information about the words and acts of Jesus but to provide the preacher with material for bringing his hearers to an authentic self-understanding. As Dr Austin Van Harvey has written:

> It is just because the New Testament writers were so concerned with

the appropriation of a new understanding of existence that makes it possible to translate the Gospel into existentialist terms, because existentialist philosophy, Bultmann believes, has developed the most adequate conceptuality for understanding human existence. It makes clear that the basic problem of man is not what he believes but how he responds to life, whether he does so authentically or inauthentically. . . . Existentialist philosophy, to be sure, does not prescribe any one concrete ideal of life, but it does show that men can only achieve authenticity by resolution and decision, and thus it helps to make what the Bible is talking about intelligible.[16]

Harvey goes on to show that the great problem for Bultmann is, on his own grounds, to show that Jesus as an actual person is necessary for the attainment of authentic self-understanding. Bultmann does, in fact, assert the historical existence of Jesus and, while dismissing the resurrection as a myth, holds fast to the crucifixion as a real historical event, but it is difficult to see that this is compatible with his general theological position or how it can be confidently affirmed in consistency with his historical relativism. His disciples Schubert M. Ogden and Fritz Buri seem to be more consistent, with their assertion that 'the validity of Bultmann's entire project depends on showing how the belief *in the cross and the resurrection* may be interpreted not as objective events but as ways of expressing an understanding of existence.'[17] Buri, it is well known, demands not only the demythologizing but also the dekerygmatizing of the gospel! In any case, the fact remains that for Bultmann and his school the elimination of the supernatural from the Gospels is not a result of their Biblical study; it is its programmatic basis.

I shall return later to a further discussion of Dr Carnley's important essay. At the moment it may be interesting to recall the reactions to current New Testament scholarship of experts who have not been trained simply in the Biblical field.

2 JUDGEMENT FROM OUTSIDE

In a previous work[18] I discussed at length the judgement made by the distinguished Roman historian Mr A. N. Sherwin-White in his Sarum Lectures *Roman Society and Roman Law in the New Testament*.[19] Here I will merely quote a few sentences from his work:

> It is astonishing that while Graeco-Roman historians have been growing in confidence, the twentieth-century study of the Gospel narratives, starting from no less promising material, has taken so gloomy a turn in the development of form-criticism that the more advanced exponents of it apparently maintain – so far as an amateur can understand the matter – that the historical Christ is unknowable and the history of his mission cannot be written. This seems very curious when one compares the case for the best-known contemporary of Christ, who like Christ is a well-documented figure – Tiberius Caesar. The story of his reign is known from four sources. . . . These disagree amongst themselves in the wildest possible fashion. . . . But this does not prevent the belief that the material of Tacitus can be used to write a history of Tiberius. The divergences between the synoptic gospels, or between them and the fourth gospel, are no worse than the contradictions in the Tiberius material. . . .

He adds, significantly:

> What to an ancient historian is most surprising in the basic assumptions of form-criticism of the extremer sort, is the presumed tempo of the development of the didactic myths. . . .
> It can be maintained that those who had a passionate interest in the story of Christ, even if their interest in events was parabolic and didactic rather than historical, would not be led by that very fact to pervert and utterly destroy the historical kernel of their material. It can also be suggested that it would be no harder for the Disciples and their immediate successors to uncover detailed narratives of the actions and sayings of Christ within their closed community, then it was for Herodotus and Thucydides to establish the story of the great events of 520–480 B.C.[20]

Perhaps Mr Sherwin-White's surprise would have been less if he had taken account of the fact that the scepticism of the form-critics was the result not of their study of the Gospels but of antecedently held dogma.

In my previous work I made some passing references to the writings of C. S. Lewis on the general credibility of the supernatural and I gave an extended discussion of the testimony borne by Dorothy L. Sayers as a result of her experience in putting the gospel material on the stage in her play-sequence *The Man born to be King*. It seemed to me that one very useful method (not, of course, the *only* method) of testing the authenticity of the material and the consistency of orthodox Christology with it would be to see whether and to what extent it was *actable* on the stage, since experienced actors develop an immediate sense of anything that lacks coherence in itself or involves impossible characterization. And it seemed to me of added importance that Miss Sayers' final text was worked out in co-operation with the actors themselves and was not, like so much writing about the Gospels, the product simply of the lecture-room and the study. Miss Sayers' experience was affirmative on both counts: the alleged inconsistencies were mostly imaginary, and the material was fully compatible with orthodox (but only with orthodox) Christology. These conclusions would, of course, be unwelcome to many Biblical scholars, by whom the incoherence of the narratives was taken for granted and whose Christology was a mixture of adoptionism and kenoticism. I was, nevertheless, surprised to be taken to task by one reviewer of my book for assuming that the views of outsiders such as Lewis and Miss Sayers could possibly be relevant to the assessment of the gospel material. For, whatever else the Gospels are not, they are certainly literature; they might therefore seem to provide legitimate matter for professional literary critics. The incident does, however, illustrate the extent to which the study of the New Testament has got out of step with literary and historical scholarship in general. I shall therefore make no apology for referring to a paper on 'Modern Theology and Biblical Criticism', which was originally read by Lewis in a theological college in 1959 and was published posthumously in 1967 in the volume *Christian Reflections*.[21]

Writing as an 'educated, but not theologically educated outsider', Lewis began by remarking on the oddness of 'a theology which denies the historicity of nearly everything in the Gospels to which Christian life and affections and thought have been fastened for nearly two millennia – which either denies the miraculous altogether or, more strangely, after swallowing the camel of the Resurrection, strains at such gnats as the feeding of the multitudes.' 'If offered to the uneducated man', he said, '[it] can produce only one or other of two effects. It will make him a Roman Catholic or an atheist.' (If Lewis had been writing after the Second Vatican Council he might have been surprised at the extent to which many Roman Catholic scholars, when released from the former tight grip of the Holy Office, have vied with their Anglican and Protestant brethren in stripping the supernatural elements from the Gospels.) He went on to commiserate with the priest who found himself forced into the late medieval conception of two truths, 'a picture-truth which can be preached to the people, and an esoteric truth for use among the clergy. But this', he said, 'is your headache, not mine.'

> The undermining of the old orthodoxy [Lewis continued] has been mainly the work of divines engaged in New Testament criticism. The authority of experts in that discipline is the authority in deference to which we are asked to give up a huge mass of beliefs shared in common by the early Church, the Fathers, the Middle Ages, the Reformers, and even the nineteenth century. I want to explain what it is that makes me sceptical about this authority. . . . First then, whatever these men may be as Biblical critics, I distrust them as critics. They seem to me to lack literary judgment, to be imperceptive about the very quality of the texts they are reading.[22]

This, Lewis admitted, might seem a strange charge to bring against men who had been steeped in the New Testament books all their lives. But this, he said, might be just the trouble; they had seriously read nothing else. 'If [a man] tells me that something in a Gospel is legend or romance, I want to know how many legends and romances he has read, how well his palate is trained in detecting them by the flavour; not how many years he has spent on that Gospel.' He went on to give three examples of this.

The first example was drawn from an article by W. Lock in the *New Commentary on Holy Scripture*,[23] in which the view is mentioned that the Fourth Gospel is 'a spiritual romance', 'a poem not a history', and that it is to be judged by the same canons as Nathan's parable, the Book of Jonah, *Paradise Lost*, 'or, more exactly, Pilgrim's Progress'.[24] Lewis found it difficult to control his contempt for the scholar who could lump together such disparate works and equate the Fourth Gospel with any of them.[25] 'After a man has said that,' he asked, 'why need one attend to anything else he says about any book in the world?' His own view of the Fourth Gospel he expressed as follows:

I have been reading poems, romances, vision-literature, legends, myths all my life. I know what they are like. I know that not one of them is like this. Of this text [sc., the Fourth Gospel] there are only two possible views. Either this is reportage – though it may no doubt contain errors – pretty close up to the facts; nearly as close as Boswell. Or else, some unknown writer in the second century, without known predecessors or successors, suddenly anticipated the whole technique of modern, novelistic, realistic narrative. If it is untrue, it must be narrative of that kind. The reader who doesn't see this has simply not learned to read.[26]

Lewis's second example was taken from a passage of Bultmann's in which the German Scholar, convinced in advance that predictions of the Lord's return in glory are older than those of the passion, described as 'unassimilated' two gospel passages which are plainly a unity. The third example, also from Bultmann, consists of an astonishing statement that the personality of Jesus has no importance for the kerygma of either Paul or John or, indeed for the tradition of the earliest Church. 'I begin to fear', Lewis wrote, 'that by *personality* Dr Bultmann means what I should call impersonality: what you'd get in a D.N.B. article or an obituary or a Victorian *Life and Letters of Yeshua Bar-Yosef* in three volumes with photographs.'

These men [he continued] ask me to believe they can read between the lines of the old texts; the evidence is their obvious inability to read (in any sense worth discussing) the lines themselves. They claim to see fern-seed and can't see an elephant ten yards away in broad daylight.[27]

Lewis's next point was concerned with the claim that 'the real behaviour and purpose and teaching of Christ came very rapidly to be misunderstood and mis-represented by his followers, and has been recovered or exhumed only by modern scholars.' This kind of theory, he observed, had been common in other branches of literature; he gave the example of Plato, who was held to have been consistently misunderstood by his successors throughout the ages and only rediscovered, as an English Hegelian of the type of T. H. Green, by Jowett and his friends. But, he said,

The idea that any man or writer should be opaque to those who lived in the same culture, spoke the same language, shared the same habitual imagery and unconscious assumptions, and yet be transparent to those who have none of these advantages, is in my opinion preposterous. There is an *a priori* improbability in it which almost no argument and no evidence could counterbalance.[28]

Lewis's third objection was concerned with the *a priori* assumption of the impossibility of the supernatural which is common to many Biblical critics. This, he rightly said, is a purely philosophical question, on which Biblical scholars as such have no more right to be heard than anyone else. And his fourth objection was an amusing one, based on his own experience of the speculations of reviewers about the genesis of his own works; from this he concluded that attempts to reconstruct the genetic process behind a work simply from the characteristics of the work itself are often very plausible – and almost invariably wrong.

Lewis recognized that the comparison of the great Biblical scholars with journalistic reviewers might seem to be lacking in respect to the former body, but he had two answers to this. First, that while the *learning* of the scholars is worthy of respect, their *judgement* seems often to be faulty. And secondly, that they labour under quite colossal disadvantages.

The superiority in judgment and diligence which you are going to attribute to the Biblical critics will have to be almost superhuman if it is to offset the fact that they are everywhere faced with customs, language, race-characteristics, class-characteristics, a religious background, habits of composition, and basic assumptions, which no scholarship will ever enable any man alive to know as surely and intimately and instinctively as the reviewer can know mine. And for the very same reason, remember, the Biblical critics, whatever reconstructions they devise, can never be crudely proved wrong. St Mark is dead. When they meet St Peter there will be more pressing matters to discuss.[29]

Finally, Lewis gave what he described as his own account of 'the hopes he secretly cherishes and the naive reflections with which he sometimes keeps his spirits up.' First, he said, he did not expect the present school of theological thought to be everlasting. He gave examples from literary scholarship, Shakespearean, Homeric, and Arthurian, and from the history of philosophy, to show how very rapidly fashions in intellectual theories can change. 'Everywhere, except in theology, there has been a vigorous growth of scepticism about scepticism itself. We can't keep ourselves from murmuring *multa renascentur quae jam cecidere*.'[30] Secondly, he remarked that, when hypotheses are linked in series, the final probability is much less than that of any of the individual members of it. He repudiated the suggestion that he was, in any pejorative sense, a fundamentalist and pointed out that his objections to the sceptical views were all based on argument. 'I do not wish', he said, 'to reduce the sceptical element in your minds. I am only suggesting that it need not be reserved exclusively for the New Testament and the Creeds. Try doubting something else.'[31]

I have devoted this large amount of space to Lewis's paper because it exposes so clearly and refreshingly the dogmatic prejudice and the questionable argumentation on which the most influential type of New Testament scholarship rests. I should not, however, wish to give the impression that all New Testament scholars of eminence are as sceptical as the Bultmannians and neo-Bultmannians. In my earlier book *The Secularisation of Christianity* I have given copious quotations from the work of the very independent scholar Dr R. M. Grant in which he reveals himself as being even more sceptical about the conclusions of the sceptical New Testament scholars than he is about those of the orthodox ones. Again, Dr C. F. D. Moule's book *The Phenomenon of the New Testament*[32] is as original and forceful a defence of the orthodox view of the life and teaching of Jesus as one could well find. Again, the writings of Scandinavian scholars such as H. Riesenfeld and B. Gerhardsson[33] give impressive defences of the substantial authenticity of the gospel records. And Fr Xavier Léon-Dufour, SJ, while accepting what one might describe as the establishment approach to the New Testament, has convincingly argued for the traditional interpretation of the gospel presentation of Jesus.[34] Nevertheless the convention persists (for it is really only a convention) in most theological faculties and many seminaries that although the supernatural elements in the Gospels, or some of them, may conceivably be authentic, it will be better for practical purposes to assume that they are not and to base whatever religion one can on the supposition that they are, if not certainly spurious, at least irrelevant. Thus, it is felt, one can hold up one's head in academic society and also be safe from the hazards of historical research. For – and this is the basic dogma – whether they are in fact authentic or spurious, it cannot ultimately matter one way or the other which they are. This is, of course, a highly satisfactory attitude for the committed Bultmannite, though he would perhaps prefer that the supernatural elements had been definitely proved to be what, as a twentieth-century man he is convinced they must be, namely certainly spurious; for then he would be delivered from the ever-present danger of relying on past events instead of achieving self-understanding as a result of his confrontation with existential demands from the pulpit each Sunday morning. As Dr Hugo Meynell has written:

> One sometimes feels not only that some theologians have retreated to a position which they have prepared in advance against the contingency that the gospels may eventually turn out to be totally unreliable as historical documents; but that they are so delighted with this position that they are now as averse to arguments for their overall historicity as they were once to the idea that they might be inaccurate in the smallest matter of detail.[35]

In any case, given (*dato sed non concesso*) that the supernatural aspects of the Gospels are not historically reliable, it is very difficult to find out just how the Bultmannites think they got into the gospel narratives. Some still appear to hold that they depend on the *Sitz im Leben* of the primitive Church and reflect its problems; that is to say, that when the Church was faced with some practical problem of Christian life it decided what it would like the answer to be and then invented a story in order to say that this answer had in fact been given by Jesus. The difficulties in this view have often been pointed out; there is much in the Gospels that seems quite independent of the special life-situation of the primitive Church, it is psychologically difficult to suppose that the Church was more concerned to invent fictions about the words and acts of Jesus than to ascertain what in fact he said and did, and some of the reconstructions are in any case highly speculative. As Dr Humphrey Palmer has trenchantly enquired:

> Were the first Christians adept at thinking up stories-of-Jesus to suit a situation in their Church? Form-critics do not show this, but take it for granted in all their reasonings. These reasonings do, however, show how adept form-critics are in thinking up early-Church-situations to suit stories of Jesus.[36]

3 MYTHS AND MYTHOPOEIA

The *Sitz-im-Leben* theory has not been abandoned, but it has been largely supplemented, if not actually displaced, by theories which attribute the supernatural element in the Gosepels not to conscious fabrication but to an alleged mythmaking activity in the primitive Church. It is in fact difficult to find out just how this activity is conceived. Sometimes it is suggested that mythological accounts were produced because that was the only way in which people knew how to write at the time. Thus Dr D. E. Nineham has written, *à propos* of the Nativity narratives:

> I want to suggest that it was basically these same questions [sc. the questions about Jesus which men have asked down the centuries] which preoccupied the earliest Christians, and that in a sense the Christmas stories were their way of answering them. Being people of a different period and of a different sort from us, they did not react to such questions as we do, or at any rate as the theologians among us tend to do. They responded by producing poetry and telling stories. . . . I do not mean to suggest that any of them deliberately sat down and made up the Christmas stories as answers to consciously-formulated questions. But equally these stories are not even attempts at sober reporting in our modern sense.
>
> To begin with, they were not really the products of individuals; they are the expressions of the *corporate* experience of Christ as it developed during the years after his lifetime. . . .

Nineham goes on to give two specific instances:

> For instance when they tell us that although Jesus had a human mother he had God – almost literally – for a father, this is the expression of their faith that, although his was a genuinely human life, what it embodied was more than human goodness and courage, even at their highest; its quality and effects were due to direct initiative on God's part. God had been uniquely active in it and revealed through it. Or again, when they talk of the Christ-child being taken down to Egypt and rescued from it, as the children of Israel had been before him, or when they describe the visit of the Magi under the guidance of a miraculous star, we are given a sort of distillation of their belief that in

77

Jesus all previous history, Jewish or gentile, found its fulfilment or condemnation (in the case of the Magi, it is not quite clear which).[37]

It is perhaps tactless to ask how Dr Nineham knows all this, but in any case there is involved a serious question of logic. There is nothing logically impossible in the events having happened as recorded, however distasteful this possibility may be to the mind of that useful theoretical construct, modern man. It is also logically possible that, in order to express some deep theological truth mythically or symbolically, the same kind of language would have been used as would have been used to describe events that had literally occurred. But, this being so, we cannot find out from the character of the narrative whether it was written as myth or as history; it will be the same in either case. St Luke tells us, in the opening words of his Gospel, that he had taken pains to verify from eye-witnesses that the material which he had incorporated in his Gospel was accurate; he certainly did not profess to be collecting edifying myths. It is, of course, logically possible that he was mistaken in his judgements just as it is logically possible that he was telling downright lies; but who are we to say this, unless we are convinced on preconceived philosophical grounds that this was the case? St Luke had access to far more material than we have and he was far better able than we are to understand the intentions of his informants. As C. S. Lewis said, in a passage that I have already quoted, 'the idea that any man or writer should be opaque to those who lived in the same culture, spoke the same language, shared the same habitual imagery and unconscious assumptions, and yet be transparent to those who have none of these advantages' is really 'preposterous'. It was with thoughts such as these in mind that I put to Dr Nineham the following question:

> Supposing that the early Christians had wished to tell us *not only* that 'though his [sc. Jesus'] was a genuinely human life, what it embodied was more than etc. . . .' *but also* that he was conceived without a human father in the way that the Church has traditionally believed, what kind of language would they have used in order to do this and how would their account have differed from that which we find in the Gospels?

Nineham's reply was revealing:

> Not only do I think that, if the Evangelists had meant to convey all that Professor Mascall suggests, they would have used exactly the same language they do use: I have no doubt that by the time these stories

came to be written down, the Evangelists did in fact believe all that Professor Mascall has in mind.[38]

What is being suggested, therefore, is that the original composers of the narratives, or the groups in which they took shape, may have known that they were telling mythical stories which had little or no historical foundation, but that by the time that the stories reached the compilers of the Gospels these latter had no suspicion of their real character and took them to be truthful accounts of historical events. This seems to me to be most implausible, for I cannot believe that Dr Nineham has had access to information that was denied to St Luke.

However, it is perhaps going too far to say that Nineham was convinced of the mythical character of the narratives. What is clear is that he thought that it is of very little importance whether they are mythical or not. He himself said that the article that provoked my enquiry was addressed chiefly to the many Christians who 'do not find it possible to accept the tradition *in toto* as sober history'.

My meditation [he said] was designed primarily for them and my point was that even where they cannot accept the tradition as entirely historically trustworthy, it can have a great deal of value and significance for them. For they can recognise that in the course of transmission it became the vehicle of insights which, in spite of their legendary form, are genuine insights because they reflect faithfully certain aspects of the total impact Christ made upon his followers both during and after the days of his flesh.[39]

Now to have carried one's listeners or readers to this point might be a useful preliminary to a fuller exposition of the Faith. It is, however, clear that Nineham saw no such further step to be important or even desirable, since he wrote as follows:

I believe the great majority of Christians today instinctively recognise the true character of these stories. They are well aware that in them they are dealing with something akin to poetry. . . .
Consciously or unconsciously, [Christian leaders] produce the effect of increasing guilt by suggesting that it is only those who accept these stories as completely historical who deserve to be called true Christians.
I would ask them to reverse their attitude. Release people from such feelings of guilt. In fact *it is not possible in these stories to disentangle the history from the poetry; it would be wrong even to try.* Help people to see

that *that does not matter*; the truth of Christianity does not stand or fall with the complete biographical accuracy of these stories. Then you will be able to help them – and very likely they will be able to help you – *to ask the right questions of these stories* and to plumb more fully their immense profundity.[40]

The qualifications in the phrases 'completely historical' and 'complete biographical accuracy' might conceivably be taken as indicating that it was necessary to preserve at least some minimal core of historicity. I doubt, however, whether their insertion shows more than Dr Nineham's habitual caution in protecting himself from the natural implications of his words. For he has told us in the same breath that it would not only be superfluous but would be positively wrong to try to disentangle this core of history from the poetic setting in which it is embedded. 'That', he says, 'does not matter'; to do this would not be 'to ask the right questions'. It is not, I think, unjust to accuse Nineham of looking on the question of historicity as entirely irrelevant, but for further substantiation of this accusation I must refer the reader to my book *The Secularisation of Christianity*.[41]

One of the problems which the mythologizing school of New Testament scholars raise but to which they seem unable to give an agreed solution is that of the way in which the mythopoeic process is supposed to have operated. Nineham seems to hold that it was a process largely akin to the writing of poetry, though he holds in addition, as we have seen, that it was the only literary technique available. Others have held that it was the result of a violent charismatic experience undergone by the first disciples immediately after the crucifixion, in consequence of which, in their attempts to recall the previous acts and words of Jesus, they had become unable to distinguish between fact and fiction. Some appear to look upon this mythopoeic frenzy as persisting until the time of the compilation of the Gospels. Dr Wolfhart Pannenberg, if I understand him correctly, holds that the resurrection of Jesus from the dead was a real event in the physical world and not just an experience in the minds of the disciples, but that it coloured their purported recollections of his earthly life so vividly as to render the gospel records of very dubious historicity.[42] And even scholars whose personal religion is traditionally orthodox seem frequently to fall almost somnambulistically into a sceptical attitude to gospel material as soon as they are on duty. Thus we find a distinguished New Testament scholar remarking quite casually, in reference to the stories of the Lord's temptations, that they are of such a kind as to suggest (except on the somewhat clumsy and tasteless view that Jesus was in the habit of retailing his private religious experiences to others) that they had been formed in the tradition of the Church as a result of later reflection upon the person and work of Jesus as a whole, and as expressions of that faith in him as Son of God, and of that understanding of him, which had been arrived at through his resurrection and what had followed it.[43]

Why, we may not unnaturally wonder, is it so 'clumsy and tasteless' to suppose that Jesus would speak to his intimate friends about his private religious experiences, especially when these were of profound significance both for his life's work and for their understanding of it?

I must make it plain at this point that I do not want in the least degree to ignore the obvious fact that in the formation of the Church's tradition the events of the Lord's pre-crucifixion life will be seen as organically related to the stupendous act of the resurrection in which it culminated and that in the accounts of these events commentary and interpretation will inevitably be embodied. We must also remember that the ancient world knew neither parentheses nor footnotes and that everything had to be incorporated into the text. Furthermore, conventions about the use in narration of direct and indirect speech were less rigid than ours, though ours are perhaps less rigid than we sometimes imagine. Nor need we be disconcerted if in the gospel account of some saying or action of the Lord there is interwoven the meaning which only later became clear to the Church under the guidance of the Spirit. 'His disciples', we are told of one such instance, 'did not understand this at first; but when Jesus was glorified, then they remembered that this had been written of him and had been done to him.'[44] But it is very different from this to assume that anything that looks like a prophecy of the passion and resurrection must be a mere *vaticinium post eventum* and that any recorded words and acts of Jesus that imply a supernatural aspect of his being must be the outcome of uncritical excitement deriving from the disciples' 'Easter experience' and have no basis in solid fact. Here, as so often, the essential point has been made by Dr R. M. Grant:

The Gospels are not simply the product of the Church. (1) Individuals, not communities, write books. (2) The evangelists regarded their function as that of bearing witness to Jesus Christ, not that of composing edifying fiction. There is no reason to suppose – though one form-critic supposed it – that there was ever a special class of 'story-tellers' in the Church. At the same time, the gospels were produced within the Church. They were not produced simply to 'meet the Church's needs' in various historical situations. The evangelists were not trying to 'make the gospel relevant'. They believed that it was relevant because they had accepted the call of Jesus. Though they inevitably wrote what they believed was meaningful to themselves and to others, they were not free to explain the apostolic testimony away.

This means that the gospels must be regarded as largely reliable witnesses to the life, death and resurrection of Jesus, and that the attitudes of the evangelists cannot be completely separated from the materials they are transmitting. For example, Christians had disputes about keeping the Sabbath; they had them because Jesus had treated the Sabbath with considerable freedom. They were concerned about divorce because Jesus had been so concerned. The life of the Church was not completely disjoined from the life of Jesus.[45]

4 THE LOGIC OF GOSPEL CRITICISM

An important and original, but much neglected, work is Dr Humphrey Palmer's *Logic of Gospel Criticism*,[46] which was published in 1968. Professor Kenneth Grayston indicated its significance in the following words:

> Generations of New Testament students have learnt conventional information about textual criticism and the synoptic problem. Much of it must have been false or misleading, and all of it insecurely based. As soon as anyone attempts a serious study of these two subjects, he learns that the ablest practitioners of them are full of doubt – the textual critics weighed down by the mass of material and the lack of agreement about its interpretation, the source critics by failing confidence in the importance of their conclusions or indeed in the conclusions themselves. At this painful moment in the history of critical study, Dr Palmer has offered an account of the logical processes implied in it. He has no difficulty in exposing the frailty of much stock reasoning and accepted opinion.[47]

This being so, it may seem surprising that Dr Palmer's book has received so little attention. This is not, I think, entirely due to the unpalatable character of his conclusions to many Biblical scholars; it is also due to the formidable appearance of his pages, packed as many of them are with symbols, diagrams and closely argued logical analyses. In actual fact, his technique is intelligible to anyone who has even the most elementary acquaintance with symbolic notation,[48] and it is precisely on account of his logical analyses that the author is able to substantiate his charges against much recent New Testament criticism. Briefly stated, his case is that, in investigating any problem of either source- or form-criticism it is essential to formulate all the solutions that are logically possible and that failure to do this will almost certainly result in the belief that one has eliminated all the possible views except one, when in fact one has overlooked other views which are equally possible and one of which may in fact be the correct one. 'As long ago as 1951', Grayston remarks, 'Butler[49] showed that the standard argument for the priority of Mark was a confidence trick, not a logical proof. This', he adds, 'does not disprove the priority of Mark, though more recently W. R. Farmer has pressed home the advantage in favour of another conclusion; but we ought to be aware of what can and what cannot be demonstrated.'[50] Of particular significance is Palmer's quiet remark that 'particular bits of evidence are sometimes said to confirm a hypothesis, meaning that they fit in with it. The trouble is that the same details may also fit in with some other hypothesis.[51] It is this fallacy, as I have pointed out elsewhere, that vitiates much of the argument in Dr Martin Werner's *Formation of Christian Dogma*;[52] Palmer points out how frequently it is to be found in the writings of Biblical scholars. On the documentary basis of the synoptic Gospels his remarks are comparatively mild, though unenthusiastic: 'The pedigree of the gospels remains unsettled because the arguments and evidence are insufficient to settle it.'[53] But – and here I quote from a summary of his argument by Professor H. P. Owen:

he reserves his sternest strictures for Form-criticism to which he objects on at least four grounds. First we have no direct access to oral tradition; so that we have no means of checking our theories of its development (pp. 175–6). Secondly, to distinguish between different units of tradition 'is not *ipso facto* to deny that they go back to Jesus and his followers' (p. 176). Thirdly, we cannot judge the reliability of the gospel material in its present literary form by an appeal to rules derived from the study of other oral traditions (pp. 180–1, 183). Lastly, the assertion that the primitive Church had various reasons (for example apologetic ones) for transmitting the tradition about Jesus does not entail the assertion that the tradition is unauthentic.[54]

Owen asserted – rightly, in my opinion – that '[Palmer's] book ought to be read by all New Testament scholars', but very few of them seem to have taken his advice. He is also right, I think, in regretting that Palmer did not give more actual illustrations of his arguments from the gospel texts and that he did not disclose how much he himself thought we can in fact know about the life and teaching of Jesus. Nevertheless, his work is admirable as a disinfectant and a therapeutic. I will close this discussion simply by quoting a few of the gentle but pointed observations which he makes in the course of his work.

A century and more of close study has not led to general agreement on gospel relationships. One explanation of this prolonged disagreement is that critics have not yet agreed what is to count as evidence. Another explanation is that the indications, though real, are contradictory: that the pedigree is 'mixed' [127f.].

The new convert does not tell his message to one person and then forget it, like a telegraph boy. He keeps on telling people, and hearing others tell. Each telling would fix the story more firmly in his mind, and widen the circle of those who knew it and could check mistakes [182].

Consideration of the general possibilities of oral development has led some form-critics to 'radical', i.e. somewhat sceptical, conclusions about the Gospel stories. I have shown that more 'conservative' conclusions could be reached by similar arguments. This suggests that the result is not determined by the arguments, but rather by the assumptions we make when applying them. If we take it for granted that early Christians would behave like telegraph operators, camp-fire raconteurs, or Boy Scouts standing in a line, we shall not place much reliance on the stories which finally got written down.

It is sometimes said that we do not know Jesus, but only what early Christians said about him. It would be better to say, that what we can know about him depends on what we think of them [183f.].

And finally, commenting on this statement by R. Bultmann and K. Kundsinn:

Form criticism begins with the realisation that the tradition contained in the Synoptic Gospels originally consisted of separate units, which were joined together editorially by the evangelists. Form criticism is therefore concerned to distinguish these units of tradition, and to discover their earliest form and origin in the life of the early Christian community.

Palmer writes:

Work along these lines has now been going on for nearly half a century. Bultmann, surveying in 1962 the progress of the movement he had helped to found, claimed that 'the soundness of Form-Criticism has been demonstrated in recent years, since it has served, and still continues to serve, as the presupposition of further research.' Unfortunately, it is quite possible for research along a certain line to be carried on even though the presuppositions on which it is based are in fact *un*sound. Where the results obtained are not open to any independent verification or check, the soundness of the method used in obtaining them can be decided only by analysis of the arguments involved, and of the assumptions which those arguments require [175].

It is this analysis, Palmer tells us, that he has tried to pursue. His judgement is confirmed by these remarks of Dr Birger Gerhardsson, who belongs to the very independent Scandinavian school of Biblical scholars:

There is no doubt that this insensitivity to criticism [sc. of the form-critics] is dependent in no small measure on this fact of their arguing in a circle. The form-critics build their own house, and consolidate their own tradition. It is easy to defend a tradition, if, when discussing the situation of the early Church, one be allowed to argue from one's own concept of the character of the gospel material, and to meet theories on the origins of the gospel material from one's own notion of the situation in the early Church. It is perhaps a little unjust to caricature the most typical representatives of the form-critical school in this way, but the caricature is not without justification. It has in point of fact been remarked that form-criticism has begun to stagnate – an observation made by *inter alia* Conzelmann and Iber.[55]

And indeed it can hardly fail to occur to any independent observer that, in spite of the immense number of its practitioners and the vast quantity of their writings, form-criticism has produced no substantial agreement on the basic questions of the character and reliability of the gospel material, beyond a general consensus that anything redolent of the supernatural, in either the words or the deeds of Jesus, cannot be historical but must be ascribed to the mythopoeic fervour of the primitive Church. And this consensus, as we have seen, is not really the outcome of critical study at all, but of a dogmatic assumption and presupposition adopted before the critical study began. There can hardly ever have been, in any branch of academic research, so colossal an enterprise productive of such meagre results. One can hardly avoid suspecting that the reason must lie in a radical defect of method. Mr E. I. Watkin has commented on the strange contrast between students of Buddhism and of Christianity in their attitude to evidence:

> Scholars . . . agree, justifiably in view of the tenacity of oral tradition, to accept as certainly authentic Buddha's teaching of the four noble truths and the eightfold path of release. And the tenets ascribed to Mahavira are also accepted as authentic. Nevertheless, although acts and teaching of Jesus are contained in Gospels composed when his apostolic disciples and closely related members of his family were still living and ruling the Church, eminent contemporary scholars pronounce the Gospel narrative the invention of the primitive community, who to all intents and purposes invented Jesus. Such gross inconsistency is not scholarship but bigoted anti-Christian prejudice masquerading as such.[56]

This is forceful speaking, but here is the same point made more mildly by another philosopher, Fr Joseph J. Sikora, SJ:

> In fact much of the knowledge gained in the current movement of Scripture study is still radically hypothetical, frequently resting on methodological canons themselves susceptible to questioning and further refinement.[57]

5 THE WRONG TOOL?

The most recent technique that has been introduced into the field of New Testament studies in an attempt to get beyond the critical impasse is that of 'redaction-criticism', whose proponents see it as providing a necessary supplement to both literary or source-criticism and form-criticism. Dr Norman Perrin of Chicago, who is one of its most enthusiastic practitioners, writes about it as follows:

> Redaction criticism is the most recent of the three disciplines to have become a self-conscious method of enquiry. It grew out of form criticism, and it presupposes and continues the procedures of the earlier discipline while extending and intensifying certain of them. The redaction critic investigates how smaller units — both simple and composite — from the oral tradition or from written sources were put together to form larger complexes, and he is especially interested in the formation of the Gospels as finished products. Redaction criticism is concerned with the interaction between an inherited tradition and a later interpretive point of view.[58]

I am not concerned here with the method as a whole; in Perrin's words, it 'burst into full flower immediately after the Second World War in Germany',[59] and its three founders were Günther Bornkamm, Hans Conzelmann and Willi Marxsen. It is obviously a legitimate study for anyone to whom it appears to offer prospects of success. I am, however, very much concerned with the principles on which it is now avowedly conducted, and in particular with those that are invoked in order to discriminate between authentic and inauthentic utterances attributed in the Gospels to Jesus himself. These appear to have been formulated independently by Dr Perrin and Dr R. H. Fuller, though Ernst Käsemann can also be quoted in their support.[60]

> First and most important [writes Perrin], we have the criterion of 'distinctiveness' (Fuller) or 'dissimilarity' (Perrin): material may be ascribed to Jesus only if it can be shown to be distinctive of him, which usually will mean dissimilar to known tendencies in Judaism before him or the church after him. . . . Then we have, secondly, the 'cross-section method' (Fuller) or 'criterion of multiple attestation' (Perrin): material may be accepted which is found in a multiplicity of sources or forms of tradition, provided always that this multiple attestation is not

due to the influence of some widespread church practice such as the Eucharist. Thirdly and lastly, we have the criterion of 'consistency' (Fuller) or 'coherence' (Perrin): material which is consistent with or coheres with material established as authentic by other means may also be accepted.[61]

The first two of these criteria, and especially the first, reveal a quite monumental degree of scepticism. It would be one thing to say that a statement attributed to Jesus is probably authentic if it is inconsistent with Judaism before him and with the Church after him, though even this would be hazardous. But to say that *no* statement attributed to Jesus can be authentic *unless* it is inconsistent with Judaism before him and with the Church after him is quite another matter, for it is logically equivalent to saying that Jesus could never have agreed with Judaism and that the Church could never have agreed with him. And this is even less plausible if it is added, as it would be (though on *a priori* grounds) by most of the modern critics that Jesus must have thought exactly like a Jew of his time. There is, however, no doubt that this is what is held, and we can quote Fuller in confirmation:

> We can, for historical purposes, eliminate from the sayings of Jesus anything which clearly pre-supposes the post-Easter situation, and which reflects the faith of the post-Easter church. For here the presumption is that their *Sitz im Leben*, their creative milieu, is in the life of the church, and not in the life of Jesus. Secondly, we can eliminate any material which can be paralleled in contemporary Judaism, for here too the presumption is that the sayings in question have (historically speaking) been erroneously attributed to Jesus.[62]

The term 'the presumption' is significant; we might well ask 'Whose presumption?' Fuller himself seems a little uneasy, for he immediately adds:

> Of course these methods are not foolproof, and one cannot help feeling that German scholars often proceed as if they were. They yield no complete certainty, for on some points Jesus *could* have agreed with the post-Easter church: but usually, in a saying of this class, the post-Easter situation is clearly reflected. Jesus might also have quoted or used with approval Rabbinic teaching. . . . [This method] may result in a reduction of the available historical data, but at least it should be reliable enough as far as it goes: and actually it turns out that it does go far enough for our purposes.

Perrin expresses no such hesitations or qualifications, but as Fuller states the position it is perhaps even more revealing. We notice the grudging phrase 'on some points Jesus *could* have agreed', with its italicised 'could', as if such agreement could be only rare and exceptional. (Incidentally, it is rather odd to say 'Jesus could have agreed with the post-Easter church' rather than 'The post-Easter church could have agreed with Jesus', but we may let this pass.) We are told that the method should be 'reliable enough as far as it goes', but how far does it go, and how do we ascertain how far? Actually it turns out (unexpectedly and by some happy chance?) that it does go far enough 'for our purposes'. We are not told what those purposes are, and we can only speculate. Fuller also tells us that 'this method of elimination . . . provides a safer course than Stauffer's principle of *in dubio pro tradito*,'[63] but safer for whom and for what? Certainly not for historical accuracy, if Jesus *did* frequently agree with the Judaism of his time and if the early Church *did* frequently agree with Jesus. It is only if we are convinced in advance that Jesus did *not* normally agree with Judaism and that the early Church did *not* normally agree with Jesus that we can accept, as giving an accurate picture, an account from which all traces of these two agreements have been eradicated. We certainly cannot, without committing a most glaring circle in the argument, appeal to an account from which all agreements have been deliberately removed, as providing evidence that the agreements were not originally there.

The attempts to buttress up this argument are most unconvincing. Perrin tells us that 'the very conception of the "historical Jesus" was foreign to the New Testament as such a conception would be to any document from the ancient world. . . . In this respect the problem is the same whether the figure be Jesus, Julius Caesar or Socrates.' But then we are told that

> the really complicating factor in the case of the New Testament, more specifically the Gospels, is that the early church, not having our sense of the word 'historical' and being motivated by an intense religious experience, saw no reason to distinguish between words originally spoken by the historical Jesus bar Joseph from Nazareth and words ascribed to him in the tradition of the church. . . . It is at this point that redaction criticism makes its impact, for it reveals to us how very much of the material ascribed to the Jesus who spoke in Galilee or Judea must in fact be ascribed to the Jesus who spoke through a prophet or evangelist in the early church.[64]

Here again we have argument in a circle. 'Redaction criticism reveals to us . . .', but it reveals this only by applying its criteria, and these, as we have seen, presuppose the very conclusion to which they profess to lead. 'No reason to distinguish . . .' – is this really true of the prologue to St Luke's Gospel, which gives a very different impression of what the evangelist at least intended to do and believed that he had done? And, to widen the question slightly, does St Paul's appeal to the five hundred brethren who had seen the risen Christ[65] suggest that he was indifferent to the distinction between historical fact and edifying myth?

Perrin himself saw a great and glorious future for the method:

> Just as it is clear that we cannot easily separate redaction from composition, so it is also clear that we must expand the concept of composition to include the composition of wholly new sayings. . . . It may well be that one day the discipline will have developed to the point where composition criticism has to be distinguished from redaction criticism as redaction criticism now has to be distinguished from form criticism, but that day is not yet. . . .
>
> What can be said to be the significance of the discipline? First and most obvious is the fact that redaction criticism is vastly increasing our knowledge of the theological history of earliest Christianity. . . . So we may confidently expect that in the course of the next few years we are going to develop major understandings of the theology of the synoptic evangelists in a way that we could never have hoped to do before the rise of this discipline.[66]

So, as Mr C. J. A. Hickling mordantly remarked, 'we are to contemplate students of the Gospels whose hope to learn from them about the Church increases in exact proportion to their conviction that they have almost nothing to learn from them about Jesus.'[67] And again:

> Perrin seems happily unaware that his heroes of exegesis could be vulnerable at any point. Moreover he himself commits at least one glaring *petitio principii* . . . , and irritatingly assumes that 'success' in exegesis vindicates the correctness of the method used to arrive at it, when there is no apparent criterion for distinguishing between success and what Farrer might have called 'Perrin-pleasingness'. And there are other short-circuits.[68]

(This last snare, as we have seen above, is one into which Palmer pointed out that no less a figure than Bultmann had fallen.) Hickling's final comment is that there is something disquieting about Dr Perrin's pugnacious enthusiasm for an approach to the Gospels which not only side-steps the purpose for which the Gospels were written – which was to preach, indeed, but to preach *history* – but also appears already a little old-fashioned.[69]

Old-fashioned, perhaps, we might comment, and not showing many signs of the glorious future prophesied for it in 1970, but nevertheless still very influential in university faculties and seminaries.

A very detailed critique of the more extreme form- and redaction-criticism was made several years ago by Dr Morna D. Hooker in an article entitled 'On using the Wrong Tool'.[70] It is significant because its author is herself a professional New Testament scholar of considerable reputation, who has recently become Lady Margaret Professor at Cambridge. It is significant in another respect because no attempt appears to have been made to reply to it. Perrin had previously crossed swords with her, in the book from which I have already quoted, for 'being convinced that form criticism has failed to make its point' and has accused her of 'being content with the assumption that may be caricatured in the words, "If it could have come from Jesus it most probably did." '[71] Dr Hooker showed considerable restraint in not characterizing Perrin's position in the words 'If it could have come from Jesus it most probably didn't'. But, while remarking that she had in fact described form criticism as 'an invaluable tool', she added that she had begun to wonder whether she was right in so describing it. She stressed its 'inbuilt circularity', which even Bultmann had admitted, though he had appeared not to have seen any harm in this, and she mentioned Humphrey Palmer with approval. And, she wrote,

The trap into which the form-critic so often falls is that he equates the *Sitz im Leben* with the *origin* of the material; the *Sitz im Leben* is not simply the 'setting' of the material but, according to Fuller, its 'creative milieu'. Now this is all right so long as by 'creative' is meant 'that which licked the material into its present shape'. But at this stage the form-critic too often makes the mistake of confusing form with content. Because he has no knowledge of earlier forms, and because he can see the relevance of the material in its present form to the life of the early community, as he understands it, he thinks he has discovered the origin of the *material*. Of course he *may* be right: but he is making an assumption on the basis of insufficient evidence. Explorers have often been misled into thinking they have discovered the source of a river –

and NT scholars have perhaps sometimes similarly been misled, though with less excuse.[72]

Dr Hooker then got to grips with the criterion of dissimilarity, which, she noted, had been used not only by Fuller and Perrin but also by Bultmann, Käsemann, Conzelmann, and others – indeed a formidable list! Her criticisms were in essence those which I have made earlier in this discussion, but they come with special force from one who is herself a practitioner in the art of New Testament criticism. The criterion, she said, 'will inevitably lead to serious distortion' and is 'a very serious drawback indeed'.

No one can seriously doubt that in some things Jesus' views must have overlapped those of the Jewish leaders and those of his followers, yet these must be set aside from our reconstruction. But to exclude details from our picture of Jesus may lead to distortion as serious as (or worse than) that which comes if we include too much. . . . We must be clear as to what this particular criterion can do; *it may* perhaps be able to give us a collection of sayings concerning whose authenticity we may be reasonably confident, but those sayings will not necessarily represent the kernel of Jesus' teaching, or be his most characteristic thought. Indeed, they would seem to offer us those sayings which the early Church treated as peripheral.[73]

Her second quarrel was based on the fact that use of the criterion presupposed a far greater knowledge of Judaism and early Christianity than in fact we possess.

Use of this criterion seems to assume that we are dealing with two known factors (Judaism and early Christianity) and one unknown – Jesus; it would perhaps be a fairer statement of the situation to say that we are dealing with three unknowns, and that our knowledge of the other two is quite as tenuous and indirect as our knowledge of Jesus himself. But one can solve $x + y = z$ only if one knows the value of two of the three 'unknowns'. . . . It could be that if we knew the whole truth about Judaism and the early Church, our small quantity of 'distinctive' truth would wither away altogether.[74]

Thirdly, the method forecloses on its own conclusions:

Such a tool is bound to produce a picture in keeping with its assumption – and that is precisely what we get: a Jesus who stands out from his contemporaries as distinctive in his attitudes, but who makes no messianic claims for himself (he cannot, because the Church will make messianic claims on his behalf), and who finds himself in opposition to the Jewish leaders. The method dictates its conclusions.[75]

Dr Hooker had no fewer than six further objections to bring against the method. Her fourth objection was that inspired prophets in the primitive Church presumably sometimes uttered sayings in the name of Jesus which have no parallel in contemporary Judaism or elsewhere in the early Church. 'So perhaps', she said ironically, 'in the small "hard core" of sayings which this method attributes to Jesus, we may again have included too much.'[76]

The fifth, sixth and seventh objections were concerned with the subjectivism which is an inbuilt feature of the method. The point was made that its users generally appeal to another criterion – 'namely that an "authentic" saying of Jesus should be "at home" in first-century Palestine.'

> To be acceptable as genuine, a saying of Jesus must at one and the same time be 'dissimilar' from contemporary Judaism, and yet use its categories and reflect the language and style of Aramaic. . . . It is difficult to know how to apply these apparently contradictory criteria simultaneously. When Norman Perrin, for example, argues that Jesus could not have used 'the son of Man' as a title because it did not exist in Judaism at the time, he is apparently using the second criterion; but if the title *had* (in his opinion) existed, he would presumably have eliminated it by applying the criterion of dissimilarity![77]

As Dr Hooker remarked, 'the old danger of looking down a well and seeing one's own reflection still exists.[78]

In the eighth objection reference was explicitly made to the coherence principle and it was pointed out that,

> when one adds the coherence principle to that of dissimilarity, it is clear that any errors in the results obtained by that method are liable to be magnified by the use of this second criterion. . . . If, for example, our core contains only 'future references to the Son of man', then any 'present' references will be automatically excluded.[79]

(In other words, the second criterion ensures that any diseases introduced by the first will be infectious.) Finally, it was observed that 'those who advocate the use of these criteria are strangely inconsistent in applying them.' Two examples were given and were very closely examined. The conclusion was the ominous but inescapable one that (the italics are Dr Hooker's own) 'the real criterion being used here is *not the principle of dissimilarity, but the scholar's own understanding of the situation.*'[80]

Dr Hooker summed up her reflections on her investigations in the following words:

> Of course NT scholars recognise the inadequacy of their tools; when different people look at one passage, and all get different answers, the inadequacy is obvious, even to NT scholars! But they do not draw the logical deduction from this fact. They go on, hammering or chiselling away with their pet tools, and using the pieces which are left as the sure foundation on which they then erect their edifice. But if *these* tools fail us because they are too imprecise, can we not find others?[81]

She then gave a catalogue of such attempts, ranging from Schmiedel to Jeremias. And in conclusion she denied that she was trying 'to offer comfort to those who have all along maintained a traditional "conservative" approach.' She suggested that she was 'being more radical than those who are commonly labelled "radical". For it seem[ed] to [her] that conservative and radical alike have both succumbed to the temptation to seek for certainty − and to believe that it can be achieved.'[82] However, she opined that any reaction from the prevailing sceptical position was likely to be in a conservative direction and said that her own assessment 'tends to be a more traditional one' but 'with the proviso that any attempt at reconstructing what lies behind our gospels is highly speculative and will in large measure reflect our own presuppositions about the material.'[83] 'All the material,' she wrote, 'comes to us *via* the Church, and is likely to have been coloured by the beliefs of those who have handed it on.'

> But [she continued] the burden of proof, to prove or disprove authenticity, lies neither on one side nor on the other. It is the duty of every scholar, in considering every saying, to give a reasonable account of all the evidence; for he is not entitled to assume, simply in the absence of contrary evidence, either that a saying is genuine or that it is not.
>
> And what tools should he use in this task? He must, alas, use the tools we have been discussing, for there are no others, and there are unlikely to be any better ones discovered. But he must not use them arbitrarily, selecting only the one which seems to give the answer he wants. Neither must he use them negatively − to blackball a saying.[84]

I must confess that I find this extremely puzzling. Dr Hooker's whole article is a systematic and devastating exposure of the arbitrary and incoherent character of the methods by which New Testament criticism has been carried on, a shattering demonstration that the main course of New Testament scholarship, as it has been developed over more than half a century, has ended in an impasse, in which it remains a moot point whether the gospel picture of Jesus retains some faint traces of historical authenticity or whether it is a fabrication constructed by the primitive Church in an attempt to give a mythical expression to an experience which it had in the days or years after the crucifixion. If there are, as Dr Hooker said, no tools other than these, then the moral would seem to be that we had better abandon New Testament scholarship altogether, for their inadequacy has been demonstrated. She did not, however, draw this conclusion, but appealed to us to go on using them, though not 'arbitrarily' or 'negatively'. But by what standards are the arbitrariness or negativity of their use to be judged?

> In the end [she wrote], the answers which the New-Testament scholar gives are not the result of applying objective tests and using precision tools; they are very largely the result of his own presuppositions and prejudices. If he approaches the material with the belief that it is largely the creation of the early Christian communities, then he will interpret it in that way. If he assumes that the words of the Lord were faithfully remembered and passed on, then he will be able to find criteria which support him. Each claims to be using the proper critical method. . . .
> They cannot all be right – though they may well all be wrong.[85]

And her last word, after admitting that to say that there are, and can be, no assured results may seem like a counsel of despair, was to repeat with the late R. H. Lightfoot: 'We do not know.'[86]

This is indeed a bleak outcome, and it leaves the modern New Testament student with something much less than the confidence and joy with which the early Church, whose writings are the object of his study, faced a confused and unhappy world. If this is all that New Testament experts can tell us, we can hardly be surprised if the ordinary Christian feels either that they have undermined his faith or that they have very little help to give him. I wonder, however, whether Dr Hooker is right in asserting that 'there are no other tools, and there are unlikely to be any better ones discovered'; perhaps what is needed is not the subtleties of the redaction-critics' criteria but the normal approaches of historical scholarship. I have already remarked that professional historians often have a greater respect for the reliability of the New Testament material than the New Testament scholars have themselves. (I suspect also that Dr Hooker may be feeling after the point which Austin Farrer made in criticizing Bultmann, that faith and evidence together can give us certainty about a historical fact that evidence alone cannot provide.)[87] Of course, if one approaches the Gospels with a predetermined disbelief in the supernatural or with the conviction that Christianity consists in being confronted with a challenge to existential self-understanding rather than with the proclamation that at a particular place and at a particular time God raised Jesus Christ from the dead, it is not surprising that one will be driven to wilder and wilder speculations as to how the Gospels became the extraordinary things that they are. Fortunately there are still some New Testament scholars who have kept their heads amid the confusion. That orthodox belief is rational and provides a far more reasonable explanation of the emergence of the Christian Church into human history is strikingly shown by Dr C. F. D. Moule. Commenting on a work in which the writer takes as his starting point what he describes as 'Christianity', Dr Moule remarks:

> Would it not be more objective to start from the *coming into existence of the Christian movement*? To do that immediately confronts the historian with the Easter-belief and demands that he account for it. But to start from 'Christianity', as 'a form of salvation or of saving truth' diverts the quest to something more subjective and more easily dissoluble.[88]

And Dr Moule's own book *The Phenomenon of the New Testament*[89] manifests a splendid application of the method which he advocates.

Some of Dr Hooker's readers have suggested that her article was wrongly named, and that what she was really attacking was not using the wrong tool but using the right tool in the wrong way. I do not think they were right; but I find it very surprising that, having so clearly shown that the tool was the wrong one, she should have ended by rather helplessly asserting that, although it was the wrong one, it was the only one we have and that therefore we must go on using it. However, one of the most deeply rooted assumptions of many modern theologians is that historical scholarship, in so far as it points to any conclusions at all, is bound to be incompatible with traditional Christian faith. Rarely indeed is it admitted, even by those who insist that all historical judgements are relative and corrigible, that in so far as they approach finality on any matter they might in fact confirm the faith, or that in so far as they appear to disconfirm it they may in fact need, and will presumably one day receive, correction. (There is also the possibility that the believer's understanding of the faith is inadequate, but that is another, though equally important, question.) Such a work as *The Historian and the Believer* by Dr Van Austin Harvey,[90] which is subtitled 'The Morality of Historical Knowledge and Christian Belief', shows how widespread and unexamined has been the assumption that an honest study of history inevitably raises a crisis of conscience for the Christian Believer. Even the type of 'perspectivism' which Harvey himself adopts at the end of his book, after exposing the weaknesses of his predecessors, manifests the same assumption. But now it is high time to return to the point from which this discussion began, Dr Carnley's essay on the Poverty of Historical Scepticism.

6 BACK TO HISTORICAL SCEPTICISM

Dr Carnley remarked that 'in [the] theological opinion concerning the uncertainty of all historical judgements there are two closely related, though slightly different, arguments.

> The first is that we are unable to achieve certainty in our judgments about the past because we can never be sure that a chance discovery of a new document will not cause us to reconsider our present judgments; the second is that we can never be sure that a future historian will not reassess the evidence *now* possessed from a different point of view and come to a different conclusion.[91]

On this second argument Carnley very pertinently pointed out that different conclusions need not be mutually contradictory, though Bultmann seemed to think that they must. They can often supplement one another to give a fuller description that any of them can give alone. And even so the fuller description can be accurate without having to be complete. Nevertheless, in spite of this obvious logical truth, 'in theological writing the assumption that there is only *one* objective history of the past is often made.'[92] Dr John Knox, the American Anglican scholar, was quoted for this view, though not for holding it consistently; Dr Alan Richardson for holding it without qualification. This was, however, only a preliminary skirmish for Carnley. A more serious assertion was that made by Bultmann and Schweitzer among others, that future evidence or more thorough consideration of the existing evidence may lead to conclusions that are not merely *different from* but *inconsistent with* those previously held. Even so, Carnley asserted,

> it does not necessarily follow that we can know *no* historical facts concerning Jesus whatsoever. It does not mean, in other words, that we must necessarily deny *every statement* in every life of Jesus or that *all* historical results 'have only relative validity'.[93]

At this point Carnley remarked that the position of the theologians whom he was discussing was 'not unlike that of some philosophers, notably C. I. Lewis and Rudolf Carnap, who have insisted that no empirical assertion can be absolutely certain.'[94] 'Indeed, John Knox says that even the "best attested facts" of the past are subject to this defect.'[95] T. A. Roberts, in his book *History and Christian Apologetic*,[96] written under the acknowledged influence of Marc Bloch, was mentioned as holding this view, which seemed however to Carnley to derive rather from philosophical empiricists such as A. J. Ayer, C. I. Lewis and R. Carnap. But, he pointed out, this position of historical scepticism had been subjected to a sustained onslaught by G. E. Moore, J. L. Austin, Ludwig Wittgenstein, Norman Malcolm and others. Briefly, the criticism is this. Admittedly, if it is *known with absolute certainty* at some date that some particular earlier event *did not* occur, then any previous claim that it was *known for certain* that it *did* occur must have been mistaken. However, if historical relativism is correct, that is to say if *no* statements about the past can be known with absolute certainty, then the statement that the event did *not* occur must itself be subject to revision, and therefore the claim that it was *known for certain* that the event did not occur must be false; the most that could be said is that someone *believed* that he knew this for certain. In other words, historical relativism cuts its own throat. Carnley thus concludes:

> It seems, therefore, that the argument which Tillich declares is 'the greatest contribution of historical research to systematic theology' and which many contemporary theologians accept and, indeed, which has led twentieth-century theology to seek a *sturmfreies Gebiet* for faith in complete independence of the alleged permanent insecurity of historical results, is a faulty one.[97]

He stresses that

> the argument for historical scepticism is a perfectly general one. It is not argued that there is a particular piece of evidence that shows that a particular statement about the past is untrue or uncertain, and that this statement cannot be asserted in the face of the available evidence.[98]

He is rebutting such an assertion as that of John Knox that even 'the best attested facts of the history of the past' are subject to future correction and that we cannot claim to know them with certainty. And he insists that 'logical possibility of error does not entail actual possibility of error'.[99] And as examples of statements that are absolutely conclusive he instances statements about the existence of King's College Chapel and the date of the outbreak of World War I. I doubt, however, whether he takes sufficient account of the fact that historians often express complete certainty about events and facts that are considerably more open to question than these. This means, of course, that, unless they were deliberately telling lies, they were rashly claiming to know facts which in fact they did not know, however strongly they may have felt certain about them and however much the available evidence may have made such certainty seem reasonable. Carnley's argument is certainly valid against the type of New Testament scholar who, for example, denies that the Resurrection can be known to have occurred, on the grounds that no statement about the past can be absolutely certain, and then, by his own handling and assessment of the evidence, claims that it can be certainly known *not* to have occurred.

As regards the fundamental New Testament question, Carnley is extremely reserved.

> It is true [he writes] . . . that the evidence concerning the person of Jesus is meagre, that once we move beyond certain fundamental assertions, such as that he was a man, lived in Palestine, died on a cross, expressed a distinctive and compelling love, we must, as historians, be prepared to accept statements as being less than completely certain.[100]

The important thing, however, is to notice the phrase 'as historians'. As Austin Farrer argued, in a passage previously quoted, it is not irrational to hold that certain truths can be known by faith, although the purely historical evidence for them amounts to something less than certainty. And it is not irrational to hold that, even if the historical evidence available at the time appears to disprove overwhelmingly the

99

affirmations of faith, further evidence or further consideration of the existing evidence will show that the alleged disproof was itself faulty. As Farrer said,

> it is possible through faith and evidence together, and through neither alone, to believe that Christ really and corporeally rose from the dead, not merely that his death on the cross had a supernatural silver lining significant for our salvation.[101]

Thus, in Carnley's words,

> The important thing is that it is not legitimate to argue that faith cannot be based on *any* historical judgements or must be *totally* independent of historical research and autonomous, because *no* historical judgement is *ever* justifiably claimed with certainty.[102]

Even on purely rational grounds and prescinding from the supernatural gift of faith, which is, as the Epistle to the Hebrews says, 'the conviction of things *not* seen',[103] there is immense evidential force in the fact that, from the earliest days and throughout the history of the Church, the Christian gospel has been preached to the world and has, for innumerable men and women, both provided an understanding of reality and has renewed and inspired their wills for authentic human living. This is not the place to develop an apologetic for Christianity. What I have tried to do is to show that the widespread modern attempts to deny or bypass the historicity of the picture of Christ that the Gospels provide or to reduce their status to that of edifying myths rests on no sure rational foundation. It is the outcome either of an antecedent bias against the supernatural or of a view of the Christian religion which is not that of the New Testament and which, by denying that Christ has come in the flesh, would have been recognized by St John as bearing the marks of the deceiver and the antichrist.[104]

The heart of the matter has been most lucidly expressed by Canon J. A. Baker. Commenting on the commonly repeated statement 'You have to start from the tradition', he writes:

> Of course. And the same is true of all past history. But it makes all the difference in the world, what you think was the attitude of those who formulated the tradition. If the early Christians regarded their own post-Easter life as the controlling element in revelation, then they may well have tailored and even invented the story of Jesus to suit this belief. But if they thought that the pre-Easter life of Jesus was of

decisive importance, then their attitude to the story will have been very different.

The first crucial point to recognize is that the choice which we are asked to make today is not a new one: it is one which the first-century church itself had to make. And there are, after all, well-known indications of their mind on this matter. Such details as the preservation of sayings contradicted by events, the retention of an unused and unusable title like 'Son of Man', the explicit declaration of intent in Luke i. 1–4, with its reference to earlier efforts on the same lines, suggest that they did regard information about Jesus as he was in his life on earth as something of vital importance that must be preserved. It is the pre-Easter Jesus to whom they looked to have their sinful and erring hearts and minds corrected and enlightened; and therefore what they wanted from tradition (and believed that they were receiving) was information about Jesus as he was. Nor is it without significance that as the process of inventing edifying material about Jesus moved further away from him in time, so it also diverged farther and farther from the original New Testament picture. In short, the tradition itself in its earliest form is a tradition that the human life of Jesus matters. To say that it does not is to contradict the only tradition we have; and is therefore most certainly not to 'start from the tradition'.[105]

7 THE RING OF TRUTH

Dr J. B. Phillips is one of the best known and most widely appreciated translators of the New Testament into modern English. He has given the following account of the impulse which led him to write his small book *The Ring of Truth: A Translator's Testimony*:[106]

What triggered off my anger (righteous, I trust) against some of our 'experts' is this. A clergyman, old, retired, useless if you like, took his own life because his reading of the 'new theology' and even some programmes on television, finally drove him, in his loneliness and ill-health, to conclude that his own life's work had been founded upon a lie. He felt that these highly-qualified writers and speakers must know so much more than he that they must be right. Jesus Christ did not really rise from the dead and the New Testament, on which he had based his life and ministry, was not more than a bundle of myths.[107]

Now it would, of course, be monstrous to suggest that the scholars whose work I have criticized in this chapter are violent and callous ogres, who take delight in destroying deeply-held beliefs in entire disregard of the happiness and even the life of their fellow men and women. And no doubt if Dr Phillip's aged clergyman had had the opportunity of consulting them they would have done their best to convince him that the mythical nature of the Gospels left them still capable of confronting him with existential challenges through which he might achieve authentic self-understanding. But the incident does at least underline the extent to which New Testament criticism, whether at first or second hand, impinges upon the lives of ordinary Christian people in a way in which, for example, Cretan archaeology or scientific cosmology does not. Few clergymen, I imagine, have been driven to suicide by the decipherment of Linear B or by black holes in the galaxies, deep as may be their respect for experts in these esoteric fields. But many of the younger clergy and some of the older ones too (for information moves upwards as well as downwards) have found their praying and their preaching alike to be paralysed by the conviction which they have acquired that, as accounts of the life and teaching of Jesus, the Gospels are radically unreliable and that they are of value only as testimonies to the mythopoeic propensities of the primitive Church. Some, of course, make heroic efforts to bring their congregations to existential self-understanding by confronting them existentially with the gospel myths, but the method seems singularly ineffective in a non-Teutonic setting. Some find themselves in the state commented on by C. S. Lewis, of having a picture-truth which can be preached to the people and an esoteric truth for the use of the clergy. Some take refuge in an unintelligent fundamentalism and retain their faith at the cost of ceasing to think about it. Others, finding themselves without a gospel to preach, suffer from what it is now fashionable to describe as an identity-crisis and wonder whether there is any place for them in the modern world. And in decisions concerning the organization and the ministrations of the Church, this same atmosphere of scepticism results in a kind of ecclesiastical pragmatism, in which everything is played by ear and contemporaneity is idolized.

The condition of virtual uselessness to which the New Testament can be reduced is well illustrated by a paper with the somewhat inappropriate title 'On the Authority of the Bible' which was read by a professor of the New Testament in 1972 at a conference on women's ministry in the Church of England. He rejected both what he described as the 'text-bandying' approach and also the 'attempt to discriminate and discern what is primary and closer to the creative thought of the Gospel, and what is secondary and to be judged in relation to what is judged primary.' Having thus swept most of the pieces off the board, he continued:

> There is a third approach to the question of what kind of appeal is to be made to the Bible for its formulations and concepts to be authoritative, which I think would be my own in relation to the particular matter with which we are concerned. *It is the kind of approach one might even make over what one judges to be central things in the Bible and the Christian religion* – and I do not think that the ministry of women is central, or indeed that the ministry of anyone is central, but that it is a secondary though very important secondary matter – such things as, for example, eschatology, the doctrine of the finality of Christ.
>
> This approach would be to take note of what is immediately in front of one, of what is pressing for recognition, of what a large number of Christians whom one honours and respects feel, of what one feels oneself to be urgent in respect of the operation of the Gosepel; and then to ask the question whether there is anything in the authoritative scriptural documents which really effectively blocks this and stands in its way; whether there is anything which is to be judged to be deeply rooted theologically and spiritually in the teaching of the Gospel and says that this is not right. *And one has to ask the question whether what appears to stand in the way does so because it is deeply rooted in the heart of the Gospel or because it is deeply rooted in the culture of the first century A.D.*[108]

Could anything more effectually devaluate the Gospels and the rest of the New Testament than the programme proposed in this passage? Note first of all the primary appeal, made twice over, to 'feeling'. Note, secondly, that no mention is made of either the 'feelings' or the arguments of those who hold the opposite view from that which is being urged. Note, thirdly, the subjectivism embodied in the phrases 'effectively blocked' and 'judged to be deeply rooted'; is it not clear that anything in Scripture which seems to discredit the desired action will be ruled out as not deeply rooted theologically and spiritually, since no indication is given as to how the judgement is to be made? Note, fourthly, the question begged in the final sentence. No account is taken of the possibility that something might be deeply embedded in the culture of the first century and also in the heart of the Gospel; we are faced with the assumption which was explicitly stated by Perrin, that Jesus could not ever have agreed with his contemporaries. And, fifthly, note the absence of any suspicion that the desired action might conceivably be deeply rooted in the non-Christian and non-religious culture of the *twentieth* century and be very far from deeply rooted in the heart of the Gospel. Finally, we must note that, according to the writer, this approach is to be made not only to what are in his view secondary matters but even to such central things as the finality of Christ. So far, then, from his programme being based on and arising out of Scripture, Scripture is allowed nothing but a late veto, and even then a veto for whose disqualification ample provision is made.

Now if the radical critics had proved their case up to the hilt or had even shown it to be highly probable, we should have to make the best of a bad job and either scrap the Church as a superstitious and parasitic corporation or do our best to transform it into something more enlightened and less pernicious before it is too late. However, when, as a reasonably well-educated outsider, I examine their arguments, as I have tried to do in this chapter, I find them unconvincing and mutually conflicting. Even the impressive appearance of a united front which is presented to the outside world turns out on investigation to be crumbling from within. And though it would be obviously unjust to accuse them of deliberate malice, it is difficult to acquit many of them of over-confidence, deafness to criticism and irresponsibility. How many of them, one sometimes wonders, when they expound their more imaginative speculations to their pupils or scatter them to the general public through the communication media, remember that what, in the small world of academic Biblical scholarship, may be no more than provocative and transient hypotheses, exposed to the ruthless judgement of their colleagues, may be taken by their more trustful but less discriminating hearers as gospel (or anti-gospel) truth which the latter are totally unable to criticize or assess? Pharmacology and finance are not the only techniques that can have unintended and calamitious side-effects.

It is time, I suggest, to have the courage to recognize that the movement which hoped to solve the problem of Christian origins by applying successively the methods of source-criticism, form-criticism and redaction-criticism has run into a dead-end from which no amount of gymnastic elaboration can extricate it.[109] (This does not mean that these three methods may not have some useful function in their limited spheres.) Dr Thomas S. Kuhn, in his celebrated book *The Structure of Scientific Revolutions*,[110] has shown how a scientific theory can sometimes be kept alive long after it is really discredited, by elaborating it with more and more special hypotheses, provided that a more adequate theory is not ready to take its place. Something like this is, I think, true of the present situation in New Testament criticism. The only trouble is that the putative successor has not yet appeared, so the special hypotheses continue to proliferate. This is, needless to say, an uncomfortable state of affairs, but there is no point in shutting our eyes to it. And perhaps the most important response which it demands from the theologian is simply that he should keep his head and not lose his nerve.

ADDITIONAL NOTE 1   THE HISTORICISM OF Dr NINEHAM

One of the most extreme examples that I have encountered of the discussion of Christian origins from the standpoint of historical scepticism is provided by the Ethel M. Wood Lecture delivered by Dr D. E. Nineham on 4 March 1975 with the title 'New Testament Interpretation in an Historical Age.'[111] Among the many authors to whom he refers in its course he makes no mention of Dr Carnley, so as he was in fact familiar with Dr Carnley's thesis he presumably considered its argument unworthy of refutation. His basic theme, for which he relies to a large extent on R. G. Collingwood and T. E. Hulme is that 'modern man is aware in a way that his predecessors have not been, of the historically conditioned character of all human experience, speech and institutions', that 'for every individual, no matter how original, what it means and feels like to be a human being and live a human life is to a large extent controlled by the presiding ideas of the cultural community to which it is his destiny to belong.'[112]

Thus stated, with the qualifying clause 'to a large extent', the claim is fairly moderate, but as Nineham develops it it becomes extreme. It is, he well observes, difficult for members of any culture to understand why the members of an earlier culture thought as they did, and there is the standing temptation to answer the questions, not in terms of the cultural assumptions of the original community, but in terms of the questioner's own assumptions. He makes the further point that 'accounts of historical events and cultures which reach us from the past are coloured by the cultural attitudes and assumptions of those from whom they emanated, and so we can never accept them at their face value. We have to treat them', he continues, 'as a court of law treats the statements of witnesses, as raw material for its own verdict.' So, he concludes, we shall 'arrive at our own verdict, an account consonant with integrity in our cultural situation.'[113]

Nineham is certainly correct in asserting that it requires no special perspicacity to see that, as he understands it, 'all this' poses considerable problems for the Christian tradition. He fails, however, to remark that, if accepted, it poses very considerable problems for historical research as such. For, in spite of the language about 'courts of law' and 'witnesses', the 'verdict' at which it arrives and the processes by which it arrives at it are, on its own principles, infected with historical relativism and coloured by the cultural attitudes and assumptions of those from whom they emanated. They may be 'consonant with integrity in our cultural situation', whatever that means, but does that mean that they are likely to be true? Nineham gives impressive examples of the way in which nineteenth-century historians misinterpreted eighteenth-century politics and post-Tridentine theologians misinterpreted the Council of Trent, through their conditioning by their own cultural setting, but he gives no heed to the possibility that his own judgement on the past is conditioned by his own.

What we find him doing in fact is appealing to historical relativism just as far as it suits him and no more. For he is anxious to maintain two propositions which are extremely uneasy bedfellows: first, that all the reports which we have about Jesus come through witnesses whose testimony was distorted by cultural attitudes and presuppositions which we cannot possibly accept; and, secondly, that Jesus' own cultural attitudes and presuppositions, which in any case we know about only through their testimony, were such as we cannot accept either. Thus we find him claiming that, as the alleged result of 'a much more fully developed historical method . . . several things have become clear', which he lists as follows:

First, that the historical truth about [Jesus] cannot be known with anything like the fulness claimed by nineteenth-century liberal scholars.

Secondly, that their supposed knowledge of him rested largely on their having yielded to the historian's arch-temptation, that of reading a story from one culture through the spectacles of another.

Thirdly, that so far as the real Jesus can be discerned, he, like the New Testament witnesses to him, belongs essentially to the culture of his time and place; there is no reason to think that the outlook of the historical Jesus will have been such as to be any more immediately acceptable today than that of, say, the historical Paul.[114]

The extraordinary 'eating-your-cake-and-having-it' character of Nineham's argument will, I think, be sufficiently evident. To change the metaphor, rarely can a conclusion have been based so explicitly on the method of sawing off the branch on which one was sitting. After all, if the New Testament writers were so incurably conditioned by their environment that we can neither share their mentality nor trust their testimony, would it not be simpler to say outright that Jesus must have been just as much conditioned by his environment as they were by theirs and leave the matter there, without any further reference to the writers and their writings at all? There are places where Nineham comes very near to suggesting this, as when he writes:

No scholar today supposes that New Testament Christianity as it stands is a possible religion for modern western man, or that the character, conduct and beliefs of Jesus, even if we knew far more about them than we do, could constitute as they stand the content of a modern faith.[115]

The words 'No scholar today' will seem to some to show a somewhat contemptuous attitude on Nineham's part towards many of his colleagues, but their application is perhaps ameliorated by the characteristic escape-phrase 'as it stands' which qualifies the 'New Testament Christianity' which he rejects. But his repudiation not only of the beliefs, but also of the character and conduct, of Jesus himself as candidates for the content of a modern faith may seem, even with the similar caveat 'as they stand', surprising from the pen of a Christian priest. There is also, in the clause 'even if we knew far more about them than we do', a suggestion that the conclusion has been virtually settled in advance of the evidence.

To pass to a further point, it is clear that to Dr Nineham, as to Dr M. F. Wiles in *The Remaking of Christian Doctrine*,[116] it is neither necessary nor desirable to hold that there was anything unique in the person of Jesus or in the action of God in his life. The concept of incarnation, which Wiles set aside on theological and philosophical grounds, Nineham would bypass on New Testament grounds by 'simply setting out to explore the nature of New Testament Christianity in the same impartial spirit in which Malinowski investigated the religion of the Trobriand Islanders or Evans-Pritchard that of the Azande.'[117] However, meeting the obvious objection that this would be begging the entire question, he insists:

> Scholars working as I desiderate would not rule out *any* possibility *a priori*. They would simply behave as characteristic representatives of an historical age, assuming as a working hypothesis the truth of its presuppositions, including its assumption, at any rate in Barraclough's modified form, that all past events form a single causally interconnected web and that no event occurs without this-worldly causation of some sort. They would then see how far it is possible to do justice to the evidence of the New Testament without going beyond those assumptions.[118]

He admits that 'in the end some such occurrence [as a unique divine intervention] may prove inescapable, but not unless and until its necessity has been clearly demonstrated.'[119]

Now all this sounds quite unsensational and Nineham claims very reasonably that 'no other procedure could really claim to be an appeal to history.'[120] But, in apparent violation of his initial position, he goes on to insist:

> These scholars should avoid the historian's temptation. I would have them be scrupulously careful to see that all New Testament language and ideas were interpreted in their own context. . . . For our purposes it is essential that the presuppositions in the light of which the text is interpreted should be the doctrine-felt-as-facts by first-century men, and not by the Fathers, the Reformers or people of our time.[121]

This hermeneutic principle is admirable and I would earnestly hope to see it applied. Indeed, in spite of Nineham's denial, it has surely been used by a great many scholars in the past. What I find difficult is to see how its application can be consistent with the principle of historical relativism to which Nineham is professedly committed. For he and his associates are twentieth-century men who, we are told, can only think as such. In fact it appears that for Nineham twentieth-century men are divided into two very unequal classes: the great mass of technologically conditioned secularized people for whom the whole conception of the supernatural and of divine intervention is meaningless, and the small sophisticated élite, who know about historical relativism, who can detach themselves, at least in thought, from the attitude of their contemporaries, can enter empathetically into the mental climate of other ages and cultures and, in the last resort, can even envisage as a remote possibility the return of the notion of the supernatural. Not that this last possibility seems to Nineham to be at all likely; for, in another of his forecasts, he writes:

> I confess I should not be altogether surprised if those who adopted such an approach concluded that, while the events of Jesus' career were such as to demand interpretation in terms of a unique – indeed literally final – divine intervention *given the presuppositions of certain circles in first century Jewish culture*, they might not have seemed to demand such interpretation given different cultural assumptions, for example to a modern western observer if such a one – twentieth century presuppositions and all – could be carried back to first-century Palestine on some magic carpet or infernal time machine.

'It may be worth adding', Nineham anxiously continues, 'that if that were the conclusion, it would not necessarily rob the events of their profound religious significance.'[122] Perhaps not, but would it rob them of it, even unnecessarily, whatever that might mean? And what kind of religious significance would it leave them? After all, religions are of various kinds; some are not worth having and some are presumably false. 'It would still be possible', Nineham goes on, 'to see the God whose hand is everywhere behind the first-century events which launched the early Christians into a relation with himself so intimate and vivid, that, given their presuppositions, they were led to posit a final and decisive intervention on his part to account for it.'[123] It would be possible, no doubt, but would it be reasonable? For it is suggested that we should admit in certain events a divine presence (a hand of God) which, as theists, we already believe to be everywhere, and that we should do this because certain people, on the strength of presuppositions which we do not share, asserted that in those events there was a special intervention of God, which we do not admit. But now, in a final concession to orthodoxy, Nineham adds: 'And it would be possible to interpret their sense of intimate and vivid relationship with God as having been exactly what it seemed to them to be.'[124] Once again, and with even more misgiving, I find myself reflecting: Possible perhaps, but would it be reasonable? Would it be reasonable to accept their interpretation if I rejected their presuppositions? Would it be reasonable to accept their interpretation if I had the twentieth-century presuppositions? If I accepted their intepretation, what presuppositions would I need to have?

Nineham gives us no help here, but passes on to his final and all-important question: 'If scholars approached the New Testament in the way I suggest, would they have any contributions to make beyond satisfying our antiquarian curiosity?'[125] (This is basically the question that Dr Fleeseman-van Leer put to Professor C. F. Evans.)[126] His answer is that 'whatever form Christianity has to take if it is to be properly integrated with any modern culture, its adherents will always find it necessary and enriching to pass over to the rock from whence they were hewn, the faith and experience of New Testament Christianity, just as they will also want to pass over to the faith of the Fathers, the Schoolmen and the Reformers.'[127] With this I would heartily agree, but I find it hard to justify on Nineham's principles. For he seems to have committed himself *both* to the position that twentieth-century men can think only in twentieth-century categories *and* to the position that twentieth-century theologians must train themselves to think in the categories of all the other Christian centuries as well. And behind this there lies the more radical contradiction on which I have already commented, that he seems to be committed *both* to the historical relativism according to which all judgements about historical events are culturally conditioned and transient *and* to the position that historical relativism itself, even if culturally conditioned in its origin, is the permanent trans-cultural truth about historical events and their impact on their observers.

Nevertheless, I agree with Nineham that 'if this process of passing over to primitive Christianity is to be truly enriching, it must be genuinely the Christianity of the New Testament to which we pass over', that New Testament Christianity must be 'displayed in its pastness, with its various doctrines, rituals and commandments exhibited in the sort of unity they seemed to form in the context of first-century cultural assumptions.' And he may be correct in his sweeping assertion that other scholars 'have interpreted New Testament accounts of the past as if they had been written by men who shared our attitude to the past.'[128] But I cannot help fearing that the promotion of his programme, if combined with his doctrine of history, would produce a generation of Christians who were completely sceptical about the Gospels as history while luxuriating in them as imaginative literature. For if the cultural difference between the first century and our own is as absolute as Nineham holds it to be, if, as he writes, 'religious beliefs and practices bear a specific meaning and are justified in relation to a particular religious community and its universe by [*sic, qu.* of] discourse, and *only* in that relation',[129] then the 'passing-over' which he advocates would necessitate a brain-washing process of an alarming kind. If, however, we hold that, behind and beneath all the diversity of human cultures, there is a continuity of rational man in an intelligible world, we shall, without rewriting the Gospels to make them agree with the outlook of our own secularized age, see them as directly relevant to our concerns. There is, I suggest, something theologically very questionable in Nineham's insistence that we should 'pass over' to the 'pastness' of the Gospel, as if there were a void between us and the life of Jesus which only sound New Testament scholarship can bridge. We may well repeat Nineham's words that 'if this process of passing over to primitive Christianity is to be truly enriching, it must be genuinely the Christianity of the New Testament to which we pass over', but discovering Christianity is not simply a matter of journeying into the past. There is something from the past that has passed over to us. And what Dr Nineham's New Testament Interpretation in an Historical Age perhaps most needs is rather less of Collingwood and rather more of the Church.

ADDITIONAL NOTE 2   REDATING THE NEW TESTAMENT

At the end of this chapter I made the provocative assertion that, although the methods of source-, form- and redaction-criticism might have useful results in their limited spheres, the movement which had attempted to solve the problem of Christian origins by their successive application had run into a dead-end from which no amount of gymnastic elaboration could extricate it. I am therefore encouraged to find that, on at least one aspect of the matter, namely the dating of the New Testament books, I have the support of a scholar whom no one could accuse of slavish adherence to tradition and whose speculations in the doctrinal realm had some years ago something like a *succès de scandale*. In his quite recent and extremely thorough work *Redating the New Testament*,[130] Dr John A. T. Robinson has written:

> What one looks for in vain in much recent scholarship is any serious wrestling with the external or internal evidence for the dating of individual books. . . , rather than an *a priori* pattern of theological development into which they are then made to fit. In fact ever since the form critics assumed the basic solutions of the source critics . . . and the redaction critics assumed the work of the form critics, the chronology of the New Testament documents has scarcely been subjected to fresh examination. No one since Harnack has really gone back to look at it for its own sake or to examine the presuppositions on which the current consensus rests. It is only when one pauses to do this that one realises how thin is the foundation for some of the textbook answers and how circular the arguments for many of the relative datings. Disturb the position of one major piece and the pattern starts disconcertingly to dissolve.[131]

And, although Robinson's chief concern is with dating, this is closely involved with questions of composition too. And on even such a firmly established idol as the two-document hypothesis of the synoptic gospels, which generations of theological students had been taught as, if not *de fide*, at least proximate to faith, he writes:

> The consensus frozen by the success of the 'fundamental solution' propounded by Streeter has begun to show signs of cracking. Though this is still the dominant hypothesis, incapsulated in the textbooks, its conclusions can no longer be taken for granted as among the 'assured results' of biblical criticism. It is far too early yet to say what new patterns or modifications of older patterns will establish themselves. The main thing required is a suspension of former dogmatisms and an admission that none of the various hypotheses so confidently advanced as overall solutions may satisfy all the facts.[132]

The conclusion at which Robinson arrives, after an extremely wide-ranging and detailed discussion, is indeed novel and sensational when judged by contemporary standards. It is that all the New Testament books were completed before A.D. 70, that all the four Gospels and Acts were coming into being concurrently from before A.D. 40 onwards, and that the Gospels are not antedated by the Pauline epistles. The foundation-stone of the whole argument is the fact 'that what on any showing would appear to be the single most datable and climactic event of the period – the fall of Jerusalem in A.D. 70, and with it the collapse of institutional Judaism based on the temple – is never once mentioned as a past fact'. 'It is,' Robinson adds, 'of course, predicted; and these predictions are, in some cases at least, assumed to be written (or written up) after the event. But the silence is nevertheless as significant as the silence for Sherlock Holmes of the dog that did not bark.'[133] And, once the most obvious explanation of the silence has been admitted, the detailed examination to which Robinson then subjects the various books individually places their growth and completion, in his opinion, safely within the period between 40 and 70 A.D. 'This,' he remarks,

> I believe, is what we should naturally expect. The notion that all the Pauline epistles, with the theology they imply, were prior to all the gospels, with the theology they imply, is not one that we should derive from the documents themselves. Laymen are always surprised to be told it, and I believe they are right to be surprised.[134]

Robinson's views and arguments on individual issues must, of course, be left to be wrangled over by the experts, but there some points of general interest that should be mentioned. He is laudably sensitive to the circularity that often characterizes arguments in this field: 'there seems', he writes, 'to be no limit to the circularity of arguments from literary dependence.'[135] And he is scathing on the topic of pseudonymity:

> There is an appetite for pseudonymity that grows by what it feeds on. Thus M. Rist, believing that possibly two-thirds of the New Testament writings are pseudonymous, says, 'This, alone, [sic] shows the influence of pseudepigraphy in the early church.' If you believe it is everywhere, you cease to have to argue for it anywhere. Perrin writes: 'Pseudonymity is almost a way of life in the world of the New Testament and also in the New Testament itself.' Certainly it is among New Testament scholars! . . .
>   There is no doubt of what Paul thought of those who circulated letters claiming to come from him (2 Thess. 2.2; 3.17): *he* knew of no harmless literary convention.[136]

But it will be of most interest to see the conclusions to which Robinson comes at the end of his investigation and what he sees as their consequences. First, he asserts that there is very little direct evidence, either internal or external, for dating the books and that both attestation and quotation are much less helpful than many have held them to be. Again, he insists, 'prophecy after the event', while not to be entirely excluded 'has to be demonstrated, and demonstrated by minute and strict criteria, rather than simply assumed.'[137] His subsequent paragraph is sufficiently important to be quoted almost in full:

This is *not* of course to say that subsequent reflection on events or the later experiences of the church have not shaped or conditioned the gospel tradition as we have it. John's looking back on the manner of Jesus' death, or of Peter's, obviously presupposes the former and in all probability the latter. Equally the predictions of the rejection, crucifixion and resurrection of the Son of Man in the synoptic tradition are clearly influenced in lesser or greater degree by the knowledge of what happened. Again, the synoptic apocalypses and the Johannine last discourses have evidently placed on Jesus' lips warnings to the church that have been conditioned by the church's own sufferings. Indeed, there is not a saying or a story in the gospel tradition that has not reached us through the sieve of the community's needs and uses. Yet it is quite another matter to say that these sayings or stories have simply been created by the history of the church and then put back into the mouth or the life of Jesus, or to say that Jesus could not have foretold what would befall his followers or his nation. Moreover, in Christian apocalyptic, whether set on the lips of Jesus or of John, there is no hint of the convention of pre-casting predictions so as to make it appear that occurrences within the readers' time were foreknown from the distant past. ... Thus there is nothing in Revelation that speaks of the fall of Jerusalem or that certainly reflects anything beyond the late 60s, just as there is nothing in the predictions of Paul in Acts that certainly reflects the situation beyond the point at which its story ends – or the subsequent organisation of the Roman Empire or of the Christian church. Whether the gospels, Acts, or the Apocalypse *were* written after the fall of Jerusalem must be assessed on the merits of each case. The argument from prophecy, like the argument from quotation, must take its place within the larger context and must in each instance be deployed with the most exacting critical discrimination.[138]

Closely connected with this is Robinson's comment on what he frankly calls 'the apparently almost wilful blindness of investigators to the seemingly obvious'.[139] Their unshakable presupposition of the late date of most of the New Testament books has, he says, prevented them from seeing the natural explanation of the absence of any mention of the fall of Jerusalem, namely that that event had not occurred when the books were written. Again, he points to 'the subjectivity in assessing the intervals required for development, distribution or diffusion. . . . Some can squeeze the whole of church history up to the conversion of Paul into a single year, others require decades for the emergence of the conditions in 1 Peter. The greater the stress on the part of the early Christian communities in the formation of the tradition, the longer the "tunnel period" tends to be.'[140] Finally, Robinson comments on what he calls 'the manifold tyranny of unexamined assumptions':

> Even (perhaps most of all) in their reactions *against* each other, different schools of critics take these over from their predecessors, and of course individual commentators and writers of introductions take them over from each other. Fashions and critical orthodoxies are established which it becomes as hard to go against in this field as in any other. . . . Some of this is sheer scholarly laziness. . . . There is also an understandable temptation to depreciate or lose patience with the lower reaches of 'mere' introductory questions of date and authorship. Those who press on to the more constructive work of building theologies of the New Testament tend to be content to assume and incorporate the foundations laid by others. . . . Their world [sc. the world of many, though not all, of the form- and redaction-critics] has been a world without fences, where words and ideas, myths and movements, Hermetic, gnostic, Mandean and the rest, have floated freely with no very noticeable tethering to time or place. Many of the circles and communities of the early church with their tensions and tendencies are frankly creations of the critics or highly subjective reconstructions.[141]

Robinson mentions specifically three of these unexamined assumptions: (1) that the writing down of traditions did not begin until *after* a considerable stretch of oral transmission, and that thenceforth the traditions were transmitted and mutually influenced almost exclusively by the processes of *literary* dependence; (2) that Greek was not spoken in Palestine from the earliest days of the Church; and (3) that 'there was an indefinite number of totally unrecorded and unremembered figures in the history of early Christianity who have left absolutely no mark except as the supposed authors of much of its greatest literature.'[142] And he asserts very emphatically that argument from development, while, if 'used with great discrimination and delimitation . . . it can sometimes help towards establishing the sequence of the New Testament documents . . . what it cannot do, except within the very broadest limits, is itself to determine the span of time over which the development takes place.'[143]

What, then, are the conclusions that Robinson draws from his investigations? First, 'that all the various types of the early church's literature were coming into being more or less concurrently in the period between 40 and 70.'[144] This, of course, rules out the view that one of the four Gospels (whether Mark or another) was first completed and was then elaborated in the others. Secondly, that the chronology of the narrative in Acts is confirmed. Thirdly, 'just as the shrinking of the span from 50–150 + to one from 50–100 + resulted in discrediting some of the extremer forms of scepticism about the Christian tradition, so a further reduction in final datings by more than half from −50 to −70 must tend to reinforce a greater conservatism.'[145] He explains somewhat anxiously, however, that this does not imply a repudiation of form- and redaction-criticism as such. 'It is merely that unexamined assumptions have tended to lead to the unwarranted conclusions that the more the documents tell us about the early church (a) the less they tell us about Jesus and (b) the longer they took to develop. But neither conclusion necessarily follows.'[146] He further asserts that 'in the same way there is no necessary correlation between the wealth of knowledge the documents can be made to yield about their setting in the life of the church and the *duration* of the period for which these processes give evidence. . . . To shorten the tunnel in principle changes nothing.'[147] Yet he feels bound to remark that 'there is less likelihood of distortion the shorter the interval. Moreover', he tells us,

> there is a critical point of transition. If one is dealing with a gap, say, of thirty years (the distance that separates us, at the point of writing, from the end of the second world war), there is a good deal of built-in control in the form of living memory – whereas if the distance is doubled the controls are much less than half as strong.[148]

He mentions the 'friendly chiding' that the New Testament theologians received from the classical historian Mr Sherwin-White 'for not recognising, by any contemporary standards, what excellent sources they have.'[149] And, on this matter of the 'shortening of the span', we may recall Sherwin-White's remark that it was precisely the presumed tempo of the development of the didactic myths as held by the extremer form-critics that caused most surprise to an ancient historian.[150] If the necessary tempo has to be raised to the degree that Robinson claims, surprise might very well give place to incredulity.

Now, whether one finds Robinson's conclusions congenial or the reverse, it would obviously be foolhardy for one who has not as detailed an acquaintance as he has both with the Biblical text and the writings of Biblical scholars to hazard a definitive verdict on the results which he claims to have established in this book. Its significance can, however, hardly be doubted or its publication ignored. For, in spite of the respectful tributes with which it is not very thickly sprinkled, it amounts to a violent revolt, from within the citadel of New Testament study itself, against the conduct of New Testament study during most of the present century. It is true that, both in the title of his work and in occasional reminders in the text, Dr Robinson tells us that all he is concerned with is the dating of the documents, but in fact and inevitably he deals with very much more. Almost all the traditional authorships are defended and so too – which is much more important – is the substantial historical reliability of the narratives. From now on, when the dogmatic theologian or the parish priest or the educated layman is told that he must abandon his most cherished beliefs because 'all modern scholars agree . . .' or because of 'the assured results of modern criticism', he will know exactly what to think.

THREE

Christology Today

In many and various ways God spoke of old to our fathers by the prophets; but in these last days he has spoken to us by a Son, whom he appointed the heir of all things, through whom also he created the world. He reflects the glory of God and bears the very stamp of his nature, upholding the universe by his word of power. When he had made purification for sins, he sat down at the right hand of the Majesty on high, having become as much superior to angels as the name he has obtained is more excellent than theirs.

The Letter to the Hebrews, 1.1–4, RSV

He is the image of the invisible God, the first-born of all creation; for in him all things were created, in heaven and on earth, visible and invisible, whether thrones or dominions or principalities or authorities – all things were created through him and for him. He is before all things, and in him all things hold together. He is the head of the body, the church; he is the beginning, the first-born from the dead, that in everything he might be pre-eminent. For in him all the fulness of God was pleased to dwell, and through him to reconcile to himself all things, whether on earth or in heaven, making peace by the blood of his cross.

The Letter of Paul to the Colossians, 1.15–20, RSV

In agreement, therefore, with the holy fathers, we all unanimously teach that we should confess that our Lord Jesus Christ is one and the same Son, the same perfect in Godhead and the same perfect in manhood, truly God and truly man, the same of a rational soul and body, consubstantial with the Father in Godhead, and the same consubstantial with us in manhood, like us in all things except sin; begotten from the Father before the ages as regards his Godhead, and in the last days, the same, because of us and because of our salvation begotten from the Virgin Mary, the *Theotokos*, as regards his manhood; one and the same Christ, Son, Lord, only-begotten, made known in two natures without confusion, without change, without division, without separation, the difference of the natures being by no means removed because of the union, but the property of each nature being preserved and coalescing in one *prosopon* and one *hypostasis*, not parted or divided into two *prosopa*, but one and the same Son, only-begotten, divine Word, the Lord Jesus Christ, as the prophets of old and Jesus Christ himself have taught us about him and the creed of our fathers has handed down.

Definition of the Council of Chalcedon, trans. J. N. D. Kelly, *Early Christian Doctrines*, 339f.

Christology is very much in the centre of the theological field today. And, while generalizations are always hazardous and I shall later on point to important exceptions, it may safely be said that there are two main features which characterize contemporary Christology. The first is the assumption that the primary need is to emphasize the reality and the normality of the *humanity* of Jesus, that traditional Christology has consistently and mysteriously failed to do this, that no special problems arise in doing it, and that when this has been done the *divinity* of Jesus can be left to look after itself, since in the last resort it can either be denied or ignored or else redefined in terms of the humanity. Thus, to give but one example, Dr John Knox, in his book *The Humanity and Divinity of Christ*,[1] asserts, 'We can have the humanity without the pre-existence and we can have the pre-existence without the humanity. There is absolutely no way of having both', and he then goes on to re-define the divinity of Jesus as simply 'a transformed, a redeemed and redemptive *humanity*'.[2] The second feature is the dismissal of the Christological decree of the Council of Chalcedon of A.D. 451 as static and abstract and as impossible to reconcile with the vigour and vitality of the Gospel portrait of Jesus; this dismissal, surprisingly enough is very commonly found among those who attribute little or no historicity to the Gospel portrait, which they hold to have resulted from the myth-making propensity of the primitive Church. Thus Dr M. F. Wiles has roundly condemned not only Chalcedon but the whole of classical Christology as resting on a 'mistake',[3] though he has been effectively answered by his colleague and neighbour Canon Peter Baelz.[4] Even as orthodox and learned a patristic scholar as the late G. L. Prestige described the outcome of Chalcedon as 'the Triumph of Formalism'.[5] Dr W. N. Pittenger, in his books *The Word Incarnate*[6] and *Christology Reconsidered*,[7] expounds what to everyone but himself is plainly an adoptionist doctrine, though he has persuaded himself that it is what Chalcedon was really trying to say. The impression that he leaves is not that he was deliberately championing Nestorianism against Chalcedonianism but that he was somehow incapable of seeing the difference between the two positions. A writer who felt less committed to the historic documents of Christendom would simply say, with Dr Wiles, that Chalcedon had made a mistake and would leave it at that. What is very clear is that a great deal of modern Christology is inspired by a mainly unconfessed and certainly uncriticized mixture of unitarianism and adoptionism.

Dr John Hick, in an interesting essay 'Christology at the Cross Roads,'[8] published in 1966, described the position held by such writers as Dr Pittenger and Dr Nels Ferré by the terms 'Degree Christology' and 'Neo-Arianism', though I think 'Neo-adoptionism' would have been a more appropriate label. He saw its fundamental defect as lying in its inability to account adequately for the uniqueness of Christ. It 'places incarnation at the top of a continuous scale which descends through saintliness to the ordinary levels of human life', whereas 'the attitude of worship demands the absoluteness of its object; and the test of this absoluteness is whether the object really (i.e. legitimately) demands our worship.'[9] Hick therefore returned to Chalcedon to compare it with the New Testament portrait of Jesus and undertook the task of 'trying to restate the Chalcedonian position in a way that can be intelligible today.'[10]

For Hick, 'the main feature of the Nicene and Chalcedonian formulae that renders them unaceeptable today [was] their central reliance on the category of substance [in Greek *ousia*, in Latin *substantia*]. They assert that Jesus Christ had two natures, being as human *homoousios* (of one substance) with mankind and as divine *homoousios* with the Godhead.'[11] Hick firmly asserted the identity involved, but he questioned the adequacy and even the intelligibility of the notion *homoousios* for our day. He wrote:

> We may emphasise what the Chalcedonian formula was concerned to emphasise in its *homoousios* by saying that Jesus' *agapé* towards the men and women whom he met in Palestine was not *like* God's *agapé* towards them (this would correspond to the Arian *homoi-ousios*), nor was it a reflection or imitation of the divine *Agapé*, but it actuallv and literally *was* God's *Agapé* acting towards them.[12]

Hick recognized that the same problem faces *agapé* here as faced *ousia* in the fifth century. Is Jesus' *agapé* qualitatively or is it numerically identical with the *agapé* of God? That is to say, is it another *agapé* than God's, though equal to it in every respect, or is it simply and literally God's very own *agapé*? In spite of difficulties, Hick opted for numerical identity as alone adequate to rule out a Degree Christology, but it appears to me that this can be done coherently only if *agapé* is identified with *ousia*, and then we are back where we started. Hick claimed for *agapé* the advantage over *ousia* that it makes it plain that 'we are not speaking of some kind of static substance but of volitional attitudes and operations.'[13] Now it is no doubt true that in common speech 'substance' has come to have static and impersonal overtones, but, in its metaphysical sense, I doubt very much whether theology can afford to dispense with it. If it has been thought of in too static a way, we ought to think of it in a more dynamic one; but I do not think we can do without it. And it seems to me that when Hick said that Jesus' *agapé* 'actually and literally *was* God's *Agapé*', he was implicitly treating *agapé* as *ousia* while at the same time raising a number of difficult metaphysical issues of which he did not seem to be conscious. That very independent thinker Professor D. M. MacKinnon, in an essay entitled '"Substance" in Christology – a cross-bench view',[14] has concluded that the notion of substance cannot usefully be discarded. He suggests, however, that *homoousios*

> is a second-order rather than a first-order christological proposition. That is to say, it is more something we say about what we say concerning Christ, than something we actually say concerning him that begins to lift the veil from the face of the God whom he discloses, with whom he is one. For that we must use the language of *kenosis*, but use it in closest relation to a reconstructed doctrine of the trinity. And for that reconstruction we shall certainly require to use ontological categories.[15]

This is an intriguing assertion, and its full explication must await that reconstruction of the doctrine of the Trinity which MacKinnon desires and perhaps intends to undertake. Its force will clearly depend on the view that is held about the relation of language to reality, but it is difficult to understand at all unless 'is more . . . than' is taken as a rather loose way of saying 'is . . . but not'. Otherwise MacKinnon is asserting that *homoousios* is both a second-order *and* a first-order term ('proposition' is an odd word to use in this context), and this would raise formidable logical difficulties. Nevertheless, it is refreshing to find a modern philosopher putting in a good word for substance. But to return to Hick, there would seem to be metaphysical problems in the assertion that Jesus' *agapé* was actually and literally God's *agapé* at least as great as those raised by the assertion that his *ousia* was actually and literally God's *ousia*. While fully appreciating Hick's attacks upon Degree Christology and Neo-Arianism, I am not happy with the substitute that he offered for the traditional Christological formulas. (This does not mean that I deny anything that he positively affirmed about the *agapé* of Jesus and of God.) And indeed in his final reflections he recommended his view for its contemporary attractiveness rather than for its superior theological adequacy. He wrote:

The assertion that Jesus' agapéing was continuous with the divine Agapéing is no more self-explanatory than the assertion that Christ was of one substance with the Father. Neither of these phrases, strictly speaking, explains anything. Each is concerned merely to point to a fact of faith; and each is concerned to point to the same fact of faith. But nevertheless I wish tentatively to suggest that the continuity-of-agapéing formulation may today be more intelligible than the oneness-of-substance formulation. Let us proclaim the *homoagapé* rather than the *homoousia*! For we know, at least ostensibly (and what better way could there be?), what we mean by *agapé*, but we do not know what we mean by substance – or at least, whatever meanings of 'substance' we isolate we then have to disavow as failing to provide an interpretation of *homoousios* which would render that term acceptable, or even genuinely intelligible, to twentieth-century Christians – let alone twentieth-century non-Christians![16]

I shall comment on only one point in this passage, namely that Hick used the phrase 'continuity-of-agapéing' and not 'oneness of *agapé*' in order to make the contrast with 'oneness-of-substance'. Presumably this is because 'continuity' was felt to indicate better than 'oneness' the dynamic character of *agapé* which Hick saw to be its great advantage. However, earlier in his discussion he had felt it necessary to insist that Jesus' *agapé* was 'actually and literally' God's *agapé*, numerically identically identical with it; and 'continuity' seems a rather weak and imprecise term to denote this.

Hick's final paragraph is in the form of two questions:

If we make this Chalcedonian claim today we shall have to face the problem which it now brings with it in ever-increasing force: what does this claim imply concerning the other religions of the world? And do the facts of history permit us to believe what it implies?[17]

His own answer to these questions is somewhat surprising; it was given in an essay which he contributed eight years later, as the summing-up contribution, to the symposium *Truth and Dialogue: The Relationship between World Religions*,[18] which appeared under his editorship in 1974. In it he showed himself to have moved a long way from the basically, and indeed obstinately, traditional position of his earlier discussion. Now he suggested that 'we should see the religious life of mankind as a dynamic continuum within which certain major disturbances have from time to time set up new fields of force, of greater or lesser extent, displaying complex relationships of attraction and repulsion, absorption, resistance and reinforcement.'[19] He had written shortly before, in answer to the question to what logical category the doctrine of the Incarnation belongs: 'I suggest that it is a mythic expression of the experience of salvation through Christ; and as such it is not to be set in opposition to the myths of other faiths as if myths were literally true-or-false assertions.'[20] So now the uniqueness of the Incarnation, which was implicit in the doctrine of Christ's *homoagapé*, seems to have dropped altogether out of view. 'In modern times . . . ,' Hick affirmed, 'the monolithic character of the traditional doctrine of the uniqueness of Christ has been modified in a number of new interpretations of the idea of incarnation – for example, the "paradox of grace" Christology suggested by the late D. M. Baillie.'[21] (Baillie would, I think, have protested against the discovery of this implication in his Christology, though his critics might have felt that it justified their disquiet.) 'The future I am thinking of', Hick said, 'is accordingly one in which what we now call different religions will constitute the past history of different emphases and variations within something that it need not be too misleading to call a single world religion."[22] But perhaps this conclusion ought not to surprise us; for I have earlier expressed doubts that the substitution of *agapé* for *ousia* as a basis for Christology can bear the weight which Hick tried to place upon it. (I stress the word 'substitution' here; that the *ousia* of Jesus and of God is *agapé* I would never dream of denying.) I believe in fact that a thoroughly Chalcedonian Christology can have a very positive attitude to the great world-religions. And I suspect that the kind of universalism in which Hick seems for the time being to have come to rest is anything but the metamissiology which its supporters believe it to be, but is far more a manifestation of the loss of conviction and confidence that is common in the world of Anglo-Saxon academic theology today.

To return to our main line of argument, many contemporary scholars have laid emphasis upon the 'heightening' of Christology which they allege to have taken place during the composition and compilation of the New Testament documents. Nevertheless, the extent and even the existence of such heightening ought not to be too hastily assumed; much will depend upon the criteria that are used for dating the documents or their components. And if one of those criteria is that anything that shows 'heightening' must be late, we are clearly in the grips of a circular argument if we claim to have demonstrated a progressive heightening because of the late date of the documents that manifest it. And it should be clear from the second appendix to chapter 2 above how little independent evidence for dating there is. However, Dr John Knox tells us that the original Christology was adoptionist 'almost by necessity',[23] but that, in view of the whole environment of early Christianity, the next step – the attributing of divine existence to Jesus – could hardly have been avoided. This, he asserts, could take only one of two forms – kenoticism or docetism – and neither of these can he accept as literal truth. Nevertheless, *as a story* kenoticism seems to him to be 'superb, indeed perfect'.[24] And, like Professor R. B. Braithwaite in the famous lecture *An Empiricist's View of the Nature of Religious Belief*,[25] it is *as stories* that the Gospel narratives interest him; it does not matter whether they are true or false. Indeed, it is better that they should be false than true. 'It is, I say again, the perfect story;' he writes, 'and in the prayers and hymns of the Church it is allowed to be the story it is.'[26] However, he continues, 'the Christian not only sings and prays; he also thinks.'[27] And to critical reflection the story is, in Knox's view, downright impossible. 'It is simply incredible that a divine person should have become a fully and normally human person – that is, if he was also to continue to be, in his essential identity, the same person.'[28] And so, Knox goes on, the Church, being unable either to reject the story outright or to recognize it as simply a story, changed it into something else in the hope of making it more credible; it turned it into a mixture of kenoticism and docetism. This began very early, as early in fact as the Pauline epistles and the Epistle to the Hebrews. 'The result is a christology, half story and half dogma, a compound of mythology and philosophy, of poetry and logic, as difficult to define as to defend.'[29]

Personally, I find Knox's account itself quite incredible, with his picture of the Church trying to make an incredible story more credible by combining it with a second story which was equally incredible. It is, however, most important to see clearly what lies behind it, for this is a presupposition common to many other modern writers as well as Knox; and, although it is highly debatable, it is rarely debated. It is the axiom that, whatever the Church and its greatest thinkers may have thought throughout the ages, it is impossible for the Son of God to be on the one hand divine and pre-existent and on the other to have really become man. Now it is not surprising that in the New Testament itself we can see a development of Christology; as Knox himself says, the Christian not only sings and prays, but also thinks. But that the primitive Church was led to accept pure nonsense I find it difficult to suppose; especially when on closer examination its thought turns out not to be nonsense at all. Knox's view seems to me to be slightly less fantastic than Martin

Werner's theory that the Church invented the deity of Jesus to console itself for the delay in his second coming;[30] but only slightly so.

It is interesting to turn from Dr John Knox to Dr John A. T. Robinson. One of the most perplexing features of Robinson's writing is the contrast between the minute and systematic method which characterizes his textual study of the New Testament and the imprecise and impressionistic style of his treatment of doctrinal issues. If we had only internal evidence to go on, we might well find it hard to identify the author of *Redating the New Testament*, which was published in 1976, with the author of *The Human Face of God*,[31] which appeared only three years earlier. In attempting a critical assessment of his celebrated book *Honest to God*,[32] I was constantly hampered by his habit of stating his opponents' positions in crude and extravagant forms and of becoming evasive at the critical moments; I found it necessary to take the book almost sentence by sentence in order to discover precisely what his argument was and to determine its value:[33] I shall not attempt anything as ambitious with this more recent Christological work *The Human Face of God*; it has received sympathetic but damaging examination from scholars as varied in outlook as Bishop B. C. Butler,[34] Dom Illtyd Trethowan[35] and Dr Colin Gunton.[36] Dr Gunton wrote:

> This is an eclectic and slippery book. So often – as, for example, in the discussion of Jesus' relation to the evolutionary process – it takes away with the left hand what has only just been given with the right, and while this may succeed in spiking the guns of heresy hunters, it neither aids the reader who would wish to understand precisely what is being said nor produces theology which is in any way original or exciting.[37]

And Dom Trethowan suggests that 'until Dr Robinson becomes clearer on what he means by God we cannot expect to find that his Christology has much to offer us.'[38] Nevertheless, a few comments on Robinson's book by a fellow-Anglican may not be out of place.

Robinson expresses considerable appreciation of Knox's *Humanity and Divinity of Christ*, which he describes as a 'beautiful little study' and as 'one of the best recent books on Christology'.[39] However, he rejects Knox's view that the Fourth Gospel is quasi-docetic and he points out that 'everyone agrees that [the author of Hebrews] stressed *both* the divinity *and* the humanity of Christ more unequivocally than any other New Testament writer.'[40] He writes very characteristically:

> It may be that we shall have to agree that pre-existence is a way of speaking that, like the language of virgin birth, can no longer be taken

literally or descriptively and is so misleading as to be unusable today. But since it is so deeply embedded in the New Testament presentation of Christ — far more deeply than that of virgin birth — it is at least worth asking what the New Testament writers really had in mind when they used it and whether they saw it as the threat to humanity that we do — and if not, why not.[41]

It will be worth while to devote some attention to this passage, as it is extremely revealing of Robinson's general attitude to traditional Christian teachings. First it must be noted that he describes Christ's pre-existence not as an alleged fact but as a 'way of speaking'. This enables his rejection of it to appear not as the denial of a truth of faith but as a preference for one way of speaking over another, a much safer position for a bishop to take up. But it leaves us entirely in the dark as to whether Robinson believes in Christ's pre-existence or not, and it carries the unfortunate suggestion that what is important in religion is not what is true but how we talk and think. This becomes more explicit in the following passage:

> If, then, we are to make any sense or use of the traditional categories in which Christian theology has spoken of the Incarnation, it is essential that we extend to it the revaluation of them to which we have now become accustomed elsewhere. For we have learnt to see the natural and the supernatural not as two layers of being that have to be joined together [we note here the standard Robinsonian technique of stating the position to which Robinson is opposed in the crudest possible form], so much as two sets of language, man-language and God-language, in which it is possible to speak of the single cosmic process. In other words, what we are talking about is not two storeys, but two stories [we note, again, no suggestion of any third possibility]. The one is natural, scientific, descriptive. The other is supernatural, mythological and interpretative. The former views the course of events in the categories of an evolutionary cosmology, the latter in terms of 'moments' like the Creation, the Fall, the Incarnation, the Parousia.[42]

To return to the passage previously quoted, we observe that Robinson draws a sharp distinction between the 'way of speaking' of the earliest Christians, which he admits to be 'deeply embedded in the New Testament presentation of Christ' though it is 'so misleading as to be unusable today', and 'what the New Testament writers really had in mind when they used it'. I think it is clear that the New Testament writers, and the primitive Church as a whole, would have admitted no such distinction and that what they 'really had in mind' was in fact what they said. The distinction has, I suggest, been manufactured by Robinson himself, so that he can reject their mode of speaking as, to use his own words, 'so misleading as to be unusable today' while claiming to share with them some underlying mental condition. And he appears to be saying that it is their 'way of speaking' that 'we' (whoever 'we' are) see as a threat to Christ's humanity, though he suggests that they did not see it as such. It seems clear, however, that, at least in the case of 'pre-existence', it is not just a way of speaking that he thinks 'we' have difficulty in accepting, but what that way of speaking has normally been taken to denote. For he expresses himself as willing to accept the term 'pre-existence' provided it is taken as meaning simply 'a life, power or activity (whether divine or spiritual) which is not as such a person', though it may '[come] to embodiment and expression (whether partial or total) in an individual human being'.[43] Then, by a somewhat breathtaking shift of position, he suggests that after all this was perhaps what the New Testament writers had in mind.[44]

Any confusion which we may now be feeling is likely to be increased when Robinson tells us that the concepts of the virgin birth (more accurately, of course, the virginal conception) and the pre-existence of Jesus were

> originally . . . separate and *alternative* ways of giving expression, in terms of the 'second' story, to the divine significance of Jesus.
>
> The New Testament writers who speak most of pre-existence (Paul, John and the author to the Hebrews) say nothing of virgin birth, while the virgin birth story as such says nothing of pre-existence. On the contrary, it presupposes that Christ is brought into existence as son of Mary and Son of God simultaneously by the creative act of the Holy Spirit.[45]

This last assertion is, of course, highly questionable, but it is in any case difficult to see why two statements should be described as 'alternative' when they are perfectly compatible and have always been recognized as such. Robinson himself discounts as 'clearly an exaggeration' Dr Wolfhart Pannenberg's claim that the two concepts stand in 'irreconcilable contradiction.'[46] As we have seen, his reluctance to reject outright the plain language of much of the New Testament has made him willing to accept the language of pre-existence, provided it means pre-existence in the mind of the Father (a pre-existence which is common to us all) and not personal pre-existence as the eternal Son. I find deeper understanding in Lady Oppenheimer's plain affirmation that 'to take one's stand . . . upon Christ's pre-existence is not just an obsolete mythological speculation, but the necessary condition of the first Christian thinkers being right about his significance.'[47]

For reasons which will, I think, now be obvious I shall not attempt a detailed discussion of Robinson's latest venture into Christology. What is very evident from it is that, while he expresses the most unqualified devotion to Jesus of Nazareth, so that, in his own words, 'it could be said, and had to be said, of that man, "He was God's man", or "God was in Christ", or even that he *was* "God for us"',[48] he finds the greatest difficulty in saying that Jesus was begotten of the Father before all worlds, and that for us men and for our salvation he came down from heaven and was incarnate by the Holy Spirit of the Virgin Mary and became man. For him, as for Pittenger and Knox, it is the humanity of Jesus that matters; whether he is personally divine is at best of secondary importance, though they hold that, in virtue of his complete self-dedication to the Father, God was active in him as in no other human being. They express great admiration for the Antiochene Christologists of the fifth century and a corresponding suspicion of, and indeed antipathy for, the Alexandrines. But, strangely enough, they have little sympathy for the point in which the Antiochenes took most pride and which constituted their chief objection to the Alexandrines, namely their unqualified and persistent stress upon the impassibility of God; Pittenger in particular is a fervent proponent of process-theology, for which the impassibility of God is anathema. It will in fact appear that the Alexandrine Christology, as developed for example by Leontius of Jerusalem, provides for genuine human experiences on the part of the divine Logos, while preserving the impassibility of the divine nature itself; it furnishes the divine Person with a human nature in which he can really suffer. But behind the whole of the modern neo-adoptionism, of which Knox, Pittenger, and Robinson are in their various ways exponents, there lies a deeply rooted assumption, which, as we have seen, is fully explicit in Knox, that humanity and divinity are not only diverse in their metaphysical basis but are also radically incompatible, in such a way that if Jesus was fully and completely man he could not also be literally and personally God. It is this assumption that I wish to deny. The insistence of these writers upon the reality and completeness of Christ's human nature is the one really strong point in their position, and it is wholly admirable. But the consequences which they claim to draw from it are, I believe, almost entirely false. Far from yielding to any Apollinarian, monophysite or monothelite doctrine, according to which if Jesus was literally divine he could not be genuinely man, I want to say that if, as I believe, the eternal God has become man, then man is what the eternal God could become; and this gives human nature a vastly nobler status than it could have on any adoptionist or quasi-adoptionist view. When Knox writes that it is 'impossible, by definition, that God should become a man',[49] he is doing what theologians of his empiricist outlook profess to abhor, namely putting logical deduction in the place of the recognition of actual fact. Indeed, I would maintain that only God, the Creator, *can*, without losing his own identity, become a being of an order radically different from his own. A donkey cannot become man, nor can an angel; but God can. It is, of course, true that thinkers such as Cyril of Alexandria and Hilary of Poitiers sometimes spoke of Christ's physical functions and sufferings as 'concessions' to our condition, but they never denied that he really ate and drank and felt pain; and it was the whole point of their Christology that, against all the protests of the Antiochenes, it provided for the divine Word, who, as all agreed, was impassible in his divine nature, a human nature in which he could and did genuinely suffer. There is, of course, a great deal that needs to be explored about the human life and experiences of Jesus in the light of our modern knowledge of anthropology, psychology, embryology, sociology and the like; the Chalcedonian formula provides a basis and a starting-point for Christological speculation, not a completed and finalized treatise on Christology. On that basis a great deal needs to be built; but it needs to be built on that basis, and not on an adoptionist basis which, even in the fifth century, the Church could see was inadequate and erroneous.

Robinson is entirely right in insisting on the human continuity of Jesus with the community and family in which he was born; in this is involved the real and not merely fictitious motherhood of Mary, whom the Council of Ephesus declared to be *Theotokos*, the mother of God. But Robinson's suggestion that Jesus' virginal conception is impossible, because natural parthenogenesis in the human species, if it occurred, would produce a female offspring,[50] invites the reply that, since Jesus was not a female, the parthenogenesis by which he was produced could not have been a *merely* natural one; and this is what the Church has always believed. What light can be thrown by modern genetic science upon the way in which the conception of Jesus presumably occurred and upon his genetic constitution is an intriguing question and inevitably a highly speculative one. The only detailed and informed discussion of it that I have seen is that given in 1964 by Fr Cletus Wessels, OP, in his book *The Mother of God, Her Physical Maternity: A Reappraisal*.[51] Such a work is necessarily somewhat ephemeral, on account of the rapidly developing character of genetic research, but it is nevertheless instructive to see how one of the most revolutionary branches of modern biological science is relevant to the supreme example of the perfecting of nature by grace and the supernatural. At least this should help us to see that orthodox Christian faith is not indissolubly wedded to discredited Aristotelian embryology.

Fr Wessels holds that 'Mary actively produced ova in the natural way and these ova, technically secondary oocytes, were perfectly natural germ cells. Only in the instant of conception did the supernatural enter the scene.'[52] He modestly adds that 'it is impossible to know with certitude exactly how the divine power accomplished this instantaneous disposition of the matter; there is found here the mystery of divine omnipotence.'[53] But he also says:

> There are two ways of reasonably explaining the presence of centrioles and the full number of chromosomes in the human body of Christ. It is possible that in the instant of conception the divine power created the centrioles and chromosomes necessary for the new organism. . . .
>
> There is, however, another possibility. The centrioles and chromosomes needed for the development of the new organism could have come from the egg-cell itself. It will be recalled that the egg-cell immediately prior to conception is a secondary oocyte which has not expelled the second polar body. . . . It is possible that in the conception of Christ the divine power, rather than expelling the second polar body, utilised its chromosomes in disposing the ovum for the generation of the new organism.
>
> One difficulty in this opinion is that artificially activated egg-cells always result in female offspring, and this is usually explained by the relationship between the X and Y sex chromosomes. Since the fruit of Mary's maternity was a male, the divine power could not utilise the full number of chromosomes she provided without at least some change in the sex chromosomes so that Christ would be perfectly normal male. [This is the question: how did Jesus get his Y-chromosome?] Such a change is possible, and so it is reasonable to hold the position that the chromosomes of the human body of Christ were

taken entirely from the ovum provided by Mary presupposing the necessary mutation of the sex chromosomes in the instant of conception.[54]

No doubt to some readers this kind of discussion will seem both over-speculative and distasteful. I can only reply that this objection is hardly available to those who insist on the literal and detailed reality of the human nature of Jesus. Others may feel that the change, by divine power, of an X into a Y chromosome or the suppression of an X and the production of a Y to take its place involves an interference with the normal process of conception that makes its product other than normally human. I do not think this is so if it is true that grace perfects nature and does not destroy it. Unless we are to be deists like Dr Wiles[55] and reject any special intervention of God into the natural process as a violation of the natural order that he has established and preserves, we must admit the possibility of a divine intervention that brings natural agencies to a consummation that they cannot achieve for themselves and so, while modifying their normal behaviour, perfects and does not suppress them. In the case at issue, a male whose Y chromosome had been produced in the way Fr Wessels suggests might well be not less genuinely human than one who had derived it from the spermatozoon of a human father. In any case, the Y chromosome seems to carry little or no genetic character but simply to determine sex. Jesus' whole genetic inheritance would seem therefore to be derived from his mother, the Virgin daughter of Israel; what is purely divine is the hypostasis in whom that genetic inheritance inheres. Robinson's fear that virginal conception would somehow weaken Jesus' organic continuity with Israel, and through Israel with the human race in general, is thus wholly groundless.

It should be added at this point that, unless Jesus is accepted as being *personally* (hypostatically) divine, the problem of his uniqueness becomes acute. Either the uniqueness has to be denied, so that Jesus is just one good man among many, or else his uniqueness has to be maintained by depriving his human nature of some one or more of human nature's normal constituents and then, by one of those *enantiodromiae* or flip-overs to which heretical positions are often subject, we find that we have switched from adoptionism to some modern counterpart of Apollinarianism or monothelitism. The assertion which one sometimes hears, that if the Incarnation means anything it must mean that there is literally nothing that distinguishes Jesus from any other male human being, would make his uniqueness unrecognizable, if not indeed nonexistent. It would perhaps be congenial to that extreme form of revelationism or supernaturalism which holds the deity of Jesus to be the object of sheer unconditioned faith, for which there can be no kind of evidential prolegomena and for which grace, so far from presupposing and perfecting nature, ignores and repudiates it. Robinson has clearly felt this temptation but, at the expense of some obscurity and ambiguity, has managed to resist it.[56] Dr John Hick, as we have seen, has in effect abandoned the uniqueness of Jesus altogether and envisages the Christianity of the future as simply one variant of a universal world-religion. Mr Don Cupitt similarly defines the only Christianity for which he sees a future as 'a family of monotheistic faiths which in various ways find in Jesus a key [note the indefinite article, not '*the* key'] to the relation of man with God.'[57]

Even among Christologists who would not admit to being adoptionists some have maintained that if Christ's humanity is genuinely real it cannot carry any indications that it is not the humanity of an ordinary man. The divine Person is there, but he is entirely *incognito*; and the act of faith by which he is recognized has no relation to anything that the experience of the senses discloses to us. However, in the Gospels themselves Jesus is seen as speaking and acting in a way that implies without argument a divine status, and this without any impairment of his complete humanity. I have pointed out elsewhere how all the Gospels, but especially St John's, can be read on two levels, one being that of historical narrative and the other that of theological interpretation, without any loss of coherent unity in the picture of Jesus which they present.[58] And I further observed that, improbable as this might seem on general literary grounds, it ceases to be puzzling if we accept the Chalcedonian doctrine that in Jesus two complete and undistorted natures, a divine and a human, are united in the one person of the eternal Son. I wrote as follows:

The Gospels . . . reflect in their very structure and their styles the divine-human character of him who is their theme. And if we do, in fact, accept the Chalcedonian definition, it would presumably be very disconcerting and perplexing if the Gospels had not the kind of duality in unity on which I have remarked. Of course, if we approach them with Arian, Apollinarian, Nestorian, Eutychian or kenotic presuppositions, we shall find them baffling and shall be forced to improvise complicated theories to explain why they are the kind of things that they are; some interesting case-studies can be made along these lines, based upon the writings of modern New Testament scholars.[59]

There are, of course, problems concerning the human nature of the incarnate Word, and in particular concerning the form and limits of his human knowledge, to which traditional Christology has not yet found satisfactory and exhaustive answers. I am not, however, convinced by the solutions offered by most of our neo-adoptionists, who allege that human nature, even if it has been assumed by the Second Person of the Blessed Trinity (though they would not admit that it had been so assumed), is intrinsically incapable of any activities beyond those with which we are familiar in ordinary life. It is, I suggest, futile for us to try to guess what it feels like to be God incarnate. Furthermore, it is psychologically crude in the extreme to suppose that, even in ourselves, the knowledge which a human mind possesses is identical in range with that which is the object of its conscious awareness at any given moment. To see this, I need only ask myself the question 'Did I know my own name five minutes ago?' St Thomas Aquinas recognized this, in his discrimination of different types of knowledge in the human soul of Christ, though his classification would not satisfy a modern psychologist. His most recent editor has remarked that 'it will appear paradoxical to contemporary theologians and exegetes that St Thomas's elaborate theology of the knowledge of Christ is worked out precisely in order to affirm the truth of his humanity.'[60]

Fr Karl Rahner, in a magisterial article on the Knowledge and Self-consciousness of Christ, has suggested, to give one example, that 'we are quite correct in attributing a direct union of his consciousness with God, a *visio immediata*, to Jesus during his earthly life, but this without qualifying or having to qualify it as "beatific".'[61] He has also skilfully handled the problem of the suffering of the impassible Logos by using a principle which he sees as applying analogically to all relations between God and his creatures, that 'he who is unchangeable in himself can *himself* become subject to change *in something else*.'[62] Rahner sees this as an advance on the common scholastic assertion that 'the change and transition takes place in the created reality which is assumed and not in the Logos.'[63] Dom Illtyd Trethowan has attacked this view as both unintelligible in itself and also contrary to the teaching of Vatican I,[64] but it seems to me to be simply a reaffirmation of the teaching of the Council of Chalcedon. A full discussion of Rahner's Christology would be a formidable undertaking, but it may be useful to list a few of its main traits. No one who had read Rahner's article 'Jesus Christ: History of Dogma and Theology' in the encyclopaedia *Sacramentum Mundi*[65] would question his fundamental loyalty to the teaching of Chalcedon; he sees it as fully compatible with an evolutionary world-view of which Chalcedon had little or no knowledge.

> The Saviour [he writes elsewhere] is himself a historical moment in God's saving action exercised on the world. . . . He must not be merely God acting on the world but must be a part of the cosmos itself in its very climax. This is in fact stated in the Christian dogma: Jesus is true man; he is truly a part of the earth, truly a moment in the biological evolution of this world, a moment of human natural history, for he is born of woman; he is a man who in his spiritual, human and finite subjectivity is just like us, a receiver of that self-communication of God by grace which we affirm of all men – and hence of the cosmos – as the climax of development in which the world comes absolutely into its own presence and into the direct presence of God.[66]

Thus, he holds, 'we are perfectly entitled to think of the creation and of the Incarnation, not as two disparate, adjacent acts of God *'ad extram'* [*sic*] which in the actual world are due to two quite separate original acts of God, but as two moments and phases in the real world of the unique, even though internally differentiated, process of God's self-renunciation and self-expression into what is other than himself.'[67] It is not surprising that Rahner saw it as a weakness that 'the average theology current in our schools today [he was writing nearly a decade before Vatican II] is only interested in the formal value of Christ's redemptive act, not in its concrete content, the inner structure of the redemptive process in itself',[68] and that he was suspicious of arguments about how God *might have* redeemed the world in isolation from the way in which he *has in fact* redeemed it. It is in line with this stress on the historic factuality, as well as with his insistence on the identity of the 'Economic' and the 'Immanent' Trinity, that he rejects the commonly held Thomist view that any one of the three divine Persons might have become incarnate[69] and maintains that incarnability is the peculiar characteristic of the Son.[70]

As regards Jesus' knowledge of himself as the co-equal Son of the divine Father, Rahner makes use of a notion which he has widely employed in other contexts, that of a pre-conscious or 'unthematic' self-awareness on the part of a spiritual being which is quite distinct from, and is antecedent to, the knowledge which it can have of itself as an object in acts of introspection.[71] It may be illustrated by the fact that, however fully I may be absorbed in the contemplation of another being, even to the point of complete unselfconsciousness and self-forgetfulness, there is at the root of this experience a primordial preconscious awareness that the experience is being undergone by Eric Mascall and not by Chairman Mao or Mrs Jacqueline Onassis. Something like this view is found in Dr Pannenberg's great work *Jesus, God and Man*,[72] though, like everything which he writes, it must be interpreted in relation to his idiosyncratic and debatable doctrine of the relation of truth to time.[73] Fr Louis Bouyer describes this view approvingly as follows:

We must not try to represent to ourselves this consciousness of Jesus, whether messianic or filial, as being essentially, and still less as being primarily, a reflex consciousness of its own identity. That was, as we have seen, the common error of the modern Christologies, whether 'descending' and Cyrilline or 'ascending' and Antiochene, and which leads them into monophysitism and Nestorianism respectively. All the difficulties which that starting-point cannot avoid accumulating vanish as soon as we recognize that this consciousness of Jesus, like every normal consciousness, was the consciousness of an object before becoming a consciousness of its own subject. The consciousness of Jesus, as the human consciousness of the Son of God, was before all else consciousness *of God*. Jesus was 'the Christ, the Son of the living God', not directly by knowing that he was, but because he knew God *as the Father*, with everything of the unique and the ineffable that that means for him according to the Gospel.[74]

In considering the theology of Rahner, and still more that of some other modern Teutonic theologians, it is important to remember that the philosophical and linguistic idioms in which they think and write are very different from those of traditional scholasticism and also from those of most modern Anglophone theologians. Rahner claims that one of his tasks has been to release the inner dynamism of scholastic theology, but he also describes his work as a transcendental theological anthropology, though with the proviso that, since Christianity is an essentially historical religion, it has aspects that cannot be deduced in an *a priori* manner.[75] In this context, it is perhaps well to distinguish between two very different meanings that can be given to the assertion that Christianity is a historical religion. It can mean that Christianity is not merely a general metaphysical theory about the nature of existence but is rooted in certain events which are alleged to have happened in particular places at particular moments of historical time; and with this I fully agree. But it can, on the other hand, mean that, because the Christian Church is a phenomenon within the changing process of human history, Christianity has no essentially permanent elements and must therefore be wholly conditioned by the various cultures within which it finds itself; and this I firmly deny. Rahner is, I am sure, clearly aware of this distinction; I am not so sure about the more radical members of the transcendental theological movement.

Robert C. Ware, in an article about the little-known Dutch and Flemish theologians of the present day (little known, because few outsiders can read the Dutch and Flemish in which they write and because little of their work, with the exception of E. Schillebeeckx's, has been translated), maintains:

> In the face of the continuing dominance of traditional dogmatic convention (catchword 'Chalcedon'), the priority of systematic Christological preoccupations with historical-ontological relationships needs to be reconsidered. The search for an adequate ontology, for a conceptual system adequate to express the saving experience of God in Jesus, deserves every priority. But the very fact of this search and the need for it, it seems to me, is enough to motivate and necessitate other directions and other accents in pursuit of systematic understanding of Jesus.

Again, he writes:

> The discovery of the pluriformity of models and concepts in the history of Christological thought is itself a liberating experience. It breaks the illusion that the finite structures of our language of dogma and worship actually encompass the reality to which they refer. By thus preventing dogmatic formulas and symbols from becoming 'taboos', the discovery opens the way to imaginative variety and development in theological expression, much as the 'model' method has done for science. Historical research in theology, too, will need to explore the various layers of meaning expressed in Christological language, concepts and symbols. This requires study of the cosmological, social and psychological, legal and economic forces which condition the formation of language in a given culture in order to arrive at the model of experience underlying a theological expression.[76]

Such pluriformity in Christology as this may be desirable, but it carries with it certain problems. Unless there is *some* community of meaning between the different systems which will allow for communication and translation, each of them will become a private activity of a little in-group, without relevance to one another or to the life of the Church as a whole. Furthermore, how are we to decide whether the conceptual scheme of any particular system is adequate to meet the needs of Christology and whether any theory stated within that system is, not only compatible with the axioms of that system, but also true in fact? Unless there is some common agreed court of appeal, however minimal and flexible, such as Chalcedon has provided in the past, we are likely to be left, not with a renewed and enlarged Christology capable of meeting the needs of the present and future Church, but with a number of competing Christologies, based on unco-ordinated and conflicting premises and methodological principles and incapable of reconciling their differences. How are we, for example, to set up a dialogue between the atheism of Dr Paul van Buren's *Secular Meaning of the Gospel*,[77] for which Jesus did not survive his crucifixion, the semantic relativism of Dr Leslie Dewart's *Future of Belief*,[78] for which there can be no stable truths about Christ or anything else, and Dr Piet Schoonenberg's contention that in Christ 'it is primarily not the human nature which is enhypostatic in the divine person, but the divine nature in the human person'?[79] I suspect that a good deal of frustration has been caused, in Christology as in other branches of theology, by the protagonists in a dispute assuming that they shared a common attitude to the basic questions of epistemology and semantics when this was in fact not the case.

2 TWO FRENCH CHRISTOLOGISTS

It is with something of a feeling of relief that I pass to consider three writers, two of them French and the third a Belgian, all of whom write in French though they appear to have had little influence on one another; they are all extremely sensitive to the outlook of the modern world, while attributing an indefeasible authority to the Council of Chalcedon. The first of these is M. Claude Tresmontant, a polymath if there ever was one. He is equally at home in philosophy, natural science, Biblical exegesis, and Christian theology. He is a loyal Roman Catholic, with nothing of the rebel about him, and he makes skilful use of the findings of contemporary science in order to relocate the problems of theology and to develop the traditional solutions in various directions. Philosophically, he is of the school of Maurice Blondel, to whom he has devoted a study and whose correspondence he has edited. (In passing, one may perhaps suggest that Blondel, who has suffered undeserved neglect in the Roman Catholic Church through unjust association with certain modernist tendencies, might have a lot to teach us today about the possibility of a dynamic Christian metaphysic.) He has written profoundly on the theme of contemporary atheism and has tellingly criticized the scientific atheism of M. Jacques Monod. He has expounded Pierre Teilhard de Chardin and has written exegetical works on the Hebrew prophets and on St Paul. And with all this he is barely fifty years old.

His recent work, of seven hundred pages, with the modest title *Introduction à la théologie chrétienne*,[80] deals in succession with God, the Incarnation, the Trinity and Man. While he is clear about the unique character of Christianity, he classes it with Judaism and Islam as a species of monotheism, in contrast with pantheism and atheism. He adroitly uses the concepts of genetics and information-theory to elucidate the contrast between creation and generation: he makes the stimulating assertion that 'the Logos is creative information itself. . . . Modern information-theory is one of the instruments at our disposal for rethinking the Jewish and Christian doctrine of creation.'[81] He remarks that, unlike biological evolution, doctrinal development does not create information but explicates it.[82] On Blondelian lines, he stresses the continuous character of creation and, more importantly, when later on he discusses Man, he sees creation as an activity of God which is not yet completed. In the second section of his work he deals with the Incarnation, recounting in detail, with many patristic quotations, the doctrinal disputes of the early centuries. Unlike most Anglophone scholars,[83] he does not hold that Christology stopped with Chalcedon and did not begin again until Schleiermacher; this is, I think, why he is able to combine an unqualified respect for the Chalcedonian definition with a recognition of its dynamic and liberating character. And – most importantly – it is in the seventh, and not in the fifth century, that he sees Christology reaching a phase of relative stability.

With the sixth ecumenical council (Constantinople, 680–681) the 'embryo-genesis' of the dogma of the Incarnation reached a stage beyond which it has hardly moved since; that is to say, the structure of Christological dogma as it was formed in the first seven centuries is ours today. We have made hardly any progress since. This does not mean that in the future the thought of the Church will make no progress in understanding what the Incarnation is. But in fact and broadly speaking Christological dogma, as it was formed at the end of the seventh century, has remained what it was until today.[84]

We shall see in a moment that for Tresmontant this relative stability achieved by Christology in the seventh century does not exclude a very striking development in theological understanding.[85] An unexpected innovation is the placing of the discussion of the Trinity after that of the Incarnation. From the historical standpoint, this involves a reversal of order, but the author justifies it by his insistence that theology is, in a genuine sense, an empirical science; in this he seems to be in line with the recent thought of both Torrance and Lonergan, whom, rather surprisingly, he does not mention, and also with Rahner, at least in the latter's approach to the 'immanent' Trinity from the starting-point of the 'economic' Trinity, revealed in God's self-communication to man.[86]

In the final section of his book, which is concerned with Man, the range and depth of Tresmontant's thought receive their fullest expression. Already, in discussing the Incarnation, he has seen Christ as subsuming into himself the whole evolutionary process:

> Present-day man recapitulates in a certain way all the previous biological and zoological evolution. In assuming man the Word of God assumed all the previous work of creation of which he is the author. He assumed all creation, recapitulated in man. In assuming the psychological and physical nature of man, the Word can be said to have assumed all the cosmic, physical, biological, and psychological preparation which has culminated in man. Thus Christ recapitulates all creation by fulfilling it and leading it to its supernatural end.[87]

In the final section the theme is amplified:

> What, according to orthodox Christianity, is the end of creation, its *raison d'être*? It is essentially the raising up of beings capable of sharing the divine life in a free and personal way, the creation of other gods, capable of receiving the communication of the Uncreated. . . .

The creation of the world and of man does not stop with the positing outside God of a being capable of consciousness, action and freedom, of what in modern languages we call a 'person'. It culminates in an intimate personal union, without confusion of natures or of persons, between created man and the uncreated God.[88]

No concession is made to the so-called 'process-theology'; in a luminous sentence we are told that 'it is precisely because God is complete, perfect and sufficient that creation is not the answer to a need but the expression of a gift.'[89] But – and here is the critical question:

How is this real, and not metaphorical, divinization of man brought about? It is brought about precisely by the incarnation of the Word. In the unique person of Jesus of Nazareth, as we have seen, God unites human nature to himself in a manner so intimate that the being constituted by this union is one person, although the two natures, the divine and the human, remain distinct, not confused or mingled or separated or diminished, but complete.

Thus it is in the Word incarnate that there is brought about the divinization of man without confusion of the natures. In this sense and for this reason the Word incarnate is the firstborn of the new creation, the new humanity, which is in process of formation for almost the last two thousand years.[90]

Tresmontant is emphatic about the sheer gratuitousness of man's elevation by grace into the life of God:

Only the Creator can know and teach what that is to which he destines and invites the created being. Philosophical analysis, which, as we have seen, proceeds by starting from experience, from the world and from nature, could not know that God invites us to such a destiny.

On the other hand, what philosophical analysis which starts from the datum which is man can discover is that there exists in man, in every man, including the man who calls himself an 'atheist', a congenital, irrepressible, indestructible desire for this destination, namely divinization.[91]

And the whole process of evolution and of human history is seen as the working out by God of this creative purpose:

The creative work is one, the creative design is one, although the moments and the times of its realization are distinct.

How the work of the creation of a being capable of sharing in the divine life is realized is the subject of Maurice Blondel's study in his trilogy on *Being, Thought*, and *Action*.

The time of human history is presented to us as the time of a long and painful apprenticeship of a humanity which emerges progressively from animality, moulded as it is from within by the destiny to which it is invited.[92]

Nevertheless, Christianity is more than the culmination of a natural historical process:

Christianity brings a new programmatization, to create a new humanity, distinct from the old, whose behaviour was governed by the biological programmatizations which are common to animals and man. . . .

According to the Christian vision of the world and of things, creation as we now know it is an uncompleted reality, a beginning of creation, a process which is on the way and is far from its end. This means that real time, what Bergson called 'duration', plays a fundamental part in the Christian vision of the world. . . .

For Christianity, the end of God's work, the work of creation, is transported not to infinity but very far ahead of us in the future. The whole Christian conception of the world and of history is finalized by this final perspective. Nothing is thinkable outside it. Christianity is essentially forward-looking. It never looks back.[93]

Tresmontant is explicit that the new creation subsists in the human nature of the Incarnate Word, who is its firstborn, and if, as must be admitted, he says little about the way in which the rest of mankind is to be re-created in him, this is perhaps to be the subject of a later volume; for all its seven hundred pages, the present work is only an 'introduction'! With a certain dead-pan realism which some of our secularizing theologians would do well to emulate, he remarks that 'in order for man to share in the divine nature, it is necessary that he should still exist' and that therefore 'the soul is not annihilated at death.'[94] But 'what is called in philosophy "the immortality of the soul" is, from the Christian standpoint, a necessary but not a sufficient condition. The soul must subsist in order to be divinized and become a sharer of the divine nature, but that is not enough.'[95] It is argued that the Hebrew conception of man, rather than the Greek, receives confirmation from modern science, original sin is interpreted as adhering to the human race rather than to the individual human being, and vigorous refutation is made of both Pelagius and Luther as misunderstanding the relation between created man and God his creator. Tresmontant's interpretation of the resurrection of the body is original and stimulating, but it is one of the very few parts of his exposition in which I find him inadequate. By downgrading, as he surprisingly does, the material aspect of the resurrection, he seems to leave the non-human constituents of the universe outside the realm of redemption. It would seem to be equally consistent with modern scientific knowledge and, indeed, with Tresmontant's own fundamental attitude and outlook to stress the final transformation in Christ of the whole of creation, matter and spirit alike. But this is a rare and puzzling lapse in a very outstanding work, in which a firm loyalty to Christian tradition is combined, without embarrassment or evasiveness, with an equally firm conviction of the dynamic and developing nature of the Church's life and thought.[96] What is it, he asks at the end of his work, that Christianity has to offer to man which nothing else can offer? 'Essentially,' he replies, 'the promise of a future, the invitation to a destiny which is supernatural, and the means of arriving at this destiny, which is sharing in the very life of God.'[97]

> Experimental science enables us to know what is now present and what has been. It cannot give us the life to come, life eternal, the life of God. Only God can give man, if he wants it, his own eternal life. That is Christianity: the communication to man of the eternal life of God.[98]

I turn now to Père Louis Bouyer, whose massive work *Le Fils éternel: Théologie de la Parole de Dieu et Christologie*[99] appeared in 1974; it is only one of many important contributions that he has made to the renewal of contemporary theology. More than half of the book is devoted to the theme of the expectation of the Saviour in the Old Testament and the fulfilment of that expectation in the New. This is due not only to his determination to build his Christology upon a firmly Biblical foundation but also to his conviction of the need to rescue Christology from a growing and excessive individualism which he sees as having characterized it in the West from the Middle Ages onwards, and also from a psychologism whose roots he discerns in St Thomas Aquinas and which he judges to have reached later on the dimensions of an invasion and to have resulted in a virtual expulsion of metaphysics from Christology. For a Biblical Christology, as he sees it, is essentially ecclesial; Jesus cannot be detached from the Church which is his Bride and his Body, the People of God, the New Israel.

This stress on the Bible makes a discussion of New Testament criticism inevitable, and Bouyer's account of its evolution and his 'critique of the critics' is of value in itself, quite apart from its relevance to the main theme of the book. He vigorously attacks Bultmann's postulate of a discontinuity between Jesus and the Church and his relegation of the Gospels to the literary category of myth and folklore. He expresses great respect for the school of Riesenfeld and Gerhardsson, who are two of the more conservative of the Scandinavian New Testament scholars, and he pointedly declares that 'the Bultmannians or post-Bultmannians, by their training, have become incapable of profiting by a whole world of data, which they are even less capable of rebutting and which show the falsity of the presuppositions from which they start.'[100] He remarks that 'fifty years ago the German historian Eduard Meyer observed that, if the history of the Greco-Roman world was treated in this way, nothing would survive of the wide agreement which has continued to unite the historians of antiquity.'[101]

I can only express admiration for Bouyer's very full and balanced exposition of the Christology of the New Testament documents. His chapter on the Resurrection and the Kerygma is masterly; it begins by remarking how few of the multitude of the books dealing professedly with the Resurrection are devoted to a really critical study of the documents and to an effort to get at the essential facts and how many are absorbed in the development of *a priori* philosophical positions for which the philological and historical critique is often a pretext or simply a façade.[102] I will quote only the following passage:

> In spite of certain inevitable hesitations of thought and still more of expression, adoptionist Christologies, far from being primitive Christologies, are only late products which can be labelled reactionary. The most immediate and sure effect of what we can call the experience of the resurrection, as the experience of the Christian faith in its first outburst, is quite different. It is a recognition (what St Paul denotes by the term *epignosis*) of what had been there in Jesus all the time and is now taken account of. He himself had suggested, and more than suggested it by his words, and perhaps still more by his actions. But God, by raising him from the dead, has in one stroke both confirmed and manifested it for those who believe in him.[103]

Bouyer shows convincingly how unforced is the development of an explicit Christology in the New Testament. There is no trace with him of Dr Knox's extraordinary contention that it is impossible to have both the pre-existence and the humanity of Jesus. And when he passes from the New Testament to the Fathers he is immune from the assumption which I have noted as endemic in English-writing theologians, that nothing of theological importance happened after Chalcedon, and which has led to the neglect of such outstanding figures as Leontius of Jerusalem and Maximus the Confessor. (It is exemplified by such standard works as J. F. Bethune-Baker's *Introduction to the Early History of Christian Doctrine to the Council of Chalcedon*[104] and Dr J. N. D. Kelly's *Early Christian Doctrines* —[105] how early, we might ask, ought 'early' to be? – as well as by Dr M. F. Wiles's *Making of Christian Doctrine*[106] and *The Christian Fathers*.)[107] Bouyer shows that it was the great strength of Alexandrine Christology that, by insisting on the completeness of Jesus' human nature and also on the fact that its metaphysical subject is the Person of the divine Word, it provided the immutable and infinite God with a human nature in which he can perform human acts and undergo human experiences. Leontius's doctrine of the *enhypostasia*, according to which the human nature of Christ, while entirely complete as a human *nature*, had no human *hypostasis* but was enhypostatized in the *hypostasis* of the eternal Word, simply clarified this, and it is ridiculous to characterize either him or the Alexandrine school in general as monophysites.[108] Like Tresmontant, Bouyer sees the importance of the sixth ecumenical council and he writes, with the clarification which it brought to Chalcedon in mind:

> Thus, as Cyril held, we can maintain that, in Christ, it is God himself who feels, suffers, and indeed is ignorant and makes human progress. Nothing, indeed, shows better the extent to which the true thought of Cyril is remote from any kind of monophysitism than his view on Christ's sharing in all our weaknesses except sin. It is an essential point of his doctrine that it was, in all truth, God himself, in Jesus, who underwent suffering and death to save us, in contrast to Nestorius and even the most moderate Antiochenes.[109]

Nevertheless, in spite of his approval of Chalcedon, Bouyer is unable to consider it as entirely successful, and he sees the separation of the so-called Nestorian and monophysite churches as a proof of this. He does not judge the separation as simply due to politics, either secular or ecclesiastical, nor, apparently to mere linguistic misunderstanding, but to the failure – perhaps the unavoidable failure – of Chalcedon to recognize genuine theological insights. (We may recall that in our own time a mixed commission of 'Chalcedonian' and 'non-Chalcedonian' – 'Eastern-Orthodox' and 'monophysite', to use the common designations

– theologians have been able to agree that their Christological differences are purely verbal,[110] and that a similar declaration has been issued by Pope Paul VI and the Monophysite Patriarch of Antioch.[111] Bouyer writes:

> It seems clear that a work of healing and of the solution of the problems in question was sketched out at Chalcedon but was not brought to a satisfactory conclusion. Thenceforth in consequence even the Christologies which can be called orthodox, in as much as they do not call in question the conciliar decisions, betray an uneasiness, an unreconciled duality, in their elaborations. This is so undeniable that we must recognize, with many moderate thinkers, that the problem needs to be reopened on a wider basis, even if we do not agree with those contemporary Catholic theologians who, following some Protestant theologians, declare the Chalcedonian solution so unsatisfactory that they propose to set it aside altogether.
>
> Nevertheless, I do not believe that it is a matter of rejecting the vision, or the successive and relatively complementary visions, of Ephesus and Chalcedon, but of recognising that the Christological problem cannot move towards a solution solely with the data that they provide.[112]

Passing to the Middle Ages, of which he is in general highly critical, Bouyer has some qualified praise for the Christology of St Thomas Aquinas, which he discusses in detail. He sees it as hitherto equalled 'neither in the richness and understanding of its delving into the traditional sources, nor in the correctness and rational coherence of its structure and its exposition, nor in the visible and almost palpable profundity with which it is rooted in a life of contemplative faith.'[113] Nevertheless, he judges it to have serious weaknesses, in particular the rigorous deductive rationality which arises from the scholastic notion of theology as a 'science'; thus, 'the chain of meditation upon mystery is periodically distorted by a web of univocal conceptualism'.[114] And, somewhat surprisingly, he accuses the Angelic Doctor of tending to forget the analogical character of the concepts which he employs. Like Rahner, he sees it as a weakness in St Thomas to have admitted that any one of the three divine Persons *might* have become incarnate, that more than one of the divine Persons *might* together have become incarnate in the same individual human nature, and that a divine Person *might* have become incarnate in more than one individual human nature; here, he says, we have entered into 'pure phantasmagoria'.[115] However, while he stresses the usefulness of the notion of *person* as *subsistent relation*[116] and praises its use by Dr John Macquarrie, he considers both St Thomas and Rahner to have overdone its employment for purposes of analytic deduction. But he finds Duns Scotus far less satisfactory than St Thomas.

I shall give only a brief indication of the topics which Bouyer discusses when he turns to the modern epoch. After an account of the scholastic controversy about the unity of the *esse* in Christ, he remarks on (1) the supersession of Christology in the strict sense by psychology and biography, (2) the arguments among Roman Catholics concerning the *ego* of Christ, which resulted in a qualified condemnation of the *assumptus homo* Christology by Pope Pius XII in 1951 in the encyclical *Sempiternus Rex*, (3) the various types of kenotic Christology among Anglicans, Lutherans, and Russian Orthodox and (4) the indications of a return to ontology at the present day.

In a final chapter, entitled 'Reflections' Bouyer gives his own views of the lines on which a modern Christology ought to develop. First of all he pleads for a correction of the individualism which has been so prominent in the Christology of the West since the Middle Ages. St Thomas' teaching about Christ's 'grace of headship' gives us a starting-point; Duns Scotus' teaching, in spite of appearances, is of no help at all. What is needed is a fuller development of the Chalcedonian teaching that Jesus is *homoousios*, consubstantial, with us in his manhood.

> All the soteriology which is enveloped in Christology, from the New Testament onwards, is linked together by the constant sense which Christology manifests of the unique relation in which we are with the Word made flesh, the Son of God become man.[117]

Both Biblical anthropology and modern psycho-physiology are called upon in support.

> How can the fact that the Son of God has become man . . . *in an individual* of our history, Jesus of Nazareth, concern us *all*, to the point that the salvation of us all depends on it and has been made possible by that alone that Jesus has done among us? That is, down to the present day, *the* Christological question; it is inevitable and yet unsolved.[118]

The other neglected truth, Bouyer tells us, is that of a certain pre-existence not only of Christ's divinity, but also of his humanity, in the life of the Trinity itself. From the standpoint of God all the temporal order is eternally present:

God is made man in time, that is to say that our human nature is assumed at a definite moment of time. But from his standpoint he assumes it eternally. Thus the Father begets his Son eternally, not only as going to be incarnate but as the Word made flesh.[119]

I must confess that I am uneasy about these last words (*non seulement comme devant s'incarner, mais comme le Verbe fait chair*). I agree, of course, that from God's standpoint his relations to all created beings, even to the human nature of Christ, are non-temporal and *in that sense* eternal. But Bouyer seems here to be in danger of confusing, in view of their common non-temporality, the necessary begetting of the divine Word by the Father with the contingent willing of his created humanity. I admit that the very possibility of the Incarnation implies a radical affinity between human nature and the Person of the Word. I agree with Bouyer, Rahner, Galot, and many others that it is peculiarly appropriate to the Son to become incarnate, and that human nature is the peculiarly appropriate nature for him to become incarnate in; and perhaps for 'peculiarly appropriate' one should substitute in each case 'uniquely possible'. I believe that many writers have virtually excluded the Incarnation from the start (John Knox is perhaps the clearest case of this) by postulating an insuperable incompatibility, or even antagonism, between God and his creatures, or between the Son and manhood. As a matter of logic, if the Word could become incarnate, then incarnability is an attribute of the Logos; and this is a fact of tremendous significance to us human beings. But it does not mean that the Word is concretely incarnate in the eternal life of the Trinity; nor do we need to assume this. Nor, I think, is it implied in the appeal which Bouyer makes to various of the Fathers and, in particular, to the much neglected Maximus the Confessor. 'The point which must be grasped above all', he rightly asserts, 'is that all the human life and all the human reality of Christ transfers and translates for us the eternal relation in which he is with the Father.'[120] And he shows himself favourable to the distinction between the essence and the energies of God, which, adumbrated by the Cappadocians and Maximus, reached its full development with St Gregory Palamas in the fourteenth century and has become part of the heritage of the Eastern Church.[121]

No modern Christology could evade the question of the development and the limits of the human consciousness of Jesus. Bouyer makes use of the notion which we have already found in Rahner, of a pre-conscious or 'unthematic' self-awareness on the part of a spiritual subject, which is quite distinct from the self-consciousness which it can have in acts of reflective introspection.

> Jesus was 'the Christ, the Son of the living God', not directly by knowing that he was, but because he knew God *as the Father*, with everything of the unique and the ineffable that that means for him according to the Gospel. When we have grasped this we are firm on the rock of the gospel-revelation. What is unique in the consciousness of Jesus of Nazareth is that it was pierced and traversed, from its first awakening, by that intuition, which was to precede, penetrate, and saturate all his states of consciousness, whatever they might be.[122]

Beyond this, says Bouyer, we are in the realm of conjecture:

> It may well be that he passed thence to the formed conviction that 'the Father' was his Father as he was naturally nobody else's, then that he had in consequence a quite unique mission in the world, and finally that this mission could be expressed only by a complete recasting of his people's expectation of the Messiah. . . . It may also be that the movement of thought in Jesus was much more rapid and intuitive. But it may, for all we know, equally well have been more sinuous, slower, or more progressive than what I have just said would allow.[123]

And, in a beautiful and moving passage, Bouyer adds:

> Without doubt, above all he learnt from his mother. By her and with her he learnt more specially all the Scripture and tradition of Israel, of which he himself would become the definitive interpreter, before the transmission, and for the transmission, of that which he alone could add, which abolishes nothing but gives to everything an unhoped-for accomplishment. . . . There was certainly, beneath all the psychological life of Jesus, a deep layer of intuitive knowledge of God and of the things of God. . . . Nearer, perhaps, to his clear consciousness, though already in the centre of his inmost consciousness, there must have been in him an inexpressible richness of ancestral memory of all the experience of Israel and of all human experience, partly, or from one aspect, intuitive, but from another aspect acquired. And he had with that, quite surely, a prophetic intuition, which it is absolutely impossible for us to delimit or circumscribe, of his destiny, his mission, and the endless repercussions which it could have. . . .[124]

May we not add that, in the part which was played in the awakening of his messianic consciousness by the teaching which he received from his mother, a key place must have been held by her memories of the events of his conception and birth?

This is indeed an outstanding work. In its scope and its competence it in no way falls short of the many earlier works by which Père Bouyer has put Christians of all denominations in his debt. I am therefore surprised that, among the vast number of other writers to whom he refers there is no mention of the man who is, in my opinion, the most constructively creative, and also one of the most judicious, of living Christologists, and whose work, while it is independent of Père Bouyer's, shows a remarkable affinity of outlook. This is Père Jean Galot sj, whose Christological writing is contained in three small volumes in French, to which I shall now turn and which I shall discuss at some length.

3   THE CHRISTOLOGY OF JEAN GALOT

I   THE PERSON OF CHRIST

The first of Père Galot's volumes, *La Personne du Christ*, has the sub-title *Recherche ontologique*; it was published in 1969.[125] While basing his thought firmly upon Chalcedon, he nevertheless emphasizes at the start that

> what was imposed at Chalcedon was neither philosophical concepts nor a particular system of thought, but rather the best way of expressing what is found concretely in Christ; it was a matter of translating the gospel datum, for it is always to this fundamental datum that the Fathers refer.[126]

Furthermore:

> If Chalcedon is the authentic expression of patristic Christology, it in no way puts an end to doctrinal research. On the contrary, it offers itself as the starting-point for new researches, since it is inscribed as a stage in the doctrinal progress of the Church, a stage which can no longer be opposed but which equally demands to be transcended.

> Thus, the formula of faith does not enter into explanations concerning what a nature is, and what a person or hypostasis is. It is not even concerned to define the act of the Incarnation, for it limits itself to declaring what is to be found in Christ. . . .[127]

Galot's special contribution at this early point in the discussion is to extend to Christology a notion which St Augustine of Hippo brilliantly devised in expounding the doctrine of the Trinity but which, strangely enough, seems never throughout the fifteen succeeding centuries to have been used in a wider context. This is the notion of 'person' as *subsistent relation* or, as Galot prefers to say, *relational being* (*être relationnel*). Stated thus baldly, the theological prospect offered may indeed seem bleak, but we shall see how dynamic and rich the notion becomes in Galot's hands and how vast is the range that it acquires. Dr J. N. D. Kelly remarks how, in Augustine's hands, it began as an ingenious riposte to certain Arian heretics:

> Basing themselves on the Aristotelian scheme of categories, they contended that the distinctions within the Godhead, if they existed, must be classified under the category either of substance or of accident. The latter was out of the question, God having no accidents; the former led to the conclusion that the Three are independent substances. Augustine rejects both alternatives, pointing out that the concept of relation (*ad aliquid relatio*) still remains. The Three, he goes on to claim, are relations, as real and eternal as the factors of begetting, being begotten and proceeding (or being bestowed) within the Godhead which give rise to them. Father, Son and Spirit are thus relations in the sense that whatever each of Them is, He is in relation to one or both of the others.[128]

Galot, appealing to the Eleventh Council of Toledo and the Council of Florence, is at pains to stress that the defined doctrine is minimal in content:

> Its intention is not to determine strictly the formal constituent of the person; it simply declares that the plurality of persons in God exists only to the extent to which there are relations bearing a certain contrast. But it thereby indicates that the reality that distinguishes the divine persons is that of relation. The natural conclusion is not only that the persons result from relations of origin, but that relation is what constitutes them. This is what theology does when it defines the divine persons as subsistent relations, as *esse ad*.[129]

And Galot makes it clear that, paradoxical as it might seem, it is precisely because *person* is relational that each of the persons can possess not just *part* of God's absolute perfection or an abstract aspect of it, but that perfection in its concrete totality, while, of course, each possesses that absolute perfection in its own 'relative', i.e. *relational*, way. We might therefore say, though Galot does not put it in these words, that there is nothing unreal or phantasmal or spectral about relational being, but that it is, on the contrary, concrete, dynamic, and intense.

Before discussing directly the person of Jesus, Galot pauses to consider the dual application of the notion of person to God and creatures. He makes it plain that there will be both similarities and differences. First the similarities. A human person cannot, any more than a divine person, be a quality of the nature, or a mode, or existence itself, or the act of existing; it must be a subsistent relation. And unless there were such similarity, we could not significantly apply to divinity the word 'person', derived as it is from the context of humanity. However, the analogy works both ways, and by projecting on to human persons the light which the word of God has shed for us on the divine persons we conclude that human persons, made in their image, are also subsistent relations.

But now for the differences. First, in God the plurality of the persons is due to their contrasted relations of origin. The plurality of human persons is due to their creation by God; each is not so unconditionally (*éperdument*) original.

Secondly, the divine nature is absolutely unique, and the divine persons are distinguished solely by their relations, since they have the same identical nature. In contrast, human persons are distinguished not only by their relations but also by the individual nature particular to each one. Galot comments in passing on a possible ambiguity in the term 'subsistent relation', which might be taken as meaning a relation deriving its reality from a substance rather than, as is intended, a relation which itself subsists as a person; he therefore expresses a preference for the term 'hypostatic relation'. He discerningly adds:

From the fact that each human person possesses his own individual nature, we easily tend to identify person and nature, personality and individuality; and then we are led to take the person as an absolute [i.e. non-relational] reality, *endowed with* relations but not *constituted by* relation. . . .[130]

The divine persons are more perfect by being mutually distinct solely through their relations and by possessing in common one identical nature. Human persons approximate to the divine persons by the fact that, while each has an individual nature, they are nevertheless essentially constituted by a relation, a hypostatic relation.[131]

Thirdly, Galot points to the difference between God's perfection, which is pure act, and that of creatures, which is progressive and incomplete:

> Human nature is not pure act, but potentiality which is being actualized; nor is the human person a completed relation, as are the hypostatic relations of the Trinity; it is a relation on the path of actualization. . . . More precisely, it is actualized by self-consciousness and self-giving, that is to say, by the activities of knowledge and love in which the person more fully becomes himself.[132]

Thus, personal development necessarily involves the extension, multiplication, and deepening of one's relations.

> But we must not confuse the hypostatic relation, which is the formal constituent of personality, with the relations which can be called accidental or occasional, that is to say, relations meshed into the concrete setting of human life with determinate persons. These relations are such as to actuate the hypostatic relation and confer more perfection upon it, but are not identical with it.[133]

So, because of their fundamentally relational character, it is by altruistic sharing and giving that human persons achieve their progressive perfection and personalization.

It is inspiring to see how Galot, starting from what would appear to be a highly abstract and academic stance – for what could seem more abstract and academic than Aristotelian logic and the categories of substance and relation? – has arrived at a pattern of human living which is vibrant with personal self-giving and altruistic love. This becomes even more evident in his discussion of human individuality. He comments on the fact that the basic characteristic of personhood has often been defined in an individualistic and even an isolationist sense. The reason for this is clear; it is that, at least in theory, there is nothing metaphysically impossible in the existence of another human being possessing every characteristic, physical and mental, that I myself possess. In old-fashioned language, human *nature*, and every constituent of it, is metaphysically multipliable and communicable; there could always be more than one instance of any given type. Nevertheless, there *is* something inherently unmultipliable and incommunicable; even if you and I were precisely alike, I could never be you, and you could never be me. The commonly heard phrase 'If I were you . . .' never in fact literally means 'If I were you . . .', it only means 'If I were in your situation . . .' or 'If I possessed most (or even all) of your qualities . . .'. There is something about me that is strictly incommunicable, and, since every constituent of my nature is in principle communicable, this cannot be a constituent of my nature. And so it is what is called my 'person', my *persona*, *suppositum* or *hypostasis*. It is this train of thought, perfectly valid in itself, that has led to the definition of person in terms of incommunicability, with its isolationist overtones. But it is less than half the truth. In Galot's words:

> Independence, self-totality, possession of one's being, the mode that consists in existing in oneself, or by oneself, existence-by-itself – these distinctive notes link up in a way with reality, but they express only one aspect of the person, and if we wished to define the essential reality of the person uniquely by this aspect, we should enclose the personal individual in himself and tend to make him into an autocratic, self-sufficient whole.[134]

However:

> The mystery of the Trinity is displayed as the most open denial of any individualistic personalism. . . .
>
> It is the same for human persons; they do not first of all exist in their separate self-enclosures (*chacune dans son quant à soi*), to enter later on into relation with others and form a community with them. Community and person are posited together; a person only exists as a relation with other persons. Its reality is that of a relational being. An 'ego' (*moi*) has meaning only in its relation with other 'egos'.[135]

And Galot remarks that 'relational being' is a better term than 'relative being' to denote what is a mutual and reciprocal relationship and not just a one-sided dependence. He sees this property reflected in the Biblical account of the creation of man as 'male and female': 'it is a community that is created, in the image of the community of the divine persons.'[136] Nevertheless for the full manifestation of the divine fecundity towards man we must turn to the order of grace:

> The mystery on which the extension of the human community is founded is wider than that of the creation of the world; this extension bears the full reflection of the divine fecundity only in the supernatural

light, by which the divine family opens itself to human persons to welcome them into its bosom. The fecundity of the first pair is the image of that vastly heightened fecundity which makes men sons of the Father in Christ.

The multiplying dynamism of relational being which characterizes the human person is thus the reflection of the dynamism of the divine persons, who, having the possibility of remaining shut up within their intratrinitarian relations, have opened themselves to the multitude of mankind.[137]

I have expounded in some detail Galot's general doctrine of the person, as otherwise it would be impossible either to understand or to assess his special contribution to Christology. He has a brief but important transitional chapter on the person in the light of psychological experience. He points out how easy it is, in virtue of the fact that it is only in consciousness that the person comes to perceive itself, to draw the false conclusion that person and consciousness are simply identical. Nevertheless the two are distinct, and the vital point is that the conscious apprehension of oneself (*la prise de conscience de soi*)[138] is 'an activity which, while it emanates from the person and bears upon the person, belongs [not to the person but] to the nature. It characterizes a spiritual nature.'[139] And this distinction is supremely important in Christology, since Christ's person is uniquely divine, while he has a genuine and unmutilated human consciousness, and with this a truly human psychology. We must not, however, suppose that self-consciousness is the sole, or the principal, manifestation of the person; that would be to encourage an unhealthy egotistic individualism. As we have seen, person as relational being has a virtually universal reference. Galot goes on to stress that it is an empirical psychological fact, quite apart from any philosophical or theological theory, that is only through its consciousness of the external world that a human subject becomes conscious of itself; the need of relationship to others for one's own self-fulfilment, he remarks, is a commonplace of empirical child-psychology. Cognitive activity is never in fact separated from voluntary activity, and relational being involves not only knowledge but also love. 'The ego fulfils itself by giving itself. It is by adhering to another person that it becomes in its fulness what it is meant to be.'[140] If this seems to be a paradox, it is the paradox of the gospel.

Essentially, of course, this is Rahner's thesis of the unthematic self-awareness which is present in all our cognitive activity, but Galot places it in a somewhat different and, in my opinion, a more satisfactory setting. He maintains that his view preserves the fundamental incommunicability of the person which other writers have stressed, while avoiding isolationism and egotism:

> The ego is indefinable precisely because it is relational; each ego is determined by its particular and unique relation to the other egos. Nature can be defined by properties, by essential notes; . . . its basic characteristic is to be common to [a number of] individuals, to carry constants which are found in each of them. In contrast, the ego is never repeated; it does not fall within a category and cannot be ranged under a general idea. . . .[141]

Incommunicability and aptitude for communion go together; 'person' and 'community' are not to be set in conflict. And, while he repudiates any desire to evacuate the Trinity of its unfathomable mystery, Galot sums up as follows:

> The progress of the discovery of human community in our day enables us to elaborate a doctrine of the person which can make it easier for us to understand the community of the divine persons. In its recognition of the person as a communitary relational being, contemporary anthropology offers an appreciable help to theological reflection on the Trinity and the Incarnation.[142]

Coming now, well after the middle of his book, to develop its professed theme of Christology, Père Galot asserts roundly that 'the definition of person as relational being enables us to solve the problem which is posed by the absence of a human person in Christ. This absence removes nothing from the human nature and does not prevent it from being complete in itself.'[143] It has, of course, always been recognized that the integrity of Christ's human nature, in the Chalcedonian doctrine, depends on the fact that person or *hypostasis* is a metaphysical entity and not a psychological one. To say, with the Apollinarians, that Christ lacked a human soul or *nous* would be to make his human nature incomplete; for soul is a constituent of human nature. So it would be to say with the monothelites that he lacked a human will or with the monenergists that he lacked a human energy, for will and energy are equally constituents of human nature. So also is personality, in the sense that that word frequently has today, for it is used to denote not just one component of human nature but the whole of human nature in its psychological aspects. 'Personality' thus understood, however, has nothing in common with person or *hypostasis* as it has been understood in Christian theology, in which it is a purely metaphysical term, whether used in expounding the doctrine of the Trinity or that of the Incarnation. The difficulty here is to make 'person' more than a purely numerical marker; that is both its strength and its limitation. As Fr Bernard Lonergan has written:

> While later developments put persons and natures in many further contexts, the context of Chalcedon needs no more than heuristic concepts. What is a person or hypostasis? It is in the Trinity what there are three of and in the Incarnation what there is one of. What is a nature? In the Trinity it is what there is one of and in the Incarnation it is what there are two of.[144]

And, while this may be sufficient and even laudable as far as dogmatic definition is concerned, since dogmatic definition should be kept to a minimum, it does not suffice as an informative and persuasive theological affirmation or as an inspiring religious watchword. It may preserve the *fides*, but what about the *intellectus* which, we are told, *fides quaerit*? This is a matter of the 'later developments', and Lonergan himself has written: 'My own position has been that the doctrine of one person with two natures transposes quite neatly into a recognition of a single subject of both a divine and a human consciousness.'[145] (I do not, however, take Lonergan as implying that nature includes consciousness and nothing else.) Galot, too, has written at length on Christ's human consciousness and has devoted to it an entire book, which we shall consider later on. But at the moment I wish to direct attention to the extraordinarily rich and deeply religious content, and to the hitherto largely unrecognized implications and consequences, which Galot has shown to be involved in the superficially bare and schematic notion of Christ's person as relational being.

As uncompromisingly as any of the radicals, Galot insists on the reality and completeness of Jesus' human activity and experience:

> Jesus' human nature is altogether similar, 'consubstantial', to ours, to use the Chalcedonian term. . . .
>
> A human existence is in no way lacking to Christ's human nature, since *person* does not consist of existence, and the presence of a divine person does not entail a divine existence for the human nature. Christ exists and lives as man; he undergoes a human experience which is no less ontological than psychological.

No more than human existence has a human manner of life been withheld from the incarnate Word. Christ has lived in the manner in which men live. . . .

What is *not* found in him is a human hypostatic relation. The Son of God enters mankind as a man, but not as a human person. The wholeness of his human nature is in no way diminished thereby.[146]

And here one of Galot's deepest insights comes into view, that it is because of the absence of a human *hypostasis* in Christ that he can be the universal saviour of the whole human race:

The unity of Christ requires the unity of his person. But the purpose of the Incarnation demands it no less, for this mystery is destined to bring about union between God and mankind. . . . The relational being of the Son of God, by being directly introduced into the human community as one of its members, fastens it directly to God. From the fact that the purpose of Christ's coming into the world is the establishment of the covenant, the Word must penetrate into the community of human persons in his quality as a divine person, as the divine relational being who weaves new relations with human relational beings.[147]

And again:

The mystery [of the Incarnation] does not consist only in the assumption of a human nature by the Word, but in the formation of a link between a divine person and all human persons. The relational being of the Son of God, which in the divine eternity is simply turned towards the Father in the unity of the Holy Spirit, orientates itself towards men and, thanks to the human nature which it assumes, involves its hypostatic relation in relationships with the human persons. It thus expresses the relation which God wishes to have with humanity.[148]

Galot is thus led to a view of God's redemptive activity of the utmost openness and amplitude. If we had to consider man without reference to his supernatural destiny and the divine plan of salvation, Galot tells us, we could recognize in him only his interpersonal relations with other men. But the Incarnation transforms this situation by establishing interpersonal relations between man and God. It is true that these relations preceded the coming of Christ and were found in pagan religions and the Old Testament; nevertheless, in the divine plan these relationships were based on the Christ who was to come. 'Thus we can say that every religion, whatever it may be, in so far as it implies personal relations with the true God, has Christ for its foundation.[149] Thus Galot sees Christ as not merely the basis of the covenant between God and man but as actually identical with it, in its relation both to God and to man, and he sums up his exposition of the Incarnation in the following passage:

> The relational being of the Son of God penetrates into humanity as a dynamic principle of transformation. We must conceive the Incarnation in this essentially dynamic perspective.
>
> The formulation 'one person, two natures', which expresses the ontological constitution of Christ, could be fastened down in an over-static view of the mystery, but it must be understood in its deepest reaches. The person of the Son of God has become man and, in assuming an individual human nature, he has not only united it to the divine nature. He has penetrated into the human community in order to bind it to the Father by his relational being and to transform it by restoring and recreating human being. It is a divine dynamism that seizes hold of a human nature to reach human persons. The Incarnation is an action, an operation, undertaken by the person of the Son, which continues without ceasing. It extends to all the human 'egos', which it wills to gather together in a relation of sonship to the Father.[150]

In the final chapter of this book, Galot emphasizes the effect of this entry of the relational being of the Word into the human community: 'He penetrates into this community as subject of love, term of love, and bond of love',[151] as 'I', 'thou' and 'we' of human relations. As 'I', as *ego*, he is the source of the filial love of the Father and of the love of the neighbour; as 'thou', he calls for faith and love, love towards all human beings; as 'we', he sets up a new relationship of all men to one another. As 'I', 'thou' and 'we', his person 'divinizes from within the human community, which is henceforth animated by a charity that starts from Christ, bears towards him, and is gathered together by him in a divine unity.'[152]

2 THE CONSCIOUSNESS OF JESUS

In the second and longest member of his Christological trilogy, which bears the title *La Conscience de Jésus*,[153] Galot addresses himself to the question which has preoccupied so many modern writers on Christology, namely that of the mental life, and in particular the consciousness and self-consciousness, of Jesus. The first of the two parts into which the book is divided consists of an extremely thorough examination of the Gospel evidence. In view of the fact that, among modern scholars, he adopts a comparatively conservative attitude in regard to the authenticity of the recorded sayings of Jesus, it should be stressed that he is by no means a fundamentalist and that he admits a considerable element of interpretation and implicit commentary in the accounts of the Lord's teaching. He does, however, deal systematically and comprehensively with the material as we have it and does not, as is so common today, eliminate or downgrade large parts of it on the basis of antecedently adopted theories about what Jesus was likely to have said and how likely it was to be true if he said it. Of the various 'self-designations' which Jesus used, Galot sees the mysterious title 'Son of Man' as most reliably authentic, if only because the Church obviously found it puzzling and let it fall into the background; indeed he suggests that Jesus used it more commonly than the Gospels as we have them record, and that it has often been replaced by less difficult designations. Showing himself well acquainted with the vast literature on the significance of the Son-of-Man sayings, Galot insists that Jesus identifies himself with the mysterious figure and that he not only fulfils but also transcends the prophetic expectations. But, he continues, while 'the way in which Jesus speaks of himself in the third person by describing himself as the Son of Man is strange and exceptional, the way in which he speaks of himself when he says "I" is no less so.'[154] Galot shows that the *Ego eimi* ('I am') passages imply a divine status, but also – and this links his discussion of the consciousness of Jesus with the theme of the earlier book – they, and many other Gospel passages, no less clearly manifest a filial relationship to the heavenly Father. Not only is this shown by the unique way in which Jesus uses the word 'Father', but more explicitly by the one passage in which he is recorded as addressing the Father by the Aramaic word *Abba*, which, so far from being a term by which any Jew would dare to approach the transcendent Father in heaven, 'was the familiar term which Jewish children used to talk to their father, more or less equivalent to our "Daddy".'[155] Indeed, writes Galot,

> one suspects at once that, in the other cases where Jesus says 'Father' in his prayer, he has most probably used the Aramaic term *Abba*. In fact, the term used in Gethsemane was that by which Jesus normally addressed the Father; it is difficult to imagine that he could have made use of two different words.[156]

And Galot remarks that, with the sole exception where he is quoting *verbatim* from the twenty-second psalm, Jesus is never reported as addressing the Father as 'God', but always as 'Father'.[157]

Galot is not, of course, the first writer to point out the peculiar intimacy of the word *Abba*; this is a commonplace among commentators and it has, for example, been emphasized strongly by Dr C. F. Moule.[158] But, while they have recognized its moral and didactic aspect, I do not think they have seen its precise *Christological* significance as clearly as Galot. Stressing that 'the audacity of the Gethsemane prayer itself helps to confirm its authenticity, and also that of the term *Abba*', Galot points out that 'the equality of nature implied in the term *Abba* is expressed in Jesus' practical behaviour; he has such a familiarity with the Father that, even in his anguish and distress, he remains on the same level with him, so that he can speak with him and ask for a change in his plans.'[159] And it is emphasized that, when St Paul in his epistles (Gal. 4. 6; Rom. 8. 15) says that Christians address God as *Abba*, this is only because they have been adopted into Jesus' own sonship: 'they do not pronounce it in their name, but in the name of Christ who lives in them by his spirit.'[160]

Thus for Galot it is the name *Abba* that provides a most significant link between the scriptural portrayal of Jesus and the Christology of the Church. In particular, it is the key to Jesus' self-consciousness. Thus Galot summarizes the first part of his book as follows:

> It is this [sc. *Abba*] that is the most apt term to indicate to us how the consciousness of divine sonship was formed in Jesus. We have seen that the *Ego eimi* is used by Jesus only in the perspective of a fundamental relation to the Father; and the key to the significance of this *Ego eimi* is found in the word *Abba*. Similarly, the declarations about the Son of Man imply a mysterious sonship in Jesus of divine origin; the force of this title can be further unveiled only by reference to the term *Abba*. The name *Abba* thus has a primordial force which illuminates all the expressions of the consciousness of Jesus.
>
> No other term could have been as meaningful to witness to the point at which the consciousness of divine sonship is, in Jesus, a consciousness that is perfectly human. *Abba* is the term used by someone who has a consciousness like that of other children, but with this difference, that in this case the father is not a human father, but is God.[161]

Having laid the scriptural foundation, Galot begins its psychological and theological interpretation by remarking that the definition of Chalcedon, unity of person and duality of natures in Christ, far from putting an end to research, encourages it by inviting a closer determination of what person and nature are. With a passing mention of his earlier work, he now limits himself to the psychological problem of the ego[162] and the consciousness of Christ, though he points out that theological principles cannot be excluded, since Christ's psychology is characterized by the presence of a divine person. The views that he considers are little known outside the Roman communion, but they are none the less of wider relevance. First he examines the theory that attributes to Christ a human ego. This was given a romantic presentation in 1927 by the elderly theologian Déodat de Basly under the figure of a 'tournament of love', in a novel entitled *La Christiade Française*. This is the story of the Triune God who wishing to be loved by a being external to himself, creates a supreme lover who is the Man-Christ or *Assumptus Homo*. Setting aside the details of the romance, it is clear that Christ's ego was conceived as a human ego, over against the Trinity; it was not the eternal Word that was the principal agent in the human actions of Jesus. A more conventional statement of the view that in Christ there is a human ego was made in 1939 by the Jesuit Paul Galtier in his book *L'Unité du Christ, Etre . . . Personne . . . Conscience*,[163] and several other writers are cited by Galot as holding the same or similar views. The controversy which ensued was damped down by the encyclical *Sempiternus Rex*, which was published by Pope Pius XII on the fifteenth centenary of the Council of Chalcedon in 1951, though a difference between two versions of the text leaves it uncertain whether a psychological, as distinct from an ontological, human ego in Christ was repudiated.[164] Without reproducing the details of Galot's own judgement on the matter, it is sufficient to say that it is evident to him that ego must be identified with person, but that this does not in the least diminish or impair Christ's human consciousness.

It is certain that Christ had a human consciousness and that therefore we must recognise, in the unity of his person, two consciousnesses, one divine and the other human. We must exclude immediately any intrusion of the divine consciousness into the human, which would result in modifying the nature of the human consciousness's apprehension (*prise de conscience humaine*) by introducing divine elements into it. . . .

From this human consciousness, which is only human, can we deduce, with Galtier, the existence of a human ego? For that to be so the human 'ego' would have to designate the human nature and not the person. . . .

That the ego designates the person does not imply that the person is fully and completely expressed in consciousness by the ego. Consciousness reveals the person only in as much as it is engaged in psychological activities; thus it does not manifest the totality of the person or show directly what the person is in itself independently of its activities. But what it reaches is the person; the ego is identically the person, or more precisely the person in its conscious expression.

Therefore, if there is in Christ a unique divine person, the ego of the human consciousness of Christ can designate nothing other than this person; it must be identical with it. In his human consciousness Christ perceives his ego, which is that of the Son of God. Thus there is in him no human ego; there is human consciousness of a divine ego.[165]

The last sentence sums up in a brief formula the essence of Galot's Christology, though if we wish to express it in a strictly theological form it would be well to substitute 'person' for 'ego': 'there is in Christ no human person, there is human consciousness of a divine person.'

To dispel any lingering doubts that Galot's Christ is perhaps not, in spite of his protestations, genuinely and fully human, it may be well to recall the central theme of his earlier book, that person, *hypostasis*, is relational being. If 'person' stood for being that was absolute, in the sense of non-relational, then to lack a human person would well imply the lack of some component of humanity; it is precisely because of its purely relational character that the person can be the totally permeating subject of the human nature in all its operations without that human nature being in the least degree impaired. To bring out the implications of this on the psychological plane, it will be necessary once more to quote Galot at length:

There is a true autonomy of Christ's human psychology, in the sense that this psychology functions according to the laws of human nature. We must rule out any mixture of the divine nature in this psychology. This is the reason why, for example, we must recognize in Christ a limited and progressing human knowledge, without the intrusion of the unlimited and eternal divine knowledge. We must similarly recognize in Christ spontaneous reactions parallel to ours, the feeling-states which are met with in every human psychology. The fact that he is the Son of God in no way prevents his experiencing a strictly human joy or sorrow.

But if there is full autonomy in the order of nature, there is at the same time total dependence in the order of the person. The human psychology of Christ depends entirely on the person of the Word. We must not set the psychological autonomy and the total ontological dependence in opposition, for the ontological dependence is translated on to the plane of the psychology. It is rather a question of reconciling psychological autonomy and psychological dependence. The reconciliation is made by the distinction between nature and person. Following the very principle laid down by the Council of Chalcedon – unity of person in two natures without confusion – we must say that the human psychology of Christ possesses a total autonomy vis-à-vis the divine nature and a total dependence with regard to the person of the Word.[166]

Resorting for once to scholastic terminology, Galot adds that the person is a true principle of operation, the *principium quod* of activity, not a mere condition of operation or a simple logical subject without real influence. It is the person of the Word that acts and directs Christ's human activity; but 'it acts by the *principium quo*, the nature, which fixes the structure of the action and makes it an entirely human one.'[167] And he explains in some detail what the relation of the two *principia* must be.

We must not, he says, view it as a dependence of the human will upon the divine will, for that would locate the dependence between the two natures instead of in the unity of the person; it would in effect introduce a dual personality into Christ. 'We must say that the incarnate Word, in his human nature, obeys the Father, but we must not say (at least if we are speaking strictly) that his humanity obeys his divinity, for that would mean that the Word humanly obeyed himself, and to obey oneself is not obedience.'[168] Nor must Christ's human psychology be conceived as dependent on the undivided Trinity, for it is the person of the Son, and not of the Father or of the Spirit, that has become incarnate and is the subject of the human nature. The classical theological principle that all the operations of God *ad extra* are common to the Trinity as a whole does not apply here; it is valid for divine operations accomplished by the divine nature, but 'when the Word acts humanly it is not a matter of a divine action but of a human action. We must carefully distinguish between a divine operation and the human operation of a divine person.'[169] Galot repeats his insistence that the autonomy of the human nature is not compromised by its total dependence on the divine person and that it is not penetrated by the divine nature, and, in spite of his disagreement with Galtier's basic position, he praises him on this point. To the question how a perfectly human life can at the same time manifest the divine status of the person who is leading it, he refers us back to the

Gospel picture of the Son whose perfect filiality is the filiality of a Son who is not a creature but is coessential with his Father, what we might describe as the *Abba*-argument.

Having established that in Jesus there is one ego, the divine ego of the Son of God, Galot next enquires how Christ can have human knowledge of his divine person. The view, widely held in the Middle Ages and later in many Roman Catholic circles, that, from the first moment of the Incarnation, Christ enjoyed the beatific vision and that in this he beheld his own divinity, is seen as unsatisfactory in several respects, not least in that it attributed to Christ in his earthly life what belongs to him only in his state of glory:

> It is important to distinguish between the intuitive knowledge of a divine ego in its intimate relation to the Father, which belonged essentially to Christ, and the state of beatific fruition, which could indeed have flowed from this intuitive knowledge had such been the concrete conditions of the Incarnation but was not given to Christ in his condition of humiliation (*dépouillement*) and kenosis and which was to be granted to him, in accordance with the divine plan of salvation, only as the crowning of his sacrifice.[170]

Galot has rather more respect for the view which assimilates Christ's awareness of his relation to the Father with mystical experience in the technical sense, but the differences seem to him to be at least as important as the similarities: 'The mystics speak of the presence of God, of fusion with God, of immersion in God. Jesus has experience of the Father and of intimacy with him; *his* mystical experience is essentially filial.'[171]

'The solution can come', Galot writes, 'only from a consideration of the ontological constitution which belongs to Christ; to account for what is exceptional in his psychology, we must take as the fundamental starting-point what is singular in his ontology.'[172] And this can only be the hypostatic union or, as Galot prefers to call it, the hypostatic unity. Karl Rahner and J. Mouroux are cited as adopting this approach, but Rahner is judged not to have taken far enough the principle of the translation of the hypostatic union into consciousness, while Mouroux is criticized for finding the point of junction between time and eternity in the soul of Jesus instead of in the person of the Word. Taking up an earlier point, Galot insists that the unity of the person of the incarnate Son is not the product of the union of the two natures but is the principle of their union: 'A static conception of the Incarnation has too much considered the person of the Word as a logical subject of attribution, whereas it is the active principle which is engaged in all the reality of the human existence.'[173] Galot is far from wishing to remove all mystery from the Incarnation, but he insists that, in view of this essential dynamism of the divine person, the question to be asked is not how a man can become conscious that he is God but how the Son of God can become conscious of himself through a human consciousness:

> We touch here upon the mystery of the hypostatic unity. The Incarnation is nothing less than the surmounting, by the person of the Word, of the distance that separates God from man. The disproportion has here been overcome. It appears that we must say that the Incarnation has brought, for the human nature that is assumed, a supernatural ontological elevation which adjusts its activity to the divine ego of the Word. This elevation allows the human activity of consciousness to be set in operation by a divine 'I' (*je*) and to perceive reflexively the divine 'me' (*moi*).[174]

Clearly we are brought up at this point directly against the question of the potentiality of nature for supernature, of created man for uncreated God, in the most challenging form. Galot does not discuss it here and there is no particular reason why he should. It will, however, be well to recognize that, like any other orthodox discussion of the Incarnation, Galot's requires a frank acceptance of the position that, so far from human nature having an inbuilt metaphysical repugnance to its assumption by God, it is precisely in such assumption that it receives its highest self-expression and fulfilment. There is no place here for John Knox's dogma that it is 'impossible, by definition, that God should become a man.'[175] Thus Galot can write that 'the structure of Christ's act of consciousness requires no extraordinary element other than that which is constituted by the hypostatic unity itself. . . . Jesus took consciousness of his divine ego as spontaneously and easily as any man takes consciousness of his ego.'[176] And at this point Galot reintroduces the theme of the relational character of the person:

> The person is a relational being. More particularly, the person of the Son is a relation to the Father. . . . When the Son humanly takes consciousness of himself, he does it as a Son, by taking consciousness of his relation to the Father. . . .
>
> Jesus does not behave like a man who in a mysterious manner feels or sees God, but as a son who has the most intimate knowledge of the Father.[177]

Basic to Jesus' self-consciousness, therefore, is this filial relationship to God the Father, a relationship which implies but does not in itself declare equality with the Father. It cannot, however, remain at this implicit stage, and Galot quotes Rahner as speaking of its 'thematization and conceptual objectivation.'[178] He does not find the notion of infused knowledge very helpful. Rather he sees Jesus' intimate contact with the Father as enabling him to assess his ego more expressly as the ego of a unique Son, a Son who is divine. But beyond this, he sees Jesus as forming his conscious understanding of himself in the whole context of the Jewish religion in which he grew up and of the prophecies which were central to it: 'What he had received in his religious education, more especially by his contact with Scripture, enabled him to translate into human concepts the content of his psychological experience.'[179]

I would add here the point on which Bouyer lightly touched, that, above all, Jesus would have learnt from his mother.[180] I would in fact lay even greater stress on this than Bouyer does, for it seems to me that what she would have been able to tell him about the circumstances of his conception and birth, unless we are quite arbitrarily to reject the nativity and infancy narratives as altogether unhistorical, must have played a predominant part in bringing him to an explicit recognition and understanding, in his human consciousness, of his unique status, both in his person and in his vocation. In any case, the question presents itself of the way in which Jesus' consciousness developed, and Galot goes on to consider it.

He stresses that such development in no way implies imperfection; to deny this would be a kind of monophysitism. 'In God there is no progressive development, but in man perfection, far from excluding development, necessarily involves it. For Christ's human consciousness, it is in the development that the perfection is found.'[181] Galot finds the story of the finding of Christ in the Temple particularly significant from this point of view, and he convincingly defends its authenticity. In it we see Jesus becoming conscious of his own status in becoming conscious of his unique relation to the Father in heaven. Remarking that it is through his contacts with his parents and other persons that a child becomes conscious of his own ego, he continues:

For Jesus, it is the intimate contacts with the Father that conditioned his apprehension of consciousness; they situated him face to face with a divine 'thou' as the 'I' of a son who had the heavenly Father for his father. . . . In this way Jesus could have a consciousness of himself which corresponded to the truth of his profound being; having no human ego, he could only take consciousness of a divine ego, and he could do this only by perceiving his relation to the Father.[182]

Behind this there lay his miraculous conception by the Holy Spirit:

This extraordinary intervention in the physical constitution of the child is prolongated by an intervention in his psychological development; psychologically as physically, the child was the son of the heavenly Father, and would develop in the truth of this sonship.[183]

These intimate contacts with the Father are of necessity mysterious to us, but Galot is insistent that there is nothing forced or violent about them, nor are they to be compared with the more exotic types of religious experience:

The contact with the Father . . . is produced in a quite simple way, in conformity with the state of life initiated by the Incarnation, and with the closest solidarity with the earthly condition of man. It might be compared with the contacts undergone in the most ordinary mystical experience, but, as has been stressed, with an entirely characteristic note of sonship.[184]

Here and in his subsequent discussion of Jesus' baptism and public life, which, interesting and enlightening as it is, I need not elaborate for our present purposes, Galot shows, in a way that I find more satisfactory than that of any other writer with whom I am acquainted, that the development in Jesus' human consciousness of a clear recognition of his unique personal status and vocation is fully compatible with the genuine and unimpaired reality of his human nature. It is true that in that human nature Jesus manifests capacities of human activity and knowledge that we do not usually see in human lives, and Galot concludes his volume by discussing such cases of 'superior knowledge', but he shows that they fall within the necessary boundaries of human nature as such. He argues also that a certain human ignorance was a necessary condition of Christ's redemptive mission. A fuller consideration of the Incarnation would need to include Jesus' miracles as well as his teaching, but this volume, as its title declares, has been explicitly concerned with his consciousness, and on this most widely canvassed of all Christological problems in recent years, Galot shows the unexhausted fruitfulness of the Chalcedonian doctrine. But to clinch the matter we must turn to the final volume of his triology, *Vers une nouvelle christologie*.[185]

3 TOWARDS A NEW CHRISTOLOGY

The volume opens with an exposition of the 'New Christology' expounded in the late 1960s by a Dutch and Flemish group, of which Galot takes A. Hulsbosch, E. Schillebeeckx and P. Schoonenberg as typical. In spite of the general similarity of their outlook, there are notable differences among them, and Schillebeeckx can indeed write on occasions in an unexpectedly traditional way. The reader should be warned that, in the expository section of this discussion, Galot writes with such restraint that he might almost be taken as sharing their position, though, as it later becomes clear, this is far from the case. What is common to them all is a rejection of the Chalcedonian Christology as, at best, unhelpful and a general dislike of the supernatural as uncongenial to the modern mind. Like all naturalistic Christologies, the 'New Christology' finds its chief difficulty in accounting for, and giving a rational description of, the uniqueness of Christ, although it is genuinely concerned with this.

Galot sees it as having three essential notes. First, it rejects any duality of the divine and the human in Christ; no divine activity is to be attributed to him, but the Creator is present in his being and his human activity in such a way that this man becomes the mediator between God and other men. Secondly, this is a 'Christology of the presence of God', in virtue of which Jesus, unlike other men, is totally penetrated by the divine presence and thus there is in him no sinful existence from which he would need to be delivered. Thirdly, this is a 'Christology of the human transcendence of Christ'; transcendence is no longer to be found in a divine person but in the human nature and the human person.[186]

This transcendence is a mystery which is addressed purely and simply to our faith. It is not objectively demonstrable. It could not be concluded from the gospel stories that Jesus does what another person could not do, while for one who opens himself to his person he is the greatest miracle. . . . Jesus adopted the religious thoughts and behaviours of his people. He is entirely the product of Israel, the true Israelite. . . .

How are we to express the difference between Jesus and ourselves? We cannot say that Christ is distinguished from other men in an essential manner, by his being, If that was so, he would not be a man among men, 'consubstantial with us', as the formula of Chalcedon says. . . . On the other hand, it would not be enough to admit an accidental or relative difference, for that would not describe Christ's transcendence.

This transcendence must rather be expressed in the terms of the World Council of Churches: 'the final meaning of Jesus Christ for the universal history of man' . . . Christ is the eschatological summit of the saving divine action and thus of the history of our salvation. But this term 'eschatological' must be understood less in the perspective of a person who is to come than in a qualitative sense: in the history of salvation, Christ is the final word of God. However, there is in him a temporal completion, the end of time.[187]

The summary just quoted is concerned primarily with Schoonenberg, who is perhaps the most extreme member of the school in question; thus, for example, he holds the extraordinary view that it is only in the human nature of Christ that the Son becomes a person – a remarkable inversion of the doctrine of *enhypostasia*.[188] Nevertheless Galot provides evidence of a wide diffusion in Holland of the abandonment of the formulas of Ephesus and Chalcedon and the substitution of the notion of the human transcendence of Christ. He remarks that the well-known 'Dutch Catechism' of 1966[189] refrained from applying the terms 'God' or 'God-man' to Christ and that the propositions adopted by the congress organized at Brussels in September 1970 by the journal *Concilium* deliberately refrained, in the face of repeated requests, from affirming the divinity of Christ. (This was the occasion when the distinguished Calvinist theologian Dr T. F. Torrance accused the organizers of trying to import into modern Roman Catholicism the worst features of nineteenth-century liberal Protestantism.)[190] Galot's judgement on the movement is clear-cut and severe. The 'New Christology', so far from providing an explanation, denies the problem which needs to be explained; it is equally incompatible with Scripture and with tradition. 'Rather than call it pre-origenist, we must call it pre-evangelical, for the Gospels show the transcendent divine sonship of Jesus.'[191] Galot is no opponent of theological pluralism, which he declares to be legitimate and desirable. Nor does he set up Chalcedon as the end-all of Christology, for he proposes to advance very definitely beyond it. But he insists that 'to put in doubt or deny the divinity of Christ is to undermine the very foundation of Christology' and that, 'if a new Christology is to be built, it can only be in the sense of a better uncovering of what is essential to the Faith, that is, the Son of God made man.'[192] And this he proceeds to do in his development of a dynamic Christology.

He, refreshingly begins his task by sweeping away the common accusation that Chalcedon, by adopting the contemporary concepts of 'nature' (*physis*) and 'person' (*prosopon* or *hypostasis*), imprisoned Christology in the narrow confines of a particular philosophical system which is totally uncongenial to the present day. Rather, he points out, it was the use of these terms and the corresponding concepts in Christology that led to their clarification and precisification when they had previously been nebulous and inexact. Scholastic theology, he admits, may sometimes have interpreted 'nature' in a very abstract way, but 'for the Council, nature is concrete, existential reality, and a hypostasis is a living person that enables us to say "One and the same Christ".'[193] What it did not do – and this was its strength – was to work out in detail what person and nature are. 'Who is this?' and 'What is this?' are questions in common speech, and Chalcedon was concerned with them. It left the deeper investigation of person and nature to the theologians; for itself, as Fr A. Grillmeier has said, it was far more concerned to protect Christian thought from Hellenization than to Hellenize it. I am reminded of the following passage from Fr Bernard Lonergan, to which I shall return later on:

> If one follows the lead of Augustine and profits by the experience of Socrates and the analysts, then one will explain the meaning of 'nature', 'person', and 'hypostasis' in the decree of Chalcedon by saying that 'nature' means what there are two of in Christ while 'person' or 'hypostasis' means what there is one of in Christ. Nor is there doubt about what is the one and what are the two. For in the prior paragraph the subject is the one and the same Son, our Lord, Jesus Christ. Of this one and the same there is the fourfold predication of opposed attributes. . . . But there is a further clarification to be added. For a nominalist the subject of the statement, namely, 'the Son, the Lord Jesus Christ' is just a proper name and two or perhaps three titles, while 'truly God' and 'truly man' involve the addition of further titles. But if one acknowledges the reality of the world mediated by meaning, then the subject of the statement is not just a proper name with certain titles but primarily a reality and, indeed, a reality begotten of the Father before all ages.[194]

This primacy of meaning over its verbal expressions, this persistence of understanding through all the relativities and imperfections of the media in which it is embodied and through which it is communicated, is the topic of the chapter on Theology and Language in my book *The Openness of Being*.[195] Galot makes the same point in the Christological context when he writes:

There are concepts that belong to the intellectual patrimony of humanity, to what we can call an essential language, which allows all men to understand one another.

It is indeed necessary, in order to determine the meaning of the conciliar declarations, to study them in the particular historical context in which they were composed. We have to disentangle from this context the precise bearing of the affirmations. Thus the formula of Chalcedon stands out in its opposition to monophysitism. But it is not purely relative to the positions adopted by Eutyches. When they affirm two natures and one person the fathers of the Council give their affirmation a general validation and express it as a truth based on Scripture which every Christian must admit. . . .

The dogma of Chalcedon therefore must not be envisaged as a pillory from which one tries if one can to get free, but as a foundation on which theology can build up its development in confidence that it is rightly orientated. . . .

And, no doubt having in mind the tendency to reinterpret the pre-existence of the Son as a metaphorical or ideal 'pro-existence', Galot adds:

The affirmation of the pre-existent divine person of the Son was not introduced after Chalcedon by 'neo-Chalcedonianism'. It is found in the profession of faith of the Council. . . . The pre-existence of the Son is clearly expressed in his birth 'before the ages as regards the divinity'.[196]

Galot is thus an unashamed adherent and defender of the Chalcedonian definition as true and irreformable. Nevertheless, he does not see it as having said all that can be said, or all that needs to be said, in Christology. It is the truth and nothing but the truth, but it is not the whole truth. What it fails to stress, and what today it is very important to stress, is the inherent dynamism of the mystery of the Incarnation. 'The affirmation of Chalcedon is made from a static point of view; it is fashioned in terms of being rather than of happening, because it wishes to tell us what there is in Christ.'[197] It was not, as Hans Küng asserts, a compromise, but a synthesis; nevertheless it remains in the ontological realm. What is missing is the movement of the Incarnation as an enterprise (*démarche*) of salvation, and it is this that needs to be brought to the forefront.

Thus, what was wrong with the 'New Christology' was not that it was dynamic, but that its dynamism was inadequate. Its proposed Christological formula, 'God is revealed in the man Jesus' expresses an essential truth but errs by defect.

> The Incarnation is not only the revelation of God in a man; it is the involvement (*engagement*) of the divine person of the Word who has become man.

To express correctly the Christological dynamism we must discern in it as the principle of unity not the man or the human being in Jesus, but the divine person. For that is what accomplishes the enterprise by assuming a human life. We cannot appreciate the character of the enterprise unless we recognize the divine transcendence of the person and the wholeness of the human condition in which it is involved; and this is what is expressed by the affirmation of the duality of the natures in Christ.[198]

Thus, Galot insists, we must take Chalcedon as our starting-point if we are to construct a satisfactory dynamic Christology, and he points to the fate of those who abandon it: 'They end up by offering a diminished Christology; they tend to reduce Christ to the human level, which fails to correspond to the image of him which the Gospel transmits.'[199] He sees in the Greek fathers, with their doctrine of the 'economy', a thoroughly dynamic Christology, which he contrasts with the static definitions of the later dogmatic treatises, and it is a dynamism whose subject is the divine Son and not a human person. And behind this he sees the texts of the New Testament books, which he expounds in some detail. Thus, he concludes, 'the Incarnation is characterized by the involvement (*engagement*) of a pre-existent divine person. These three elements: involvement, divine person, pre-existent person, give the mystery its true bearing.'[200] And he elucidates his teaching in such statements as these:

> The person of the Word . . . does not only manifest itself in a man and does not restrain itself to acting in him; it has willed to be this man who has lived among us. . . . A divine person has accomplished human actions and has felt human emotions; it is, in all reality, God who has eaten and drunk, who has suffered and undergone the experience of death. . . .
>
> A divine person is necessarily pre-existent, but I wish to stress that this pre-existence gives a very special value to the involvement. . . . Eternity is thus introduced into human existence.

Pre-existence is not a luxury of theological speculation, which we could set aside in the interest of simplification. It concerns us because it affects the relation of Christ to mankind.... He who possesses eternity in its fulness in common with the Father has the power to make men share in it by communicating eternal life to them.

Furthermore, it is in the pre-existence that there is situated the decision of the redeeming Incarnation, the act of love which has brought about the coming of the Son among men. The mystery is governed by a divine attitude; it is the expression of a divine dynamism which dominates all the earthly life of Jesus by being anterior to it.[201]

Here, I think, is the answer to those who, like Robinson, are content to reduce the pre-existence of the Son to a merely psychological existence as an idea in the mind of God. It will also be clear that Galot's insistence on the personal deity of Jesus does not in the least detract from the genuine reality of his human activities and experiences. Indeed, one of Galot's chief complaints against the 'New Christology' is that it weakens the human influence of Jesus upon us:

Not only does the 'New Approach' remove from Christ his supreme greatness but it deprives him of that which allows him to exercise on our life the most profound transforming influence, that of a new creation. The Saviour described by Schoonenberg acts on us only as an example. Thus, paradoxically, the Christ who it was hoped would be more living in us becomes much less living; being only a man essentially similar to us, he has at his disposal only those means of action which belong to men in their interpersonal relations.[202]

Galot has thus skilfully turned the tables on those whom we might, by a political metaphor, describe as his adversaries of the left, but it would be mistaken to take his work as merely a brilliant *tour de force*. For, however mistaken we may judge their basic Christological assumption to be – and this would apply specially to such writers as Pittenger and Robinson, the latter of whom appears to have considerably influenced Schoonenberg – they were concerned with a quite fundamental Christian truth, that of the genuine humanity of Jesus, and this should be recognized although, in their fear of anything approaching to docetism, they drifted into Nestorianism, adoptionism, or even some kind of sophisticated twentieth-century psilanthropism. Galot, in the remainder of his third volume, by his careful adherence to the Chalcedonian understanding of *hypostasis* and *physis*, does, in my judgement, make his case thoroughly good. He would, I think, even have strengthened it if he had made more explicit use of the argument of his first volume and had not restricted himself to a few footnote-references. But this is to anticipate.

More surprising than the neglect of Galot by the left is the opposition from some quarters on the theological right. (May I interpose that the political analogy seems to me to be of very limited usefulness; I am more concerned with the contrast of right and wrong, or true and false, than of right and left.) Dom Illtyd Trethowan, in an appendix to his book *Mysticism and Theology*,[203] has attacked Galot for virtually denying the impassibility of God and for endorsing Karl Rahner's formula that the immutable *in se* becomes mutable *in alio*. Trethowan is one of the most outstanding writers in English on philosophical theology, but his praiseworthy defence of the divine impassibility against various eccentricities in the contemporary theological scene[204] has perhaps led him to underestimate the subtlety of the Christological problem. In any case, his criticism of Galot was based on a comparatively brief article published shortly before Galot's third volume. But, again, I am anticipating.

Having stated his plea for a dynamic Christology, Galot embarks upon its exposition in a succinct but systematic chapter entitled 'The Dynamic Face of God' (*Le visage dynamique de Dieu*). He begins by asserting frankly that the divine dynamism poses a problem and that it is a problem in which each of the three divine persons is concerned in his own way. Scripture makes it plain that not only does the Son humble himself in becoming man, but also the Father gives his Son to us and for us, and the Holy Spirit, in making Mary the mother of God, depends on her consent and co-operation.

> This element of dependence is not exclusively proper to the action of the Holy Spirit. It appears in the *démarche* of the Son who assumes 'the condition of a servant', and in the gesture of the Father who sends his Son in response to the sin of man. But in the Holy Spirit it is manifested more immediately under the form of co-operation and covenant, in the very act of the Incarnation.[205]

Galot is emphatic that neither of the terms of the problem is to be belittled or suppressed. He is attracted by Rahner's famous phrase that God, while immutable in himself, becomes mutable in another, but he judges it to contain much obscurity:

All ambiguity is not absent; one wonders whether mutability, in affecting the Word, can dwell exclusively in something other than him. Either mutability intrinsically qualifies the Word, and then it is found in him in some way, or else it is purely extrinsic, and in that case does it truly affect him?[206]

Nor is Galot satisfied with attempts made by H. Mühlen and Hans Küng to identify God's immutability with his moral faithfulness and stability which Scripture attests. Scripture itself, he asserts, bases this faithfulness upon a metaphysical persistence in the order of being. On the other hand, Scripture does not see it as a static immobility like that of Aristotle's unmoved mover, but as a free and infinitely adaptable vitality.

If we force ourselves to translate into a principle the indications of Scripture on the subject of the mutability which results from the divine immutability itself, we can say that, God being in himself the fulness of life and energy, there is nothing strange in his displaying life and energy in the most intense and varied fashion in his relations with men. If he is pure act in his own interior, how could he be motionless outside? He who in himself is infinitely active, is infinitely capable of a superabundant activity outside himself, including an activity that enters the world and accepts its conditions in complete freedom.[207]

It is this broad notion of the sovereignty and the freedom of God that, according to Galot, makes sense of the whole mystery of the Incarnation:

The Word has truly become flesh. . . , not *although*, but *because* he was the eternal being; his fulness of being, being fulness of energy, grounds a capacity for becoming. . . . The divine person of the Word has thus experienced what it is to be man. He has experienced it through the human nature, but he has truly experienced it in as much as he is a divine person.[208]

It is here that I could wish that Galot had explicitly harked back to his first volume *La Personne du Christ*, for he could thus have removed any flavour of artificiality and schematism that could attach to a sentence such as that last quoted. The notion of person as pure relational being carries with it the consequence that the divine Word is in the most unqualified sense the subject of the total human life of Jesus, while that human life is entirely conducted in the faculties and energies, physical and psychological, of the human nature. The fact that the person is divine requires no amputation of the human nature, such as the Apollinarians and the monothelites demanded, nor any limitations on its exercise, sin only excepted; and sin is a frustration of human nature, not an expression and expansion of it. We do indeed see in Jesus wonders, both of consciousness and of activity, such as we have seen in no other man, but this is not because his human nature is, so to speak, mechanically manipulated by his deity. It is because, in its human perfection, it is spontaneously, not artificially, responsive to its divine person; and, in his relational being as the eternal Son, that divine person is perfectly and filially responsive to the person of the eternal Father.

With this I feel sure that Galot would agree, and I think his argument would have been still more strengthened had he made a more explicit use of the truth that time is not an antecedent receptacle in which both God and creatures are immersed but is a mode of existence of finite created beings. It follows from this that, if God becomes man by uniting a human nature to his timeless divine hypostasis, he necessarily acquires a temporal and developing finite mode of existence, but this temporality and mutability does not become a quality of his divinity as such. I might perhaps quote the following passage from the chapter on God and Time in my book *The Openness of Being*:

> A God to whom, in his timelessness, the whole spatio-temporal fabric of the world is eternally present is not less but more concerned with the world than would be a God who was entangled in it. For the latter kind of deity would be limited in his experience at each moment to the particular stage in its development that the world had reached at that moment, while the former, in his extra-temporal and extra-spatial vision and activity, embraces in one timeless act every one of his creatures whatever its time and space may be. Difficult, and indeed impossible, as it is for us to imagine and feel what a timeless existence is like, we can, I think, understand that a God to whom every instant is present at once has a vastly greater scope for his compassion and his power than one would have who could attend to only one moment at a time.[209]

These words were written with direct reference to God's relation to the world as its creator and sustainer in the order of nature, but the truth with which they are concerned must be the necessary prolegomenon to that entry of God into the finite order which is involved in the Incarnation and the order of redemption. It is perhaps because Galot has neglected to give a thorough discussion of the relation between eternity and time that he has seemed to such critics as Trethowan to compromise the divine impassibility. But, when that has been said, it must be added that the precise point of the Chalcedonian doctrine of the Incarnation is that, without detriment to the divine impassibility and immutability, it provides the divine Word with a finite nature in which he can be mutable and passible. But – and this needs the strongest emphasis – this is entirely dependent on the Chalcedonian doctrine being taken in the strictest form, without the subtraction from the human nature of even the most insignificant of its constituents or their transference to the divine person. The person is totally divine, the nature is totally human. And this involves, as Galot stresses, that, although there is the most radical difference between the self-existent creator and the creature which is totally dependent upon him, there is no antagonism but rather compatibility between them. As I have said before, a horse or a cat could not become a man, nor could one man become another man; only God the Word, on whom man totally depends and in whose image he is made, could become a man. There appears also at this point, though I do not think Galot has explicitly mentioned it, the weakness of kenotic theories of the Incarnation; for, in place of a complete human nature assumed by the divine Word, they substitute a divine nature scaled down to the dimensions of a human one.[210]

It is, I think, relevant at this point to draw attention to a certain deficiency in the famous Letter of Pope Leo to Flavian (the 'Tome of Leo'), which was in fact commented on at the Council of Chalcedon itself. I have discussed it at some length in my book *Via Media: An Essay in Theological Synthesis*[211] and will deal with it as briefly as possible here. Leo, as is well known, states with admirable lucidity the doctrine of the two natures, a divine and a human, which coinhere in the one divine person of the pre-existent Son. He is also clear that, while the two natures each preserve their unconfused reality, they are not on the same footing, since the Son was begotten as divine by the Father from all eternity while he was born as man from the Virgin Mary at a moment in time. It is, however, when he applies the consequences of this doctrine that Leo lays himself open to criticism. In a famous sequence of antitheses he distinguishes between the acts and utterances of Jesus recorded in the Gospels which are to be attributed to the human nature and those which are to be attributed to the divine. 'It does not belong to the same nature to weep with feelings of pity over a dead friend and . . . to raise him up alive again by the command of his voice. . . . It does not belong to the same nature to say "I and my Father are one" and "My Father is greater than I".... ' Now the first thing that strikes us about this passage is that, while Leo professes to be classifying the activities of the divine Son under the respective headings of his humanity and his divinity, all those that he mentions under either heading are comprised within the sphere of the incarnate life. We might expect that the activities which fell under the heading of divinity would include those cosmic creative operations by which the Son 'through whom all things were made' sustains the universe in being. There is, however, no mention of these at all. All the activities mentioned are in fact exercised within the sphere of the Incarnation and are mediated through the human nature taken from Mary. Christ uttered the words 'I and my Father are one' with the same lips as the words 'My Father is greater than I'; he walked on the surface of the sea with the same feet that were weary after tramping the roads of Galilee. What Leo has classified as acts of the human and of the divine nature are respectively such as any ordinary man could perform and such as could be performed only by one who was God as well as man. But they are all alike acts performed in the human nature; and we might in some cases find it difficult to decide whether an act which, as we should say, is supranormal is possible to Jesus simply in view of his Godhead or in view of his perfect humanity. When, for example, he stills the storm, is he exercising the authority of the Creator or the authority over the lower creation which man lost through the Fall and which is now restored in the Second Adam? It is very much to the point that at Chalcedon itself, in spite of the general enthusiasm for Leo's Tome, certain bishops from Illyricum and Palestine objected to some phrases in it as savouring of Nestorianism, until their misgivings were allayed by Aetius of Constantinople, who produced similar passages from Cyril of Alexandria. Among these was the following:

> There are some sayings which are in the highest degree God-befitting; others befit manhood; and others there are which, as it were, hold a middle rank, demonstrating that the Son of God is at once God and man.[212]

The incompleteness of Leo's discussion is shown by the fact that he makes no mention of this third category of Cyril's, yet it is really the key to the whole matter. For the whole of the incarnate life is the life of God-made-man, and Christ's acts are the acts of God-in-manhood. Some of them may show more clearly than others that the personal subject of these acts is not a man but God; none of them, however, are acts of the divine nature acting independently of the human, for any such acts would, like the act by which the divine Word sustains the universe, fall outside the sphere of the incarnate life altogether. In fact, all the acts of the incarnate life are, in various ways, *theandric*, acts of a divine person in a human nature; and the fact had been stated perfectly plainly long before the time of Leo in a letter of Athanasius to Serapion, the importance of which was pointed out by G. L. Prestige.[213] Here, in marked contrast to Leo, Athanasius wrote:

> When he willed to declare himself God it was with a human tongue that he signified this, saying 'I and the Father are one'. . . . He stretched forth a human hand to raise Peter's wife's mother when she was sick of a fever, and to raise up from the dead the daughter of the ruler of the synagogue when she had already expired.

It is in fact of central importance not to misunderstand the term *theandric*, applied to certain of Jesus' words and acts. It must not be taken as meaning that in those words and acts the divine *nature*, as such, is directly involved, but that the human nature as the medium (the *instrumentum conjunctum*, a Thomist would say) of the divine person, while remaining perfectly human, is seen as manifested in an altogether unique way, and this not because as nature it is (except for its perfection and sinlessness) different from any other human nature, but because its person, its ultimate metaphysical subject and relational being, is not human but divine.[214] This involves the principle, which I have repeatedly stressed, that the total dependence of created human being on the uncreated self-existent deity makes the incarnation of God the Son in human nature not impossible or unfitting, but wholly right and proper. It is indeed supremely wonderful and unpredictable, but that is another matter. As St Thomas says, 'Of all the works of God the Incarnation most greatly surpasses our reason; for nothing more wonderful could be thought of that God could do than that very God, the Son of God, should become very man.'[215] 'Surpasses our reason', but does not contradict it; rather, enlightens and ennobles it. We are far from Dr John Knox's dogmatic denial, which rules out the Incarnation, in any real sense, from the start. It is, however, significant that the Council of Chalcedon, while it gave formal approval to the Tome of Leo, as it did also to the three synodical letters of Cyril, altogether ignored those statements in it which had upset the bishops from Illyricum and Palestine.

We must return to Galot, though I do not think this digression has been irrelevant. Still under the heading of 'The Dynamic Face of God', he passes from what he has somewhat paradoxically called 'the dynamic immutability of God' to consider 'the face of God' *tout court*. Here he attacks as inadequate the common scholastic formula that the relation between God and his creatures is real in the creatures but only 'logical' (*rationalis*) in God. While not entirely devoid of truth, this seems to Galot to be inconsistent with the conditions of the Incarnation itself:

> Even before the relations [with mankind] established by the Word made flesh we must consider those implied at the beginning by the initiative (*démarche*) of the Father; the Father has been able to send his Son through love for us, only because he was establishing with men a real relation of love.[216]

On the other hand Galot rejects the view of some modern theologians who conceive a relation to external beings as belonging to the very essence of a God who is love; for this, he holds, would lessen God's love by making it less fully free:

> Scripture underlines the gratuitous character of the divine love. It is freely that God has established relations with men and has willed to be love for us. And it is precisely this freedom that constitutes the mystery of novelty in God himself; this novelty is formed in the relations which the Father, the Son, and the Spirit decide to set up with mankind. These relations, which are fully real, arise from a sovereign divine will, which is not identical with the divine nature since it arises freely.[217]

And Galot drives his point home in a short section on the divine compassion as it is revealed in the Gospels.

Thus, although he does not put it in precisely these words, Galot's view might be stated by saying that, in addition to logical relations and necessary real relations, he also postulates voluntary real relations, and he sees these, and not only logical relations, as included in God's relationship to the world. Some such distinction as this seems to me to be needed, and Galot makes an important advance on Rahner's simple concept of God as mutable *in alio*. Certainly a Christian theologian should be as deeply concerned with God's compassion as with his impassibility, but I am not sure that all theologians have been. Galot is one who has, and in his later work *Dieu souffre-t-il?*[218] he has carried his thought a stage further by making a fundamental distinction between the necessary order of God's being and the free order of his will. Immutability and impassibility belong to the former, but creation and redemption to the latter, in which love and suffering are really and not just verbally implicated. 'In God suffering belongs not to the order of necessity and of essence, but to that of free initiative.'[219] This involves no imperfection in God; just the opposite. 'He is sovereign, and sovereignty consists in acting in the freest manner, and in *not* being imprisoned in an inaccessible altitude.'[220]

> People too easily suppose that any kind of suffering would destroy the principle of the divine impassibility. But a God who suffers remains the impassible God. There is no contradiction between these two aspects of God, because impassibility is a property of the divine nature, while suffering concerns solely the free love of the divine persons for men.[221]

This is extremely impressive, but I think that Galot's exposition needs supplementing by some reference to the divine infinity. I have argued elsewhere that, if we correctly understand the relation between the infinity of God and the finite character of his creation, we shall see that his compassion in no way detracts from his impassibility, not because the compassion is in any way fictitious or minimal but because, in all its reality and intensity, it is infinitely exceeded by the fulness of his beatitude.[222] In any case Galot would be the first to maintain that this loving relation of God to man which pertained before the Incarnation is very different from the experience of human living on the part of the divine Word which is set up by the hypostatic union. And indeed, under a title which, by a remarkable coincidence, anticipates that of Dr Robinson's book – *Le visage humain de Dieu* – he develops the theme that 'in Christ God takes a human face',[223] but in very different terms from Robinson's. He is every bit as emphatic as any of the proponents of the 'New Approach' upon the totality and reality of the human experience of Jesus; indeed his complaint against them is that they fail to safeguard it adequately. But he is equally emphatic that the subject of this human experience is the divine Word himself. Thus he writes:

> To bring this human experience into full light it is not helpful to withdraw into the shade the divine person of the pre-existent Son of God or to question its reality as the 'New Approach' does. The denial of the divinity of the person not only fails to make Christ more human, it prevents one from recognizing the value of the human experience which the Incarnation constitutes. That value resides in the fact that a person who is God has willed to undergo and experience the existence which is proper to man. . . . In his solidarity with the poor of this

world, Jesus has been more intensely poor than any other man whatever, since in him an infinitely rich person was living an ontological poverty.[224]

I am, however, not altogether happy with the way in which Galot describes the divine *démarche*:

The Incarnation . . . presents the sole case in which a human existence was first of all expressly wished by him who was going to live it. Christ is the only man who has lived his human life in virtue of an antecedent personal commitment. . . .

   This experience deserves more than another the name of 'adventure', in view of the distance that exists between the divine person of the Word and the new existence on which he entered. . . . The Incarnation is the great divine adventure, that of a human existence deliberately faced and totally lived.[225]

With all that Galot goes on to say about the way in which the incarnate life of Christ acquires its redemptive character from the totality and reality of his human life I am in full agreement, but, in spite of its arresting vividness, I am uneasy with the suggestion in the passage from which I have just quoted that the decision to become incarnate was made by the divine Word at some moment or moments in time; this seems to envisage God as himself within the time-process and to be almost reminiscent of the 'tournament of Love' of Déodat de Basly! It is of course difficult for us not to think of God as making his decisions in time, although we know that he makes them in eternity; but, even when we concede to the limitations of our time-bound minds, we can surely think of his purposes as stable and persistent, rather than as arising from a change in his own will.[226] For what is spoken of here is not a decision taking place within the human mind of the incarnate Lord, but of a decision alleged to be made by the divine Word in his pre-incarnate state. It would be wrong to attribute too much importance to a few paragraphs which in no way affect the general tenor of the argument, but I must record my impression that Galot has for once succumbed to a sense of the dramatic and also that, as on an earlier occasion on which I have commented, he has surprisingly shown a rather inadequate understanding of the relation of time to eternity. (Père Bouyer, as we saw, avoided this particular snare, but in doing so fell into another.)[227]

   In the few remaining pages of his book Galot has admirably expounded the truth that, in the Incarnate Christ, everything is mediated in the context of his perfect, but humanly perfect, human nature, with the limits, weaknesses and temptations that even (or should we say, especially?) a perfect human nature must experience. Schoonenberg's proposal to eliminate the Gospel miracles is repudiated, but the miracles are seen not so much as direct manifestations of divine omnipotence as 'witnesses, by anticipation, of the marvellous transformation which [Jesus] will accomplish in his human nature in his quality as the glorious Saviour after his redeeming sacrifice.'[228] And, in line with the whole previous discussion, humanity is seen as no obstacle to deity, but as its medium and instrument:

> To grasp the divine in Christ, we must look less for external activities of an extraordinary kind than to the interior of his human soul. It is man as such, with all his spiritual resources, who bears the transparency of God. It is he who makes God seen. In this sense, the Incarnation is the highest exaltation of man, the supreme demonstration of his nobility.
>
> My purpose is not to analyse all the expressions of the divine in Jesus, but to underline the principle that the human was not an obstacle but a way of revelation. . . .
>
> There is no contradiction or repugnance, but a fundamental harmony between the Word who is in the beginning and the man who he becomes.[229]

'A more dynamic conception of God', Galot repeats, 'favours the discernment of the true dynamism of the human existence and the human psychology of Christ',[230] and, reproducing almost word for word a sentence from his second volume, he sums up a brief but luminous discussion as follows:

> The essential problem of the psychology of Christ is not to know how a man has acquired consciousness of being God, but how the Son of God has humanly acquired consciousness of his divine identity, in the way in which a human consciousness awakens and progressively develops.[231]

I would in fact suggest that, as far as the Gospel evidence is concerned, a great deal of light has been thrown on this problem by Galot's second volume and, as far as the basic theology is concerned, by his first. But he always seems too modest to refer very much to his own work.

His last few paragraphs are devoted to the wider aspects of the Incarnation, as also was the conclusion of his first volume. Accepting

Robinson's description of Christ as 'the man for others',[232] he remarks that 'he is not for others only in the sense of a love that gives itself to them, but is the man destined to cure all humanity spiritually and to impart to it eternal life.'[233] And, in order to be not only the saved but the Saviour, to be the author of the new creation, he must be a divine person. Galot makes a striking application of the famous phrase of St Gregory Nazianzen,'What has not been assumed has not been cured.'[234] The Cappadocian father, writing against the Apollinarians, coined the phrase in order to argue for the completeness of Christ's human nature; Galot adopts it in order to argue for the deity of the person who assumes it. He remarks that 'today, in the presence of the "New Approach", the principle reminds us that if there is no divine person to assume a human nature, there can be no salvation: nothing has been cured, for nothing has been assumed.'[235] If, however, we locate the Chalcedonian formula in the perspective of a dynamic Christology, we see the promise of a glorious elevation of human nature itself. For, Galot writes:

> By entering into human becoming, the Word confers on this becoming a new value. . . . His person outstrips the becoming in which it is involved; it bears it up, dominating time by eternity.
>
> In the human becoming of Jesus, the absolute being expresses itself with its unlimited capacity of becoming, and in consequence with the universality of all the becoming of the creatures. . . . The person of the Word possesses a universal stature, embracing all the domain of becoming, that is to say, all the beings that become and all the journeying of their becoming.[236]

And he has done this by accepting the conditions of an individual human life, lived in a particular place and time and yet outstripping those limitations.

> To enter into becoming is to become the subject of a history. To enter it as the Son of God is to make himself the subject of universal history, to be involved in the recapitulation of the history of mankind. . . . As Son of man and servant, he represents a whole people. In fact, he bears in himself the destiny of all mankind, and he confers on history its truest and most definitive meaning, that of a total rule of God over the human community.[237]

And it is in this light that Galot is able to give an orthodox interpretation to Teilhard de Chardin's doctrine of Christ as a new principle of evolution of the universe. Furthermore, he sees the Incarnation as having already transformed the interpersonal relations of mankind:

We must recognize the full reality of the relation established by God with the world in the Incarnation. This relation includes something new for God himself. . . .

On the other hand, the entry of a divine person into human personal relations raises these relations to a divine level. Henceforth, all the human egos are put in contact with a divine Thou. The whole human community is thus bound to the community of the divine persons.[238]

And Galot's last word is to demonstrate by implication what he has many times explicitly affirmed in the course of his argument, that the traditional Chalcedonian Christology, when interpreted and developed in a dynamic theological setting, has a far nobler estimate of man and offers him the hope of a more glorious destiny than the desupernaturalized Christologies of the 'New Approach'.

If we are willing only to consider Christ as a man, a human person, we can no longer take account of this elevation of all human persons and their community to a divine level. The affirmation of the divine person of Christ is not a luxury, nor is it a theological speculation without bearing on our human existence. Our existence would be quite different from what it is at this moment if we had not been placed, by the Incarnation, in the presence of a divine person who, having become man, converses with us and calls us into intimacy with him.[239]

And here Galot concludes his trilogy. Clearly, he has left us with a great many questions unanswered in the realms of missiology, ecclesiology, sacramental theology and spirituality, to mention only a few, though his strictly Christological task is, at least relatively, complete. How is Christ's univeral presence to mankind in virtue of his incarnation in human nature related to his presence in the Church to those who have been baptized into his body? In brief, what difference did my baptism make to me? How should Christian missions today envisage their task? (I have in mind specially Fr Rahner's essay on 'Anonymous Christianity and the Missionary Task of the Church'[240] and Fr Raymond Panikkar's book *The Unknown Christ of Hinduism*.[241] It is no condemnation of Père Galot that he has not answered such questions as these; rather it is to his credit that he has given us a new sense of their relevance and a fresh light upon them. Nor does the occasional occurrence of some questionable detail detract from the unity of his theme or the magisterial competence with which he handles it. In his three modest volumes he has achieved two most impressive results. He has shown that the Chalcedonian doctrine of the two natures and the one divine person, so far from being an outmoded relic from an obsolete world of thought, is far more capable of coping with the religious questionings and demands of the present day than the 'New Approaches' which have been hastily improvised to meet its imagined requirements. Secondly, he has shown that the Chalcedonian formula is no conceptual fossil, devoid of sensitivity and vitality, but is capable of growth and development in the dynamic context that can nourish it today.

4 LIGHT FROM LONERGAN

This has been a long discussion, but even so it has made little or no reference to many of the best-known writers on Christology of recent years, Barth, Tillich, and Pannenberg to mention only three. My excuse, if excuse be needed, is that they have received exhaustive criticism from scholars many of whom are far better acquainted with their works than I am. My chief purpose has been to bring into prominence some writing that is much less well known to the English-reading public but is, in my opinion, of equal or indeed of greater importance. And here there is one point which can hardly be stressed too strongly. If one is to understand the work of any modern theologian and to criticize it fruitfully and constructively, it is essential to acquaint oneself with his metaphysical and epistemological presuppositions, his theories of being and knowledge. If one neglects to do this, one is in grave danger of radically misunderstanding him and in even more serious danger of looking for flaws in the superstructure of his edifice while totally failing to observe signs of imminent collapse that may be present in its foundations. This is a neglect to which English scholars are particularly prone, with their frequent impatience with metaphysical subtleties. It has led to inadequate and sometimes inaccurate assessments of Bultmann, in spite of the searching philosophical analyses of Owen, Schmithals, and Malet,[242] none of whom, we may note, is himself English. It has led to misunderstandings of Pannenberg's attitude to the historicity of the Gospels, which depends on his very idosyncratic doctrine of the nature of truth.[243] It has led also to rather futile discussions of Leslie Dewart's programme for the dehellenization of dogma, which depends on an equally idiosyncratic (though different) doctrine of the nature of truth.[244] And this will be a suitable place for some further remarks on the work of Fr Bernard Lonergan.

Lonergan, no less than Dewart, has demanded a very radical refashioning of Christian theology, to take account of the intellectual orientation – the 'differentiation of consciousness', to use his own term[245] – of the modern world. His proposals inevitably invite criticism and I have myself ventured to suggest places in which some elucidation is desirable.[246] Like Dewart, he pleads for a 'removal from theology of the many limitations of Hellenism.'[247] However, he interprets this dehellenization in a very different way from Dewart, whom he criticizes quite drastically. He condemns Dewart's views on truth as 'not defensible' and describes his rejection of propositional truth as seeming to be 'less "coming of age" than infantile regression'.[248] And, while he writes: 'I am of the opinion that the Christological systematization, from Scotus to de la Taille, had bogged down in a precritical morass',[249] he confronts Dewart with the following issue, which is very relevant to our present concern:

Dewart roundly asserts that no Christian believer today (unless he can abstract himself from contemporary experience) can intelligently believe that in the one hypostasis of Jesus two *real* natures are united. . . . Let me put the prior question. Does Dewart's Christian believer today accept the positive part of the Nicene decree, in which neither the term 'hypostasis' nor the term 'nature' occurs? If so, in the part about Jesus Christ, does he observe two sections, a first containing divine predicates, and a second containing human predicates? Next, to put the question put by Cyril to Nestorius, does he accept the two series of predicates as attributes of *one and the same* Jesus Christ? If he does, he acknowledges what is meant by one hypostasis. If he does not, he does not accept the Nicene Creed. Again, does he acknowledge in the one and the same Jesus Christ both divine attributes and human attributes? If he acknowledges both, he accepts what is meant by two natures. If he does not, he does not accept the Nicene Creed.

What is true is that Catholic theology today has a tremendous task before it, for there are very real limitations to Hellenism that have been transcended by modern culture and have yet to be successfully surmounted by Catholic theology. But that task is not helped, rather it is gravely impeded, by wild statements based on misconceptions or suggesting unbelief.[250]

I have quoted on a previous page[251] a passage from Lonergan's essay on the Origins of Christian Realism, concerning the adoption of the terms 'person' and 'nature' by Chalcedon. Elsewhere in that essay he writes:

> The distinction between persons and nature[252] is added to state what is one and the same and what are not one and the same. The person is one and the same; the natures are not one and the same. While later developments put persons and natures in many further contexts, the context of Chalcedon needs no more than heuristic concepts. What is a person or hypostasis? It is in the Trinity what there are three of and in the Incarnation what there is one of. What is a nature? In the Trinity it is what there is one of and in the Incarnation it is what there are two of.[253]

Lonergan's point is plain. It is that, in using the terms 'person' and 'nature', Chalcedon was not committing the Church to any particular philosophical interpretation of them, but was using them 'heuristically', with just sufficient content to identify the objects to which they are applied. Later developments, as he says, may put them in further contexts, but that is not a matter of the dogmatic definition. On the other hand, they are not mere labels with no intelligible character, as they would be for a nominalistic philosophy. They are instruments of the human spirit, which is endowed with intelligence and insight and functions in a climate of meaning. They are rooted in reality by their application to God and the Christ. And Lonergan has said explicitly that Chalcedon takes Nicene orthodoxy for granted. And, although he does not appear to make this point explicitly, a further involvement in reality is provided by the fact that, when all has been said that has to be said about analogical predication, what is one in the Trinity is two in Christ, and what is one in Christ is three in the Trinity.

Lonergan's loyalty to Chalcedon is all the more impressive when one recognizes that for him theology is far from being a simple logical process of drawing new conclusions from old premises by a set of deductive syllogistic principles. As he expounds it in his monumental work *Method in Theology*, it is an enterprise of the human spirit, ultimately motivated by love and involving conversion on the intellectual, moral, and religious planes. As he says in an essay on Philosophy and Theology,

> When theology is seen as an ongoing process, its contextual structure

accords not with the rules of deductive logic but with the continuous and cumulative process ruled by a method. It is a context in which similar questions are assigned successively different answers. It is a context in which incoherence is removed, not at a stroke, but only gradually, while this gradual removal only tends to bring to light broader and deeper problems. It is a context in which the intelligibility attained is, in general, that of the possible and not that of the necessary. Finally, it is a context in which developments no less than aberrations are not historically necessitated but only historically conditioned; they are the steps that *de facto* were taken in given situations and either legitimated or not by the situations and their antecedents.[254]

To carry the matter further would involve us in nothing less than a full analysis and critique of Lonergan's theory of theological method and is quite impossible here. It should, however, have been useful to see how such an original and, in many ways, radical thinker sees Chalcedon as not a stumbling-block but a signpost for later developments in Christology. And, in view of his reputation for subtlety and complexity, it is refreshing to read the following passage with which, in an earlier essay written in 1959, he summarized a defence of his Christology against certain criticisms made by Fr A. Perego:

Consider, then, the following series of questions and answers that, were they not so elementary and so obvious, might be included in a catechism.

Q   Who suffered under Pontius Pilate?

A   Jesus Christ, his only Son, our Lord.

Q   Did he himself suffer, or was it somebody else, or was it nobody?

A   He himself suffered.

Q   Did he suffer unconsciously?

A   No, he suffered consciously. To suffer unconsciously is not to suffer at all. Surgical operations cause no pain, when the patient is made unconscious by an anaesthetic.

Q   What does it mean to say that he suffered consciously?

A   It means that he himself really and truly suffered. He was the one whose soul was sorrowful unto death. He was the one who felt the cutting, pounding scourge. He was the one who endured for three hours the agony of the crucified.

Q   Do you mean that his soul was sorrowful but he himself was not sorrowful?

A   That does not make sense. The Apostles' Creed says explicitly
    that Jesus Christ, his only Son, our Lord, suffered under Pontius
    Pilate.

Q   Do you mean that his body was scourged and crucified but he
    himself felt nothing?

A   No, he felt all of it. Were our bodies scourged and crucified, we
    would feel it. His was scourged and crucified. He felt it.

Q   Is not Jesus Christ God?

A   He is.

Q   Do you mean that God suffered?

A   In Jesus Christ there is one person with two natures. I do not
    mean that the one person suffered in his divine nature. I do mean
    that the one person suffered in his human nature.

Q   It was really that divine person that suffered though not in his
    divine nature?

A   It was. He suffered. It was not somebody else that suffered. It
    was not nobody that suffered.

Such is the doctrine we have all believed from childhood. Still, as an
object of faith, it is apprehended, not in terms of an understanding of
the nature of the subject and of consciousness, but in the more
elementary fashion that rests on our own experience of ourselves as
subjects and as conscious. There remains, then, the theologian's task
and it consists simply in making explicit what already is implicitly
believed.[255]

I think that this is entirely correct and that it provides the answer to
those who accuse the Chalcedonian Christology of committing the
Church to a particular philosophical doctrine or system.[256] It also, I
think, provides the answer to those who, on the grounds that Christ is
the profoundest of all mysteries, are prepared to commend Chalcedon as
having demonstrated the bankruptcy of rational theology or as having
quite rightly (in their view) promulgated a self-contradictory dogma
and thus made clear the futility of human attempts to apprehend the
divine incomprehensibility. There is a small work on Christology,
reconstructed from notes of lectures given by Dietrich Bonhoeffer in
1933, in which this attitude is expressed in a characteristically German
Protestant form. Bonhoeffer was insistent on the fact that Jesus is the
revelation of God in the fullest possible sense; but he vigorously denied
the possibility of understanding the revelation and the legitimacy of
trying to do so.

The Incarnation [he wrote] is the message of the glorification of God who sees his honour in being man. It must be observed that the incarnation is primarily a real revelation of the creator in the creature, and not a veiled revelation. Jesus Christ is the unveiled image of God.[257]

He even wrote: 'Against liberalism, it must be said that in its own way there is no thought-product less Greek than the Chalcedonian Definition.'[258] But here is his assessment of the nature of the Definition and its achievement:

In the Chalcedonian Definition an unequivocally positive, direct statement about Jesus Christ is superseded and split into two expressions which stand over against each other in contradiction. . . .

The question 'How?' succeeds in making itself impossible simply in the asking. It is directly connected with objectifying thought. Objectifying thought takes the question 'How?' out of itself, but it cannot answer the question of how the union of God and man is achieved. If the question 'How?' is consistently and relentlessly put to Christ, the result will be the Chalcedonian Definition, in which the question 'How?' has made an end of itself. All that remains is a pointer to the question 'Who are you?' The Chalcedonian Definition is itself ultimately the question 'Who?'[259]

Bonhoeffer was perhaps right in holding that Chalcedon did not answer the question 'How?' about Jesus, but on less sure ground in holding that the question cannot or ought not to be asked. 'How?' is, in any case, a very ambiguous word; there are, as modern logicians would point out, a great many kinds of 'how'. And, so far from the Definition being itself the question 'Who?', it is *inter alia* that question's answer. Furthermore, 'Who?' and 'How?' are not the only questions. There is also 'What?'; and, in its two-nature doctrine, Chalcedon answered precisely that. It used its language with extreme simplicity and restraint, 'heuristically', as Lonergan would say; and for this very reason after fifteen hundred years most of its potentialities are still unrealized. In comparison, the mutilated Christologies of the 'New Approach', with their amputation of Christ's deity, are sterile and impotent, deficient in that very relevance to the contemporary situation which they claim to manifest. I can illustrate this by a striking example.

Several years ago I listened to a broadcast from a university of a religious service which was commended for its highly contemporary character. In it extreme emphasis was laid upon the humanity of Jesus to the entire neglect of his divinity. The climax came with the recitation of Sydney Carter's poem *Friday Morning*, with its refrain

> It's God they ought to crucify
> Instead of you and me,
> I said to the carpenter
> A-hanging on the tree.

After this various religious leaders were asked to give their comments. Their chief anxiety was to defend the author from narrow-minded accusations of blasphemy, and to emphasize the intensity of his concern with the problems of human suffering and his refusal to gloss them over by uttering conventional religious platitudes. But it did not occur to any of them, any more than it occurred to Dr John Robinson when he quoted this same poem in his book *But that I can't believe!*,[260] to suggest that the carpenter hanging on the tree was in fact God and that in his crucifixion he was sharing our sufferings. But then all these commentators were *avant-garde* adherents of the New Approach; not one was an old-fashioned Chalcedonian. And I think there is a lesson to be learnt from this about true contemporaneity. Fr H. A. Williams, CR, in a university sermon at Oxford, has asserted that 'obviously the major task of Christian theology during the second half of the twentieth century is a radical reappraisal of traditional Christologies and an attempt to think out afresh what is the form in which we can most adequately express the relation we believe to exist between man and God.'[261] The second half of the twentieth century is already more than half over and there has certainly been no lack of such radical reappraisals. What I suggest we now need is a radical reappraisal of the *un*traditional Christologies, a radical reappraisal of the radical reappraisals. The present essay is a modest contribution to that task.

APPENDIX 1 THE CONCEPTION AND ANIMATION OF CHRIST

I have referred above[262] to Fr Wessels as one of the very few writers who have paid attention to what one might call the genetic and embryological aspects of the Incarnation in recent times, and in particular to the question of Jesus' chromosomes. A further point concerns the time of the appearance of his human soul in his embryonic body. St Thomas Aquinas accepted the contemporary view that the moment of animation of a normal human embryo is not identical with the moment of conception but is considerably later. Present-day embryologists, while using a different vocabulary, would agree on this and would say that the embryo does not become fully human until many days after the fertilization of the ovum by the spermatozoon. Now there are bound to be *some* differences between the case of the incarnate Son and that of other human beings, though they will not be such as to impair the genuineness of his humanity, and St Thomas holds (and is not alone among Catholic theologians in holding) that in Christ, unlike other men, conception and animation were simultaneous, on the double ground that the hypostatic union must have taken place at the moment of conception and that the divine hypostasis could not become the subject of a nature that was not yet fully human.[263] Fr Wessels agrees, and writes:

> If the human soul is ordinarily infused at a later stage of development, then [sc. in the case of Christ] all the intermediate stages were accomplished instantaneously. At the end of the generative action there was a perfect human nature united personally to the divine Word.[264]

I fully agree that the hypostatic union (that is, the assumption of created being by the person of the divine Word) must have taken place at the moment of conception, so that, to give a dramatic illustration, it was symbolically right that, in the Graham Street Pageant of the Holy Nativity which some older readers may remember, Mary was preceded by an angel bearing a white light from the event of the Annunciation to that of Christ's nativity, since from her utterance of her *Fiat voluntas tua* onwards her womb was the tabernacle of the eternal Word. But I would raise the question whether the appearance of a human soul may not have taken place at a later moment. This would not involve the distasteful notion that, until that moment, the divine Word was the subject of a sub-human or non-human organism, for from the moment of conception the embryo was genuinely, if incompletely and not yet fully operatively, human. It was not merely potentially human, in the sense that human was one of the things that it might become while it might equally well have become something else, equine or piscine or scarabean, for example. It was, physically though inchoatively *human*; and it would in due course either become manifestly and operatively human or it would become nothing at all. (This fact about a human embryo is, of course, a very relevant consideration in discussions about the legitimacy of abortion.) I suspect that the older view was influenced by an unduly static view of human nature, or even by the preformationist view that the fully developed physical organism was contained in a microscopic state inside the embryo; if this was so, it would have been ready from the start for partnership with a human soul. An alternative view might be that in all cases animation takes place at the moment of conception (or at any rate by the time that twinning of the embryo becomes impossible), although the soul's capacities can develop and manifest themselves only *pari passu* with the development of the body. What I find difficult to suppose is that in the case of Christ there was a complete lack of co-ordination between the development of the soul and that of the body until the moment when in any other human being animation would have normally taken place, so that a fully adult mental life was being lived in association with a merely embryonic brain. And I find it almost as difficult to suppose, as an alternative, that immediately upon conception the body was instantaneously brought to the state of development that it would normally have attained some weeks later. Conceivably this difficulty may be due to a lack of imagination on my part; I find it difficult to *imagine* the instantaneous transformation of water into wine at Cana, but I have no doubt that it took place. And I fully accept that God may for good reasons produce supernatural and even miraculous effects. But I also believe that grace perfects nature and does not destroy it or contradict it; and some of the text-book theories about the animation of the embryonic body of Jesus seem to me to have this negative character. There is in any case no question as to what is *possible* to divine omnipotence; it is only a question as to what is (as St Thomas would say) *conveniens*. We are concerned with what is, in the strict theological sense, a mystery; that it raises problems for the human intellect is not surprising. What is more important is that it should stimulate our wonder and our awe; and this, as I see it, is precisely what such a speculation as this can do.

One aspect of this matter is the question of the character and development of Christ's knowledge and especially of its content in his pre-natal state. It has been generally accepted by Christian thinkers that consciousness is a function of the whole human being, with body and soul in intricate and reciprocal interaction, and it is in line with this view and not in opposition to it that one recognizes the importance of modern discoveries about the way in which mental and cerebral development go together. Catholic thinkers as different in their general outlook as Karl Rahner and Jacques Maritain[265] have felt obliged to face the implications of these discoveries for Christology. I would heartily endorse the judgement passed on St Thomas' treatise on Christ's manhood in the *Summa* by its most recent editor, Fr Roland Potter, OP: 'Whatever is transient and of a period long past is amply counterbalanced by the many insights which follow from the pervasive application of enduring principles at once theological and anthropological.'[266]

The traditional assertion of the theological manuals that each human soul is the product of a direct and immediate creative act on the part of God will obviously have its bearing upon questions about the soul of Christ. The difficulties often felt about the assertion seem to me to arise from a misunderstanding about the notion of creation itself. I have discussed this in detail in Appendix 4 of my book *The Openness of Being* and therefore shall not repeat my argument here.

APPENDIX 2   A VOICE FROM EASTERN ORTHODOXY

The present chapter was virtually complete when there came into my hands the extremely impressive work *Christ in Eastern Christian Thought*,[267] by Dr John Meyendorff, who holds the chair of Church History and Patristics in St Vladimir's Orthodox Theological Seminary at Crestwood in the State of New York. Although published in 1969, and simultaneously in Paris under the title *Le Christ dans la théologie byzantine*,[268] it has attracted little attention in the Eastern hemisphere, although it is a work of deep scholarship and of genuine ecumenical importance. Its title is rather misleading, for it deals entirely with the period after Chalcedon, and therein its importance largely lies. For, as I have previously lamented, we in the West have suffered drastically in our Christological thinking from the assumption that Christology, so far as anything of importance is concerned, stopped at Chalcedon. With Meyendorff's book and the more recent second volume of Dr J. Pelikan,[269] there is even less excuse than before for that assumption. For Meyendorff, Chalcedon neither manifested the bankruptcy of Greek theology nor spoke the last word on the subject; for all its providential stature and its inalienable authority, it needed for its clarification and precision that subsequent period of vigorous, not to say turbulent, controversy whose climax came in the Fifth Ecumenical Council in 553 and which did not really find a point of relative stability until the Seventh in 787.

I am encouraged by the support which I find from Meyendorff's book for the position which I have taken up in the present chapter. With a wealth of evidence from the patristic writings, he shows that the post-Chalcedonian development was a genuine clarification of the Chalcedonian teaching and not, as has sometimes been held, a narrowing down of an area which Chalcedon deliberately left flexible and undefined. If such was in fact its intention, it was conspicuously unsuccessful in achieving it, in view of the persistence of the Nestorian and monophysite schisms to which Père Bouyer has drawn attention.[270] It is true that the Chalcedonian definition, when it declares that the two natures of Christ 'coalesce' or 'run together' into one *prosopon* and one *hypostasis*, does not explicitly state that this one *prosopon* and *hypostasis* is the pre-existent Logos, so that it remained possible for someone who wished, for example, to hold with Leontius of Byzantium that the two natures themselves formed a composite hypostasis to claim that he was not in fact transgressing the verbal expressions of the definition. However, if the definition does not say in so many words that the *hypostasis* of Christ is the Logos, it is explicit that Christ himself is; so the objection is a mere quibble. Furthermore, it is important to remember that the Chalcedonian definition, in the narrow sense of the passage beginning with the words 'In agreement, therefore, with the holy fathers. . . ', quoted above on page 120, is only a small section of the whole Chalcedonian decree, and that the latter explicitly recognizes the authority of the Nicene and Constantinopolitan Creeds which affirm unambiguously that the eternal and consubstantial Son of God the Father has become incarnate of the Holy Spirit and the Virgin Mary. As a matter of history, subsequent councils were necessary in order to rule out evasions and distortions of the Chalcedonian doctrine, and it is here that Meyendorff's book is fascinating and illuminating; but I do not think there can be any real doubt as to what the Chalcedonian doctrine was.

It is interesting to note the sympathetic remarks which Meyendorff makes in the last few pages of his book on the trinitarian and Christological teaching of Fr Karl Rahner. He quotes with approbation the following passage which Rahner wrote in an essay 'Considerations générales sur la Christologie', which was published in 1965:

> Because, in the Incarnation, the Logos creates by assuming and assumes by stripping himself, we can apply here, and even in a radical and specifically unique manner, the axiom which is valid for every relation between God and a creature, that the creature's nearness and its remoteness, its dependence and its autonomy, do not vary in inverse but in direct proportion. . . . By the very fact that God himself exists, the existence of Christ's human nature receives in the most radical manner its own value, its autonomy, and its reality.[271]

Meyendorff's own reflections are given in the concluding paragraphs of his book; these must be quoted at length:

> The real basis of Nestorianism was precisely the idea of competition and mutual exclusion of divinity and humanity. The overcoming of that Nestorian tendency – which was at the root of all the criticism directed against the neo-Chalcedonism of the fifth council – thus leads inevitably to recovering the importance of considering the Logos as the hypostasis, the 'uniting unity' and the source of Christ's human existence. And, in turn, this 'open' understanding of hypostasis – as the Person which, while pre-existing in divinity, *assumes* also humanity as its own, without making it less human – challenges the old Thomistic notion of God's immutability, and also leads to the real distinction in Trinitarian theology between essence and hypostasis: for immutability, if the hypostatic union is taken seriously, can be the property of the nature, or essence, of God but not of his hypostatic existence, which did change when the son of God 'became flesh'. Thus Karl Rahner arrives at challenging the Latin idea that the Persons of the Trinity are internal relations in the divine essence, for, indeed, if such were the case, the divine hypostasis of the Logos could neither be the subject of change and passion, nor be seen as the existential centre of his human nature. A sound Christology implies, for Rahner, the

return to a pre-Augustinian concept of God, where the three hypostases were seen first of all in their personal, irreducible functions, as Father-God, Son-Logos, and the Spirit of God, and not only as expressions of the unique immutable essence.

For if one identifies the being of God with the essence *only* – as it was done in the West since Augustine – this essence loses its absolute transcendence, incomprehensibility, and immutability. Meanwhile, the distinction between the transcendent essence, the personal or hypostatic existence and the life *ad extra* of God, makes it possible to give a full meaning to apophatic theology, which the Greek fathers cherished so much. . . . [A quotation from Rahner follows.]

It is quite evident, therefore, that Karl Rahner's thought implies not only a return to pre-Augustinism but also a return to the basic presuppositions of the Christological thought analysed throughout this [sc. Meyendorff's] book. This coincidence cannot be explained only by a reference to Rahner's own patristic formation; it also shows the astonishing relevance, for our own time, of the patristic view of the Christian message. It is by facing the challenge of modern thought that contemporary Western Christian theology, in the persons of its best representatives, may discover its authentic roots. The ecumenical significance of this discovery is incalculable.[272]

This approval of the work of a modern Roman Catholic writer on the part of a leading Eastern Orthodox is indeed encouraging, but its details call for some qualifications. I agree with Rahner's rejection of the Thomist view that any one of the three divine Persons might have become incarnate,[273] and with his assertion that to affirm that only the Son is incarnable does not exclude the Father and the Spirit from the Incarnation but, on the contrary, gives each of the three Persons his particular role in the work of God's self-communication to man. On the other hand, it must be remembered that St Thomas argues vigorously that it was much more 'suitable' (*convenientissimum*)[274] that the Son should be incarnate rather than either of the other Persons; and I do not think that he ever contemplates the likelihood of God doing something 'unsuitable'. Augustine is indeed often alleged to be the father of the 'Western' view that in God the one essence is primary and the three Persons are merely modifications within it, but this view is certainly not dominant in the *De Trinitate*. What do seem to be original in Augustine, at least relatively, are the various 'psychological' analogies (mind-knowledge-love, memory-intelligence-will, memory-understanding-love), and these imply a definite order of derivation comparable with the 'Eastern' view of the Father as the 'source' (*pege*) in the Godhead. Again, if it is true that Augustine was the first Latin father to make explicit trinitarian use of the Aristotelian category of *relation*,[275] it can also be claimed that he learnt it from St Basil and St Gregory Nazianzen,[276] who are as Greek as it is easy to be.

Some comment may be needed on Meyendorff's assertion that 'immutability, if the hypostatic union is taken seriously, can be the property of the nature, or essence, of God but not of his hypostatic existence, which did change when the son of God "became flesh" [French edn, *mais non celle* [sc. *propriété*[*de l'hypostase, puisque le Logos "devint" chair*].' As intended, this is correct, and it is the strength of the Chalcedonian doctrine that, in spite of protests from Antiochenes that the Alexandrines were making God passible, it provided the impassible Logos with a complete human nature in which he could genuinely suffer and die. And Meyendorff is formally right in using the term 'theopaschite' to characterize Chalcedonian orthodoxy; Jesus suffered and he was personally God, just as Mary is *theotokos* because she bore Jesus and he was personally God. However, if it is right to use such terms as 'passible' and 'mutable' of the incarnate Logos, it must be noted that the term 'mutable' is specially liable to misunderstanding. The change (*mutatio*) which it implies is change, 'mutability', in the human nature which the Logos assumes, not a change undergone by the Logos in the act of assuming it; to hold otherwise would be to fall into the error of the kenoticists, who substituted a mutilated divine nature for an integral human nature in the incarnate Lord. I have previously referred with approval to Dr Weinandy's contention that, when God is the subject ('The Word became flesh', John 1. 14), *becoming* does not involve *change*.[277]

Meyendorff's strictures on Augustinianism come from the standpoint of a committed and erudite priest of the Orthodox Church. It has, however, been attacked quite as severely from a very different angle by the Scottish Calvinist theologian Dr T. F. Torrance in his recent book *Theology in Reconciliation*;[278] for him, Augustinianism is a particularly obstinate and insidious embodiment of the essentially Greek-pagan dualism which in his opinion has incessantly dogged Christian thought, life, and worship down the ages. He is himself a fervent defender of St Cyril of Jerusalem and the Council of Chalcedon (as also of St Athanasius and the Council of Nicaea), and he maintains what to many will be the surprising thesis that 'the theology most relevant to the post-

Einsteinian world is that of classical Patristic theology, although of course it needs to be recast in the idiom and style of our own era.'[279] Nevertheless, his attachment to patristic theology, while vehement and learned, is somewhat limited in its range. He has little use for the Cappadocian doctrine of the Father as the *arche* or *pege* in the Godhead, for the trinitarian theology of St John of Damascus or for the later Byzantine distinction between the divine *ousia* and *energeiai*, all of which he condemns as manifestations of the hated dualism. It is perhaps a sign of the greatness of Augustine that he comes under assault from standpoints which would seem to be opposed to each other even more sharply than they are to him, but it is at least a hopeful sign that the fathers are once again being taken seriously and that this is happening in the ecumenical field.

ADDITIONAL NOTE 3 'THE MYTH OF GOD INCARNATE'

The present work was almost in the hands of the printer when there appeared a symposium entitled *The Myth of God Incarnate*,[280] containing essays by several of the scholars whose writings I have already discussed. Its topic is so closely related to my own that at least an interim assessment seems to be desirable. The symposiasts, seven in number, are, from Birmingham, Dr John Hick, Dr Frances Young and Dr Michael Goulder; from Oxford, Dr Maurice Wiles, Dr Dennis Nineham, and Mr Leslie Houlden; and Mr Don Cupitt from Cambridge. Their general thesis, as stated in the preface, is that a major theological development is now called for as a result of growing knowledge of Christian origins. It 'involves a recognition that Jesus was . . . "a man approved by God" for a special role within the divine purpose, and that the later conception of him as God incarnate, the Second Person of the Holy Trinity living a human life, is a mythological or poetic way of expressing his significance for us.'[281] They admit that there is nothing new in this, but they claim that in England the traditional doctrine has long been something of a shibboleth, exempt from reasoned scrutiny and treated with unquestioning literalness, and that it now calls for adjustments which are not likely to become generally accepted without further ecclesiastical trauma but which will help to make Christian discipleship possible for our children's children.[282]

A certain anxiety about the title of the book was shown at the time of publication, and it was pointed out that the word 'myth' does not necessarily mean in this context what its common usage suggests, namely a story that is untrue. Had this been thought of before, some misunderstanding might perhaps have been prevented, since the title of a book is what makes its first impact on the public, and common usage is what interprets that title to the public's mind. As to what precisely the word 'myth' does imply, the symposiasts themselves do not appear to be agreed; it is not until the eighth essay that Dr Wiles tries to clear up the confusion and comforts the reader with the assurance that 'the power of the myth will not be undermined by its being more widely recognised for what it is'.[283] They are, however, agreed that, whether or not the notion of God becoming man was taken literally by the Christians who first applied it to Jesus, it is certainly not to be taken literally today. None of them would hold it to be true in the classical sense of truth as the correspondence of the mind with fact. Some of them would apparently ascribe to it some kind of poetical or symbolical or mythological 'truth' as being psychologically or spiritually or morally beneficial to the religious consciousness so long as any suggestion of factual assertion is carefully excluded. But even on this, agreement seems to be doubtful and it is not clear whether, *even as myth*, the image of Jesus as God incarnate is held to be edifying or pernicious. Dr Wiles, in his book *The Remaking of Christian Doctrine*,[284] had already repudiated the doctrine of the Incarnation as inconsistent with his particular form of deism, according to which God never does anything at any one time that is genuinely different from what he does at any other; and he does not recant this view in his essay on 'Christianity without Incarnation?' in the symposium, though he concedes that it is 'reasonable for us to see the doctrine [of the Incarnation] as an interpretation of Jesus appropriate to the age in which it arose'.[285] Dr Hick, in contrast, accepts the myth as giving 'definitive expression to [Jesus'] efficacy as saviour from sin and ignorance and as giver of new life',[286] though on the understanding that Jesus is not to be given exclusive priority over other saviours in other religions. And Dr Young, in an account which is deeply moving as a testimony to her own personal religion, explicitly renounces any notion that the Christian religion is in the last resort intellectually coherent and commits herself to two incompatible 'stories', derived respectively from the 'scientific' model of contemporary culture and the 'mythological' model of religious faith, the story of a *man* who lived as the 'archetypal believer' and the story of *God* being involved in the reality of human existence.[287] How near she is in fact to Chalcedonian orthodoxy, in which the two 'stories' are not incompatible but reconciled!

It is hardly an exaggeration to say that the only point on which the symposiasts appear to be agreed is their rejection of the Incarnation as a truth of fact. On its respectability when considered as a myth they range from the whole-hearted self-commitment of Dr Young, through the hospitable but not exclusive welcome of Dr Hick, to the detached attitude of Dr Wiles and the violent rejection of Mr Cupitt. In Mr Cupitt, indeed, this negation becomes a kind of metaphysical obsession. For him, the heart of Jesus' message is the *disjunction* between God and man. 'The doctrine of the incarnation unified things which Jesus had kept in ironic contrast with each other, and so weakened the ability to appreciate his way of speaking, and the distinctive values he stood for.' 'The assertion that deity itself and humanity are permanently united in the one person of the incarnate Lord suggests an ultimate synthesis, a conjunction and continuity between things divine and things of this world.'[288] All the moral weaknesses of the Church through its history, all its political compromises, all its lapses into worldliness, all its dubious accumulation of power and wealth are in Mr Cupitt's eyes the direct and inevitable consequences of the scandalous dogma that Jesus of Nazareth is God incarnate. In four thunderous charges 'the Christ of Christendom' is demolished, and with him the addressing of prayer to Christ in the liturgy, the development of Christian art in both East and West, and the doctrinal basis of the World Council of Churches; almost the only really sound Christian believers down the ages were, it seems, the iconoclasts! How odd, then, it must seem to Mr Cupitt that most of the great Christian social reformers have seen the traditional Christian doctrine of the Incarnation as the warrant for their assaults upon the entrenched injustices of the social structure and have never suspected that it was their cause! And how much odder still that his fellow-symposiasts show no signs of reaction for or against his polemics!

The way in which the false belief that Jesus was God incarnate got into the Church is another question on which the symposiasts are not agreed. For Dr Goulder its twin roots were the Galilean eschatological myth taught by Jesus and the Samaritan myth of gnostic type;[289] for Dr Young it emerged from the tangled mass of Hellenistic religion. She does admit, however, that 'there does not seem to be a single, exact analogy to the total Christian claim about Jesus in material which is definitely pre-Christian.'[290] If, nevertheless, we inquire how the Church came to apply supernaturalist categories to Jesus, Dr Goulder has the answer:

> Jesus died on the cross, and for a period beginning two days later his disciples had experiences of seeing him, which convinced them that he was alive, raised from death and exalted to God's presence in power. Without such conviction it is impossible to explain the survival of the church . . . Paul was taught of it at his conversion . . . and it is the presupposition of every New Testament document. . . . We are not obliged to accept the first Christians' supernaturalist account of what happened: indeed, as historians, we shall be bound to prefer a naturalist account if one can be offered, and this I shall attempt briefly below.[291]

So far, so good; but why did the first Christians give this supernaturalist account? It all goes back to Peter, who, Dr Goulder tells us, conveniently belonged to a psychological type whose beliefs are strengthened rather than weakened by their apparent refutation and who cast about for means to refute the refutation. On Easter Sunday morning he achieved this resolution, 'a conversion experienced in the form of a vision. The amazing "truth" dawned on him, to solve all his problems: Jesus was not dead after all – he had risen again, he was raised to God's right hand in heaven, he would soon return to establish his kingdom in power.' And so, by corporate 'hysteria' (Dr Goulder's own word) within a small community assisted by candlelight, 'it seemed as if the Lord came through the locked door to them, and away again'.[292] So belief in the resurrection arose; no other hypothesis is even mentioned.

To what extent it is imperative, or even desirable, for the Church today to lay stress upon the importance of Jesus is another question on which the symposiasts appear to differ, though not all have expressed themselves upon it. Those who have – Dr Hick, Dr Wiles, and Dr Nineham – certainly seem content that Jesus should take his place with other great figures of world religion on more or less equal terms. That he is unique or outstanding in any way that is more than accidental and empirical, if indeed in any way at all, inevitably appears doubtful if he is in no way different metaphysically from other men. For Dr Hick, Jesus is simply *one* point at which the Logos – God-in-relation-to-man – has been manifested; he is of supreme concern to *us*, but others may be of equal concern in other cultures. And this raises by implication a further question which underlies the whole symposium, though only Dr

Nineham, in his epilogue, brings it fully into the open. If it is doubtful whether Jesus is really relevant to other *cultures* than the Judaeo-Hellenistic to which he belonged, may it not also be doubtful whether, even in the Judaeo-Hellenistic culture, he is really relevant to other *epochs* than that to which he belonged? If, as traditional belief has held, he is literally God incarnate, and in him the particularity of a human life has been assumed by the universal Creator, it is understandable, though profoundly mysterious, that he has a universal relevance to all time and space. But if, as the symposiasts hold, the notion of God incarnate is a myth, congenial to minds of the first century but uninteresting to those of the twentieth, and if the Jesus to whom it has been applied was simply a man who lived nearly two thousand years ago in a culture vastly different from ours and whose words and deeds are accessible to us, if at all, only through documents which we are repeatedly told are biased, inaccurate and historically unreliable, it is difficult to see that it is really worth our while to demythologize him.

Finally, is not the title of the symposium semantically confusing, however elastically the word 'myth' is understood? One might describe the Lucan narrative of Jesus' birth as a myth, if one did not accept it as historical; one might indeed describe the whole Gospel as a myth if one believed it to be mainly fiction. And in either case one might judge the myth to be edifying or demoralizing, exciting or dull, important or trivial, and so forth. For it is to *narratives* that the word 'myth' properly applies. But the sentence 'Jesus is God incarnate' does not recount a narrative; it makes a straightforward assertion, though it is one with which a great deal of narrative is connected. The assertion is indeed both startling and mysterious; it raises many problems, of which the classical discussions of analogy provide one indication. But once its meaning has been ascertained it must be either true or false in the old-fashioned sense in which truth is the correspondence of the mind and its assertions with reality. And no introduction of more esoteric senses of 'truth', however useful or useless they may turn out to be, should be allowed to obscure this primary question.

I am inclined to think that the ultimate achievement of this book will be to have made it quite clear where you are likely to end up once you abandon the traditional doctrine of the Incarnation. Many people today appear to suppose — and this may include even some of the symposiasts — that you can abandon that doctrine as a hangover from the first five centuries and still retain belief in Jesus as unique among the sons of men, as morally impeccable, and as the universal saviour of the human race. Dr Hick and Dr Nineham have shown how tenuous and fragile that supposition is. I have argued elsewhere in the present volume that the traditional doctrine of the Incarnation, so far from being static and fossilized as many imagine, offers unlimited opportunities for creative advance. But I fear that the seven symposiasts lead us only into the desert.

FOUR

Character and Collegiality Relationship as a Principle in Theology

This chapter is the outcome of a hunch that some of the recent emphases and insights that have appeared in the realm of ecclesiology may help to open up a new and more fruitful approach to some of the most obstinate problems in the movement for Christian unity, namely those connected with the Church's ministry, besides providing a deeper understanding of the nature of Christian existence itself. At the same time I wish to stress the tentative character of these remarks and to offer them merely as suggestions for further criticism and development, without implying that they represent a fully worked out position and still more a confession of faith.

It has, I think, become more and more widely recognized in recent years that the effect of a sacrament upon the individual recipient should be thought of less as the imparting to him of some quasi-physical object or quality which he did not possess before than as the setting of him in a new relation to the Church which is Christ's body or as the renewal and intensification of a relation which had been previously set up. Whatever may have been true a century or more ago, I do not think that any Roman Catholic theologian today would accept the antithesis asserted by F. D. Maurice in his statement that the 'Romanist' of his time 'makes it appear that the blessing of baptism is not this, that it receives men into the holy Communion of Saints, but that it bestows on them certain individual blessings, endows them with a certain individual holiness', and in his insistence, again with the 'Romanist' in mind, that 'a man . . . does not by baptism, faith or by any other process, become a new creature, if by these words you mean anything else than that he is created anew in Christ Jesus, that he is grafted into him, that he becomes the inheritor of his life and not of his own.'[1] Again, Fr Karl Rahner, in his essay 'Forgotten Truths concerning the Sacrament of Penance', maintains that the essence of absolution is the reinstatement of the penitent in his true status in the Church and not only his reconciliation with God or the abolition of his guilt.[2] As regards the Eucharist, the whole meaning of the liturgical revival has been the recovery of the truth that the Eucharist exists for the building up and maintenance of the Body of Christ and not just for the sanctification of the communicant as an isolated individual. Even so 'existentialist' a theologian as Fr E. Schillebeeckx has insisted that, while the medieval theologians were not formally in error when they described the effect of a sacrament as an 'adornment of the soul', it has been realized more clearly in the last few decades that 'the reality perceived is fundamentally an ecclesial effect' and, in the case of baptism, confirmation, and holy orders, has identified this 'ecclesial effect' with the 'character' of the sacrament.[3] Fr Bernard Leeming, in his weighty *Principles of Sacramental Theology* (published, we might notice, before the Second Vatican Council), defines a sacrament as 'a permanent and effective sign of Christ uniting the recipient in a special way to his Mystical Body. . . '.[4] And, on an even more authoritative plane, Vatican II itself, in its Constitutions on the Church and the Liturgy, explicitly expounds the essential nature of the sacraments as incorporating and maintaining the individual recipients in the corporate body of the Church.[5]

In the light of this new emphasis, which clearly goes a long way to meet the strongly felt objection of Protestants to what seems to them to be the 'materialistic' and even 'magical' nature of Catholic sacramental theology, the mysterious 'character' which is alleged to be imparted in certain sacraments will be thought of much more as a *relation* to Christ and his body the Church than as a *quality* acquired by the individual Christian. I would stress as firmly as possible that this does not involve any weakening or watering down of the notion of character but if anything a strengthening of it, for the new relation is every bit as concrete and indelible as any new quality could be; it 'makes as much difference' (or more) to the recipient. And this is specially true if the second term of the relation is a permanent enduring supernatural entity, such as God, Christ, or the Church.

Again – and this affects particularly the sacrament of Holy Order – it is more and more widely understood that, while the notion of 'apostolic succession' represents an important aspect of consecration to the episcopate, the essence of consecration or of ordination consists not in the tactual communication of a new quality but in the reception of the consecrand or ordinand into the organic body of the episcopate or presbyterate respectively, that is to say, in a new relation – a membership-relation – to the existing ministerial organism and a new relation – a ministerial relation – to the organic body of the Church. Dr Hans Küng writes as follows:

The apostolic succession is not an individualistic mechanical succession of an individual to his predecessor but the entrance of an individual into a community. As a corporate body the college of bishops likewise succeeds the college of the apostles as a corporate body.[6]

He quotes Fr Karl Rahner to the same effect:

> An individual bishop is not the successor of an individual apostle. He is only in the line of succession from an apostle insofar as he belongs to the Church's episcopate, which in turn, as a body, succeeds the corporate apostolic college.[7]

Thus the concept of character as relation rather than quality coheres easily and naturally with the concept of consecration as incorporation rather than contagion; and, as we shall shortly see more fully, it is equally consistent with the very fruitful notion of collegiality. However, before passing on to this I would comment on two points.

1. While strongly endorsing the assertion of Küng and Rahner that the consecration of a bishop ought to be thought of not as the succession of an individual to his predecessor but as his entrance into a community (a view for which I myself pleaded in an article in the *Church Quarterly Review* in 1951 and which I repeated in my book *Corpus Christi*),[8] I am less happy with the assertion that the college of bishops *succeeds* the college of the apostles, unless the word 'succeeds' is defined in a very special sense. I would far rather say that the college of apostles *expands into* the college of bishops or that the college of bishops *is* the college of apostles, in an enlarged and transformed condition. And I do not think it is necessary on theological grounds to hold a particular view of the way in which the transformation occurred; that is a question for the historians, if they are able to solve it. Nor need there, or indeed can there, be complete identity of functions. There are admittedly certain functions of the apostles which by their nature cannot be exercised by anyone of a later generation in the precise way in which the apostles exercised them; the most obvious is that of being literally eye-witnesses to the earthly life of Jesus. On the other hand, it may well be argued that the duty of preserving and transmitting the Church's tradition without distortion, which was seen as one of the central obligations of the bishop in the early Church, is nothing less than an analogical expression of the function of 'eye-witness' in the only form in which it could be exercised after the first Christian generation, or, from an even wider perspective, that it is the collegiate episcopate as a whole, transcending each generation and embracing all, that expresses through each of its members its function as the eye-witness of the risen Christ. I do not want, however, to make too much of this point. What I want to maintain – and neither Küng nor Rahner seems to me to be quite sufficiently explicit on this – is that, whatever may be the precise relation between the

apostolate of the first generation and the episcopate of the later Church (a relation which, for example, the prayer for the consecration of a bishop in the *Apostolic Tradition* of Hippolytus certainly suggests is very close),[9] the college of bishops itself must not be thought of as a purely earthly body with a membership totally changing from generation to generation, but rather as a continuing organism, into which new members are incorporated by consecration but which they do not leave by death. That is to say, just as we have in recent years learnt to see the Church of God as not merely an earthly institution but as a steadily growing organism, of which the earthly part is only the lowest level or fringe, so we must think of the episcopate (and of the ministry as a whole) as a steadily growing organism within the Church, to which, by its sacramental nature, it is in indelible relation. Whether as applied to the individual bishop or to the episcopal college as a whole, the notion of succession, in the sense of *substitution*, must be discarded in favour of that of *incorporation*. If it is objected, as it sometimes still is, that to view the ministry in this way is to exaggerate the status of the ministry by placing ordination on the same theological level as baptism and making the ministry a kind of super-church within the Church itself, it must be replied that the precise opposite is the case. For this view sees the ministry as organically integrated with the Church and as living and growing with and within it; while views of the ministry which see its basic nature as less deeply theological are more, and not less, likely to allow it to develop a parasitic autonomy.

2. My second remark will be a brief one in support of my assertion that the notion of character as relation is not less concrete than the notion of character as quality. I merely wish to remark on the use of the notion of relation by St Augustine in his trinitarian theology, which we had occasion to consider earlier in connection with Père Galot's Christology.[10] In order to give full weight to the equality of the Persons in the Godhead without dividing the unity of substance (that is to say, in order to avoid subordinationism on the one hand and tritheism on the other), the great African doctor adroitly turned to his purposes the Aristotelian doctrine of the 'categories' or 'predicaments'. In Aristotle, one of the ten categories is that of 'substance', and the other nine, which include both 'quality' and 'relation' are 'accidents'.[11] In order to avoid tritheism and to keep within the accepted terminology of Latin theology, for which *substantia* was the official equivalent of the Greek *ousia*, Augustine could not describe each of the Persons as a substance; on the other hand, to describe them as accidents would be to fall into

Sabellianism or worse. He therefore, with inspired ingenuity, withdrew 'relation', for trinitarian purposes, from the class of accidents and, taking Person as identifiable with it, placed it on the same level as substance,[12] maintaining that nothing is to be said of God according to accident, but only according to substance or relation. He thus propounded the notion of 'subsistent relation', which was to be enthusiastically developed in the West by the Medievals.[13] I do not want to press the parallel but only to remark that there is a respectable precedent for the view that relation can be even more concrete in its connotation than quality. And that the notion of person as subsistent relation is not a lifeless theological fossil has been strikingly shown by Père Galot.

To return to our main theme, it has become increasingly recognized in all branches of Catholic Christendom that both the Church as a whole and its differentiated organs should be understood in terms of the organic conception which is denoted by the term 'collegiality'; its moral aspect has been indicated by Cardinal Suenens in the closely related word 'coresponsibility'.[14] It is, of course, easy to suggest that the notion of collegiality has been improvised and acclaimed in the Roman communion simply in order to enable diocesan bishops to secure within the areas of their several jurisdictions more individual spontaneity and more independence from the central authority of the Pope and the Curia in Rome. It was indeed rumoured shortly after Vatican II that one extremely conservative and inflexible cardinal archbishop had made use of his increased independence in such a way as to prevent his diocese from adopting the reforms that had been decreed by the Ecumenical Council and endorsed by the local national hierarchy, and that Rome had become so timorous of interfering with diocesan bishops that appeals of his clergy against his directions were simply ignored.[15] One need, however, only read the Constitution on the Church to see that it was very far from the Council's intention to make every bishop a virtual pope in his diocese. Nor, on the other hand, was its purpose to convert the episcopate into a committee on the model of a secular society, making decisions for the government of the Church by a majority vote.[16] In contrast to both these concepts, the doctrine of collegiality is based upon the fundamental theological nature of the Church as the People of God and the Body of Christ. Just as the local Church is seen as neither a self-sufficient entity nor a mere component of the universal Church, but as the local manifestation of the life of the whole body – the fulness of the Church concentrated, as it were, to a point – so the individual bishop is seen as being the local focus through which in this or that place there is manifested the universal episcopate, to which Christ has committed (whether directly or indirectly, whether explicitly or implicitly may be a matter of controversy) the ministerial, pastoral, liturgical, and teaching functions which primarily inhere in him as the Apostle and High Priest of our profession.[17] This is not an altogether easy concept to grasp or to express in legal and constitutional terms, and there has been throughout the Church's history an understandable, though deplorable, tendency to substitute for it a conception of official status derived from some secular source, whether that of the administrative officials of a society or of the ministers of a government, monarchical or democratic as the case may be. Nevertheless, the episcopate is a *collegium*, not a committee nor a secretariat. It has, of course, its organizational and governmental and administrative aspects, and it is these that are the rightful province of canon law. Nevertheless, its fundamental *theological* nature, like that of the Church itself, escapes the sieve of canon law altogether. It is well known that the Roman Catholic Pontifical Commission for the Revision of the Codex of Canon Law has run into so many difficulties in its well-meaning attempt to provide a *Lex Fundamentalis Ecclesiae*, as a theological prolegomenon or axiomatic for the whole system of canon law, that some have been led to question whether it is really feasible, or indeed theologically sound, to include theological and canonical elements in the same theoretical structure at all. Such despair may be excessive, but the fact remains that, although canon law can deal with those aspects of the Church's life which can be expressed in terms of rights, privileges and duties, penalties and rewards, *theologically* the Church's structure is much more like that of a living body differentiated into mutually interfunctioning vital organs than like that of a society composed of individual members, though it must be repeated that no comparison does full justice to its unique nature.

It is this conception that, I believe, lies behind St Cyprian's famous sentence *Episcopatus unus est, cujus a singulis in solidum pars tenetur*,[18] which I would translate as 'The episcopate is one thing of which each part is drawn together by each of the others into the whole.' The alternative rendering that some have adopted, namely 'Every bishop's office is identical, so each individual bishop possesses the whole of it by himself'. seems to me to be quite out of line with Cyprian's thought and also to lose the parallel with the following sentence, which begins 'The Church also is one (*Ecclesia quoque una est*)'. For, as Dr John Meyendorff has argued, Cyprian's concept is that there is basically no plurality of episcopal sees, but only one, the Chair of Peter, and all the bishops, each within the community of which he is president, sit together upon it.[19] I think, with Fr Bernard Schultze, SJ,[20] that Meyendorff, with other disciples of Dr Nicolas Afanassieff, goes too far in contrasting 'universal' and 'eucharistic' ecclesiology, as if the two were contradictory and not complementary, but as regards St Cyprian I believe he is right. His view is confirmed by Charles Gore's judgement that for Cyprian 'the episcopate which belongs to each bishop belongs to him as one of a great brotherhood linked by manifold ties into a corporate unity.'[21] However, the precise nature of St Cyprian's ecclesiology is not essential to the present argument, though I think it is clear that he did not hold that each bishop was an absolute monarch in his own diocese. Whether the episcopate, in correlation with its collegial nature, has a divinely constituted head in the person of the Bishop of Rome is, of course, another question and needs to be settled separately. The Constitution *De Ecclesia*, in the chapter on the Hierarchy, bears manifest signs of a very tough tussle between the view that the Pope's authority, however great or little it may be,[22] belongs to him simply in virtue of his position as Head of the episcopal college and another view which sees him as possessing, quite apart from this and over and above it, an entirely different independent authority of a purely personal kind. The former view, which appears on the whole to be dominant in the Constitution, does not seem to be ultimately irreconcilable with the remarks about the Papacy expressed by Lord (Dr A. M.) Ramsey in his well-known book *The Gospel and the Catholic Church*.[23] There is room and need here for further exploration even after the very considerable advances made by the Anglican/Roman Catholic International Commission in the agreed report on Authority in the Church.

In the light of this concept it becomes easier to understand the otherwise puzzling fact that the traditional rite for the consecration of a bishop clearly purports to confer at one and the same time and in one and the same ceremony both the sacramental character and the pastoral office (what later theology distinguishes as the *potestas ordinis* and the *potestas jurisdictionis*), although the bishop may later be translated to another see and although he may retire from the exercise of pastoral and administrative functions altogether. *Theologically*, it appears to be the case that the pastoral *episcope* over the whole Church belongs to the college of bishops as a whole, and this coheres with the interpretation of consecration as the incorporation of the new bishop into the universal episcopate; we may recall that, when Christ commissioned the twelve Apostles, he is not recorded as having assigned to each of them a local sphere of jurisdiction and pastoral activity. Nevertheless, this universal *episcope* has to be exercised in this, that, and the other place towards human beings who live under conditions of space and time, and this fact about our situation while we are *in via* is itself of theological moment and is not just an accidental and practical inconvenience. It is therefore right and necessary that to each bishop (or, conceivably though not ideally, to a group of bishops) a particular limited sphere should be designated within which he should exercise the *episcope* of the universal episcopate. (It is well to remember that, although normally a bishop's flock consists of the Christians in a particular geographical area, it is the Christians and not the geographical area that have been committed to his pastoral care.) All that canon law can take account of is, of course, the rights and duties that pertain to him in that individual sphere; but this does not alter the fact that it is the universal episcopate that he is exercising; and canon law itself, if it is not, as has frequently happened in the history of the Church, to become parasitic upon the Christian body, can at least take note of its own limitations. And any attempt by an individual bishop to seal off, as it were, his diocese from the rest of the Church and administer it as his sole responsibility will be an offence against the nature both of the Church and of his own episcopate. A similar offence will be committed if one group of bishops, whether a national group or any other, tries similarly to seal itself off from the rest of the Catholic Church. This, again is recognized in *De Ecclesia*, in the statement that, 'together with the office of sanctification (*munus sanctificandi* [i.e. the function of celebrating sacraments]), episcopal consecration confers the offices of teaching and ruling (*munera docendi et regendi*)'. It adds, as we should expect, that these offices, 'of their nature, can only be exercised in hierarchical communion with the head and members of the college',[24] though even here it is significant that the phrase is 'head and members' and not only 'head'. And, together with its emphasis upon the supremacy of the Roman Pontiff, the Constitution declares that 'the order of bishops succeeds to the college of the Apostles in teaching and pastoral government, and indeed in it the apostolic body continues unbroken.' Again, 'this college, in its multiple composition, expresses the variety and universality of the people of God; as collected under one head it expresses the unity of the flock of Christ.'[25] Nevertheless, we are told that 'individual bishops, set over particular Churches [and, no doubt with a prudent eye upon the practices of the early church and indeed of some of the uniate churches today, the Constitution does not say how this "setting over" is achieved], exercise their pastoral government over the portion of the

People of God committed to them, and not over other churches or over the whole Church. But, as members of the episcopal college and lawful successors of the Apostles, they have each, by Christ's institution and command, a responsibility for the universal Church, which, even if it is not exercised by an act of jurisdiction, nevertheless makes a very great contribution to the universal Church.'[26] Thus the twofold function of the bishop, as exercising the episcopate of the universal Church and yet as designated to its exercise within a particular portion of the People of God as its father and shepherd, is held in a delicate and integrated equilibrium, which is none the less impressive in spite of the Council's inability to achieve a definitive account of the nature of the Petrine primacy. The second aspect of the bishop's office will appear more clearly when we now go on to consider the relation of the bishop to his diocese.

Analogous to the collegial nature of the universal nature of the universal episcopate, though not in all respects identical with it, is the collegial nature of the presbyterate of a single diocese. (I use the words 'presbyter' and 'presbyterate', in accordance with Latin usage, to denote the second order of the Sacred Ministry, since 'priest' and 'priesthood' [*sacerdos* and *sacerdotium*] would include the episcopate as well.) 'The presbyters,' *De Ecclesia* tells us, 'as trained fellow-workers with the episcopal order and its aid and instrument, are called to the service of the People of God and together with their bishop form one presbyterate, although entrusted with different duties.'[27] The presbyters, then, with the bishop, form an organic collegium, and, just as each bishop functions not as an isolated individual but as the local organ of the universal episcopate, so each presbyter, in his ministerial, pastoral, liturgical, and teaching activities, functions not as an individual free-lance nor as a mere delegate of the bishop, but as the local organ of the diocesan presbyterate, this presbyterate being not a mere committee of equals but an organic body consisting of the presbyters with and under the bishop, who is their father in God. The *locus* of the presbyter's functions is normally the parish, as the *locus* of the bishop's functions is normally the diocese; nevertheless, one must allow for abnormal, though not for that reason illicit, spheres of functioning of both bishops and presbyters. And, again in an analogous and not a purely univocal way, we must see the parish priest and his people as together forming yet a third type of collegium, as the local manifestation of the universal people of God; it is perhaps unfortunate that *De Ecclesia*, in spite of its insistence on the priesthood of the faithful as a whole[28] and on the need for the closest mutual confidence and co-operation between priests and people,[29] does not develop this point, though the gap is filled in two other conciliar decrees, *De Pastorali Episcoporum Munere* (§28) and *De Presbyterorum Ministerio et Vita* (§8). And again we may quote from St Cyprian, this time from a letter written to his presbyters and deacons. 'At the very beginning of my episcopal office', he writes, 'I decided to do nothing on the basis of my own opinion alone without your counsel and the agreement of the people (*nihil sine consilio vestro et sine consensu plebis mea privatim sententia gerere*).'[30]

I suggest, therefore, that the presbyter is the local organ of the diocesan presbyterate in the parish, in a way analogous to that in which the bishop is the local organ of the universal episcopate in the diocese. (I am here using the words 'parish' and 'diocese' in the widest sense, to include those legitimate but non-typical spheres of ministry in which a presbyter or bishop may be exercising his various functions.) And, since the diocesan presbyterate is centred or focused in the bishop, it is itself organically inherent in the universal episcopate at, so to speak, one remove. This has consequences for the doctrine of holy orders. Consecration to the episcopate is the incorporation of a man into the organic body of the universal episcopate by a group of bishops (conceivably, though not normally or ideally, by a single bishop) acting as its local agent and organ for this purpose. Ordination into the presbyterate is, in its immediate reference, the incorporation of a man into the diocesan presbyterate by the bishop, acting (not necessarily, but at any rate normally and typically) together with presbyters of the diocese. Nevertheless, because of the organic membership of the bishop in the universal episcopate and because of the resulting mediated organic relation of his diocesan presbyterate to the universal presbyterate, a man cannot be made a member of the diocesan presbyterate without *ipso facto* becoming a member of the presbyterate of the universal Church. Thus a bishop, while consecrated *into* the universal episcopate, is consecrated *for* a particular diocese; while, in contrast, a presbyter, while ordained *into* the diocesan presbyterate and *for* a particular parish, is *ipso facto* incorporated, *via* the ordaining bishop who is a member of the universal episcopate, *into* the presbyterate of the universal Church. He cannot become a presbyter of the diocese of Canterbury or of Wagga Wagga without becoming, by that very fact, a 'priest in the Church of God'.[31]

If this perspective is correct, it would appear that what is needed in order to regularize the status of ministers who have not received episcopal ordination is *their sacramental incorporation by a bishop into the presbyterate of his diocese*; this will bring about *ipso facto* their integration into the universal presbyterate of 'the Church of God'. The word 'sacramental' needs to be emphasized; this whole discussion is set within the context of the Church as a sacramental organism, the People of God, the Body of Christ, and not as an organization to be thought of primarily in juridical, managerial, or constitutional terms. It is certainly not sufficient for the bishop or his secretary to sign a document authorizing Mr So-and-so to act as a presbyter of his diocese, or to address him in a tactful and felicitous speech of welcome. On the other hand (and here I would stress the point made earlier in this chapter about the basically *relational* nature of sacramental 'character') what the bishop has to do in a unification rite is not primarily to impart to the non-episcopally ordained ministers some *quality* which they have not previously possessed, but, by a sacramental (or quasi-sacramental)[32] act, to receive them into his presbyterate. This should be done by a rite including prayer for the Holy Spirit and the imposition of the bishop's (and, appropriately, of his presbyters') hands. Along these lines it should be possible to overcome some of the difficulties (there are others) that have hitherto dogged attempts to find a satisfactory formula in a unification-rite to express the relation of the ministry to both the local and the universal Church, to devise, for example, a formula that professes to admit the recipient into a ministry wider than that of the local united Church of Lanka or Nigeria. What matters is not 'the Church of Lanka' or 'the Church of Nigeria' or 'the Church of England', which are, as such, man-made organizations, but the presbyterate of the local bishop, which is organically inherent in the ministry of the universal Church. If a man becomes a member of *that*, he will *ipso facto* become, if he was not already, a 'priest (presbyter) in the Church of God'.

It should be added here that this concentration upon the episcopate and the presbyterate in no way belittles the significance of the Church itself, as the People of God and the Body of Christ; on the contrary it presupposes it and depends upon it. The indelible ontological relation which is the 'character' of holy orders is a highly complex one, involving as its constituents sub-relations to the episcopate, the presbyterate, the Church as a whole, the ascended Christ and, indeed, the human race in its totality and the whole created universe; its full description would require a lengthy treatise and would, no doubt, raise further problems than have yet been envisaged. As Fr Karl Rahner has observed, 'in theology to settle one question, even correctly, raises three new questions that remain to be settled.'[33] Nevertheless, this very fact is a strength and not a weakness. For, if the character imparted by a sacrament is considered simply as a *quality*, the almost inevitable suggestion is that it is a private possession or privilege of the individual, even if, like wealth or hereditary dignity, it is held to carry with it obligations towards God and other people. But a *relation* is essentially outward-looking and directed to others, it necessarily places its subject in a communal setting, and, when its subject is a person, it is dynamic and fertile in its consequences.[34] And once again I would stress that there is nothing in the notion of relation as such that is impermanent or unsubstantial; this appears clearly from St Augustine's application of it to the Persons of the Trinity. Both qualities and relations *can* be fictitious or ephemeral; neither *need* be.

It will be well at this point to repeat that the three instances which I have taken — the Pope with the other bishops, the bishop with his presbyters, the parish priest with his layfolk — while they all exemplify the notion of collegiality, exemplify it analogically and not univocally, and that the differences are not less important than the similarities. For, to go no further, the Pope is himself a bishop, in a sense in which a bishop is not a presbyter or a presbyter a layman. And, while a man becomes a presbyter or a bishop by a *sacramental* rite of ordination or consecration,[35] he becomes a pope by a *canonical* process of election. Nevertheless, the notion of collegiality is of deep theological significance and it permeates the Church throughout its being. It coheres with the fundamentally personal nature of the Church as the People of God, united with one another and with Christ in deeply human relationships, and not as a mere collocation of individuals endowed with private qualities.

There are one or two related topics on which a brief comment may not be out of place. Clearly, in the view of the Church's structure which I have been defending, the diocese on the one hand and the Church universal on the other are the basic ecclesial communities, with the bishop as the link between the two. He is both the local symbol and agent of the fatherhood of God and is also one member of the universal collegiate episcopate. He represents both his diocese to the universal Church and the universal Church to his diocese. The primitive custom, by which the bishop was chosen by his flock and then accepted and consecrated by neighbouring bishops gave expression to this two-sided truth; the extent to which Christian disunity and involvement with the secular power have obscured its understanding and impeded its practical implementation are too obvious to need much description here. It is, however, not improper for there to be intermediate ecclesiastical groupings between the diocese and the universal Church. The development of patriarchates and provinces, even if it has been largely conditioned by political and cultural influences, is natural and useful, in spite of the abuses to which it is subject. Furthermore, the limitation of our human imaginations being what it is, and the convocation of representative gatherings of the whole Church or the whole episcopate being inevitably infrequent and cumbersome, intermediate organizations and gatherings can be an effective reminder that the Church is something wider than the local diocesan or parochial community. It is interesting to see how, as a result of the cautiously decentralizing policy of Vatican II, the Roman communion is encouraging the formation and active functioning of national or quasi-national episcopal councils, to deal with matters affecting areas larger than the diocese but smaller than the Church as a whole, and, with the 'shrinking' of the earth through speedier means of travel and more efficient media of communication, the desirability and feasibility of such developments is obvious. Nevertheless, it is vital to recognize that such organizations are artificial and relative in a way that the diocese is not; and this remains true even when we have given full weight to the fact that the number and distributon of dioceses themselves has been determined largely by historical and sociological considerations. And these organizations carry with them the danger that the essentially supra-national and supra-cultural character of the Church may be overlaid and obscured. The 'separated' Churches of the East, such as the Armenian and the so-called 'Assyrian', furnish striking examples of this, though history goes far to excuse as well as to explain it. The Eastern Orthodox Churches, too, with their admirable determination to be identified with the lives of their peoples, have not entirely avoided the snare of nationalism. And certainly Anglicanism is in no position to be critical of other Christian communions on this score, as is evident on consideration of the monuments inside Westminster Abbey, the transplanted synthetic version of an already obsolescent phase of English religion in the so-called 'National Cathedral' at Washington, D.C., or the titles of 'the Church of England in Canada', only recently discarded, and of 'the Church of England in Australia', still in force. And, in our increasingly bureaucratic world, with its proliferation of administrators and administrative organizations, the ever-present temptation of ecclesiastical synods and councils is to consider themselves as quasi-parliamentary legislative bodies, whether they owe their constitution and composition to autocratic or to democratic action, rather than as contrivances of a strictly relative and intermediate character, between the fundamental theological entities of the diocese and the universal Church. Dr J. V. Langmead Casserley, writing in 1965, bitingly commented on the deplorable fact that there was then evident a passionate desire for membership of a united national church in most of the reunion schemes then being canvassed and very little desire for membership of the Church universal;[36] it is no doubt difficult for many Christians to have an imaginative awareness of anything much larger than their local or national community, but it is here that a proper understanding of the nature of the diocese and of the bishop should provide a bridge. The justification for provincial and similar organization is the wholesome principle of 'subsidiarity', which, although it is not mentioned by name in the documents of Vatican II, undoubtedly underlies many of their provisions. It was declared by Pius XII to be 'valid for social life in all its organisations, and also for the life of the Church without prejudice to its hierarchical structure.'[37] It has been briefly defined by Dr Küng as follows: 'What the individual can accomplish on his own power should not be done by the community, and what the subordinated community accomplishes should not be done by the superordinated community. The community must respect the individual, the superordinated community the subordinated community.'[38] It must not, however, be construed simply as individualism given as much rope as can be safely allowed it, and still less as a corporate form of authoritarianism. (I am reminded of W. E. Gladstone's words, inscribed in letters of gold on the pedestal of his bust in the entrance of the National Liberal Club: 'The principle of Toryism is mistrust of the people qualified by fear; the principle of Liberalism is trust of the people qualified by prudence'!) In its application to the Church, no illustration derived from the secular realm can be altogether adequate, though some may be valuable and suggestive. The Church's nature is essentially bipolar, for it is founded on the two facts of the Fatherhood of God and universal redemption in Christ; and the two poles are the diocese with its own personal father in God and the universal episcopate.

Here, however, I must draw attention to the point made quite early in this chapter, that 'the college of bishops itself must not be thought of as a purely earthly body with a membership totally changing from generation to generation, but rather as a continuing organism, into which new members are incorporated by consecration but which they do not leave by death.'[39] Whereas the last paragraph has expounded the relational structure of the Church and its ministry geographically or in space, now we must remind ourselves that that structure also extends historically or in time. This is the basis both of respect for tradition in the doctrinal sphere and of devotion to the saints in the religious sphere, and its vivid recognition is the great safeguard against both ecclesiastical bureaucracy and synodical government conceived on the model of parliamentary democracy. It provides the justification for the solemn personal obligation laid upon, and accepted by, a bishop at his consecration, to preserve and maintain the faith which he has received, an obligation which cannot be evaded by the consoling reflection that these matters are now democratically settled by the General Synod or the General Convention.[40] For, in the unity of the Body of Christ, the previous earthly generations are not our predecessors; they are our contemporaries. And we shall be guilty of a grossly untheological secularization of the relational and corporate understanding of the Church and the minstry if we limit our perspective to that part of the Church which is militant here upon earth.

The extent to which a defective understanding of the theology of the ministry can lead to serious practical consequences can be instructively illustrated by two animated controversies of the nineteen-sixties. The Revd John Livingstone, in a pamphlet entitled *Reforming the Bishop*,[41] commenting on the proposed rite of unification in the Anglican-Methodist reunion scheme, remarked that 'the proposed form of service, seen through Anglican eyes, implies that the bishops of the Anglican flock . . . make them [the former Methodist ministers] – not as one would expect elders with delegated episcopal powers to work under them in their own dioceses (for this is what ordination rites are for) – but valid elders independent of any bishop', and that the subsequently conse-crated bishops would not be 'fellow members of their own episcopal college . . . but a separate body of men in episcopal orders who do not constitute an episcopal college, since they are responsible to the Metho-dist Conference rather than to the Christian episcopate as a whole.'[42] It is in fact difficult not to feel that Anglicans in recent years have been so obsessed with the one very important question of ensuring that the ministers of a reunited church shall have received valid orders that they have assumed all other questions about the ministry to be irrelevant. Indeed – and here we touch directly upon the central theme of this chapter – they have conceived the character of holy orders entirely as a quality communicated to the individual minister and not as a permanent relation between him and the corporate ministry of the Body of Christ.

The extent to which it is assumed, by others if not by themselves, that Catholic-minded Anglicans look upon a priest as little more than an enchanter endowed with certain magical powers is shown by the fact that it has been seriously suggested (though not, I think, by themselves) that they cannot on their own principles have any objection to a joint Eucharist concelebrated by Anglican and Free-church ministers, on the sole ground that, as long as one of the men who repeat the dominical words has been ordained by a bishop in the apostolic succession, the bread and wine will be converted into the Body and Blood of Christ.

But, quite apart from questions about the validity of sacraments, there is a serious and urgent question about the concept of the ministry, and especially of the episcopate, which is offered to non-Anglicans for their acceptance. The image of the bishop as the efficient administrator of a large area, largely cut off from any effective contact with his lay people and even seeing his presbyters only at long intervals and for brief spaces of time, but nevertheless acceptable as an influential figure in regional and national affairs, is alluring to some non-Anglicans and repulsive to others, but it is a totally false picture of what a bishop essentially is and of what he ought to be seen to be. And reports embodying proposals for reforms of one kind and another are not invariably reassuring in this respect.

Mr Livingstone was writing just after Mr Leslie Paul had produced his famous Report on the Payment and Deployment of the Clergy, and he remarked that Mr Paul had taken 'clergy' as meaning lower clergy and had discussed the ministerial structure of the Church while scarcely mentioning the bishops. Some devastating strictures were passed on the report from a strictly non-theological angle by the professional sociologist Mr Bryan Wilson,[43] who, in spite of Mr Paul's protests,[44] continued to maintain that Mr Paul's proposals could only bring the Church into closer conformity with the unreligious society of the contemporary world.[45] Mr Livingstone went to the heart of the matter from a theological standpoint in the remark that 'Mr Paul should have started with the bishop and his diocese, and looked at parishes and regions after this and not before.'[46] He made similar criticisms of two other commissions of the day, the Arbuthnot Commission on the redistribution of bishops in South-East England and the Hodson Commission on Synodical Government. He pleaded for smaller dioceses, corresponding roughly in area to the new London boroughs and containing from thirty to fifty parishes each, in order to make the diocese a real pastoral unity. He pointedly condemned the Hodson

Report for 'trying to balance prelacy with federal democracy'. 'The bishop', he wrote, 'is meant to represent his diocese to the universal episcopate and the episcopate to his diocese. He should be at the same time chosen by the episcopate and elected by the diocese. . . . There are basically three units of pastoral government – the parish priest with his people, the bishop with his synod, and the episcopate, whether provincial, national or universal.'[47] I am not sure that 'chosen by the episcopate and elected by the diocese' is necessarily the right order, or just what in practice the difference between choice and election would be, but Mr Livingstone was clearly concerned, as the reports of the commissions which he was criticizing were not, with the theological and pastoral nature of the bishop's and presbyter's office and not primarily with economy of resources and administrative efficiency. Those reports are, of course, now of mainly historical interest, but they are, though this was not their conscious purpose, written for our learning. Since their appearance a number of ecclesiastically important events have taken place: the Lambeth Conference of 1968; the setting-up of the Anglican Consultative Council, with its meetings at Limuru in 1971, in Dublin in 1973, and in Trinidad in 1976; and the inauguration of the General Synod of the Church of England in 1970. While the reports and resolutions of Lambeth 1968 and the resolutions of the A.C.C. cannot be described as theologically exhaustive, they have at least shown a tendency to move away from a purely pragmatic attitude to the episcopate; and it is encouraging to notice that the report entitled *Bishops and Dioceses*, which was produced in 1971 by a working party for the General Synod with highly practical questions in view, gave to its first chapter the title 'A Theological Understanding of Episcopacy'. Again, the impressive Agreed Statement on the Ministry (*Ministry and Ordination*, the 'Canterbury Statement'), issued by the Anglican/Roman-Catholic International Doctrinal Commission in 1973, is an almost entirely theological document. The following passage will show how close its view of the ministry is to that which I have outlined above:

In the ordination of a presbyter the presbyters present join the bishop in the laying on of hands, thus signifying the shared nature of the commission entrusted to them. In the ordination of a new bishop, other bishops lay hands on him, as they request the gift of the Spirit for his ministry and receive him into their ministerial fellowship. Because they are entrusted with the oversight of other churches, this participation in his ordination signifies that this new bishop and his church are within the communion of churches. Moreover, because they are representative of their churches in fidelity to the teaching and mission of the apostles and are members of the episcopal college, their participation also ensures the historical continuity of this church with the apostolic church and of its bishop with the original apostolic ministry. The communion of the churches in mission, faith and holiness, through time and space, is thus symbolised and maintained in the bishop. Here are comprised the essential features of what is meant in our two traditions by ordination in the apostolic succession.[48]

It will be well at this point for me to remind myself as well as my readers that it is not the purpose of the present chapter to give a comprehensive and exhaustive discussion of the nature of the Church's ministry. That purpose has been to show, by some particular illustrations, the relevance of the view that sacramental character consists in a relation rather than in a quality. In doing this, I have hoped to allay some of the fears which are evident in unity discussions on the evangelical side, that the Catholic view of the ministry is superstitious and materialistic, since it appears to conceive of the priest as a kind of magician endowed in his own right with supernatural powers. On the other hand, I have also tried to show that the understanding of the character of priesthood as relational does not imply that priesthood is essentially subjective or fictitious or merely functional, but that it is real and ontological, since a relation can be every bit as real as a quality. I have already mentioned the way in which the realistic understanding of relation has been used by St Augustine in triadology and by Fr Jean Galot in Christology; I shall briefly suggest two further uses of it in concluding this chapter.

The first is in connection with the notion of *Blessing*. It is, I think, true that, in both Catholic and Protestant circles, the blessing of a person or an object is often thought of as the imparting of a quality, though opinions would differ widely about the nature of the quality, the manner, and the agent of its impartation, and its permanence when imparted. In particular, in Catholic circles the quality would be thought of as imparted by the priest ('Please, father, will you bless my statue of St Joseph of Cupertino?'), even when it is taken for granted that the primary agent of the blessing is God himself, while in Protestant circles the quality would be thought of as imparted by God in response to prayer ('Pastor Jenkins, will you ask for the blessing on our meal?'); though it should be observed that the indicative form ('I bless . . .') is virtually unknown in both the Roman and Eastern Orthodox communions and that the forms regularly used are precatory ('May God bless . . .' or 'Do thou, God, bless . . .' or 'We ask thee, God, to bless . . .'). My present point is, however, that, whatever the *subject* of the verb 'bless' is or may be assumed to be, the *object* of the verb is taken as being a created person or thing. However, recent scholarship has shown – and this is of special importance in understanding the Eucharist – [49] that, in Judaism, the object of a blessing is not any of God's creatures, but the Creator himself. It is he who is 'blessed' and is 'given thanks' for creating the good things of the world and bestowing them on man, and until man has blessed and thanked God for them he cannot without irreverence use them for his own purposes. Thus the Hebrew word *berakah* is rendered in Greek by both *eulogia* and *eucharistia*, 'blessing' and 'thanksgiving'; for in Judaism the operations are identical. The *blessed food* is the food that has been recognized as coming from God, and for which and over which God has been thanked and blessed and praised;[50] the *blessed man* is the man who has been recognized as receiving his being from God and as responding to God in self-dedication and gratitude. It is not accidental that the eucharistic canon is prefaced by the words *Eucharistomen to Kurio, Gratias agamus Domino Deo nostro*, 'Let us give thanks to the Lord our God', since the Church is about to praise God for his work of creation and redemption over the food which he gives us of the Body and Blood of his incarnate Son. But there is one point which it is essential to emphasize if we are to see the full realism of this in its Christological context.

I have been at pains to maintain that a relation *can be* as real and objective as any quality; but this does not mean that every relation *is*. And, while we must certainly not disparage the institutions of the Old Dispensation, we must never forget the central theme of the Epistle to the Hebrews, that those institutions were essentially preparatory, prophetic, figurative and, in the last resort, ineffectual foreshadowings of the one perfect and effectual reconciliation of man to God which was brought about by the death, resurrection, and entry into heaven of the incarnate coessential Son of the Father, Jesus the Messiah. In the Old Dispensation the blessings of God are, in their interior and only partly conscious meaning, a praising and thanking of him for the anticipations of what he would one day do, far more than for what he had already done. In contrast, the relation to God expressed and enacted by a blessing pronounced within the Body of the Ascended Christ has an objectivity and a reality that far transcends those of the blessings of the Old

Israel. This is specially true of the sacraments and supremely of the eucharistic meal of the Body and Blood of Christ. The Jewish *Amen*, the prayer that 'this may be so', has become the Christian *Amen*, the triumphant proclamation that 'this is so', that this has now come to pass.[51]

The second application that I would suggest of the principle of relation as objective reality is in connection with the eucharistic presence. There has been in recent years a good deal of criticism of the adequacy of the concept of transubstantiation, not only, as one might have expected, outside the Roman communion but inside as well,[52] partly because of the changed, and therefore misleading, connotation that the term 'substance' has acquired in modern usage but also because it is felt to be unable to do justice, even when carefully explained, to the nature of the Christian Church as a community of men and women living in personal relationships with one another and supremely with Christ and the Father. Thus, attempts have been made to reformulate the eucharistic presence in terms such as transignification, transfinalization and transvaluation,[53] which are felt to have a more personal and dynamic character than transubstantiation. I find myself, however, agreeing with Pope Paul VI[54] that, legitimate as these attempts may be in themselves, they cannot make up for the healthy realism carried by the term 'substance'. If, as I believe to be the case, substance has been conceived in insufficiently dynamic and personal terms in the past, we should conceive it more dynamically and personally, but I do not think that we can afford to dispense with it. To these adverbs I would add a third one, 'relationally', and it may comfort those who wish their theology to be in line with modern scientific thought to remind them that, whereas for Newton and his successors the universe was made up of tiny inert particles, immersed in receptacles of space and time that were antecedent to them, and related to one another by purely extrinsic relationships, the universe as the scientist of today conceives it is a vast fabric of constantly changing and interweaving patterns of energy, reacting in a structure of spatio-temporal relationship which is subsequent and not antecedent to the entities that it relates. I cannot attempt to follow up these suggestions here, but I will content myself with indicating that eucharistic theology is one of the areas in which the principle of relation as objective reality might be both illuminating and ecumenical.

Finally, I would suggest, very tentatively, as a subject for investigation, the possible theological utility of the advances in the logic of relations initiated by Bertrand Russell and A. N. Whitehead, especially with regard to polyadic relations. If handled with the subtlety with which St Augustine handled Aristotle's *Categories*, this might be helpful for triadology and especially the *Filioque* dispute – or, of course, it might not.

Notes

FOREWORD

1. *New Blackfriars*, LVI (1975), 563f.
2. Edited by Morna Hooker and Colin Hickling (SCM* 1975).
3. Cf. her article, published elsewhere, 'On using the Wrong Tool', which I have discussed in ch. 2 infra.
4. *What about the New Testament?*, 239.
5. Ibid., 240.
6. Cf. p. 37 infra.
7. It is interesting to compare these remarks of the Revd Dr T. M. Parker: 'I well remember my alarm and horror, when, turning over to the Honour School of Theology after my History Schools [in the late 1920s], I looked at the far less rigorous standards of proof apparently required in dealings with Old and New Testament history. In those days at least this was very largely taught and written about by scholars who, whatever their eminence in philology and philosophy, had very little idea of history as a professional historian understands it, and often were visibly prejudiced by their particular ecclesiastical background' (Foreword to G. Dix, *Jurisdiction in the Early Church, Episcopal and Papal*, (Faith House 1975, 6). How far is this true fifty years later?
8. Cf M. B. Reckitt, *Maurice to Temple: A Century of the Social Movement in the Church of England* (Faber 1947).
9. Cf., e.g., G. R. Dunstan, *The Artifice of Ethics* (SCM 1974).
10. *Faith and Society* (The Church Union 1955).
11. (CUP 1953). Here, to give a glaring example, Raven's indiscriminate condemnation of all thinkers who distinguish between the natural and the supernatural led him inadvertently to take a statement which Professor Dorothy Emmet wrote about Emil Brunner as referring to St Thomas Aquinas (I, 73).
12. E.g. *Honest to God* (SCM 1963). Cf. my critique in E. L. Mascall, *The Secularisation of Christianity* (Darton 1965), ch. iii.
13. E.g. P. van Buren, *The Secular Meaning of the Gospel* (SCM 1963); G. Vahanian, *The Death of God* (New York, Braziller, 1957); W. Hamilton, *The New Essence of Christianity* (Darton 1966); T. J. J. Altizer, *The Gospel of Christian Atheism* (Collins 1967); H. Cox, *The Secular City* (SCM 1965).
14. Cf. J. B. Metz, *Theology of the World* (Burns Oates 1969); 'Political Theology', *Sacramentum Mundi*, ed. K. Rahner et al. (Burns Oates 1968–), V, 34ff. (with bibliography); and *Encyclopaedia of Theology*, ed. K. Rahner (Burns Oates 1975), 1238ff.; Peter Mann, OSB, 'The Transcendental or the Political Kingdom? Reflections on a Theological Dispute', *New Blackfriars*, L (1969), 805ff., LI (1970), 4ff.
15. Cf. G. Gutierrez, *A Theology of Liberation* (SCM 1974); James H. Cone, *Black Theology and Black Power* (New York, Seabury 1969); *A Black Theology of Liberation* (Philadelphia 1970); Edmund Hill, OP, 'Black Theology', *New Blackfriars*, LIV (1973), 244ff. J. L. Segundo, *The Liberation of Theology* (C. Gill 1977).
16. Longmans 1958.
17. SPCK. Most of the documents here assembled are the products of bilateral conferences involving Roman Catholics, Anglicans, Lutherans, and Calvinists.

18. As examples of really constructive and theological ecumenical thinking I would mention the three Agreed Statements of the Anglican/Roman Catholic International Commission on the Eucharist (Windsor 1971), Ministry (Canterbury 1973), and Authority in the Church (Venice 1976), especially the last of these. These deserve (and need) to be made the material for continuing sympathetic and critical discussion and not merely to be treated as final proposals to be assessed from established denominational standpoints.

* SCM = SCM Press throughout.

CHAPTER 1

1. 'A Page from the Past', *Theology*, LXXVI (1973), 648.
2. *The Christian Mind* (SPCK 1963), 3f.
3. SCM 1974.
4. 'The Theology of the Catholic Revival', in *Northern Catholicism: Centenary Studies in the Oxford and parallel Movements*, ed. N. P. Williams and Charles Harris (SPCK 1933), 130f.
5. 'One Jesus, many Christs?', in *Christ, Faith and History: Cambridge Studies in Christology*, ed. S. W. Sykes and J. P. Clayton (Cambridge 1972), 142f.
6. 'The Outcome: Dialogue into Truth', in *Truth and Dialogue: The Relationship between World Religions*, ed. John Hick (Sheldon Press 1974), 151.
7. Op. cit., 131.
8. *Summa Theologiae*, I, i, 1 ad 2.
9. 'Recent Higher Degrees in Theology', *Theology*, LXVIII (1965), 431ff.
10. A. N. Sherwin-White, *Roman Society and Roman Law in the New Testament* (Oxford, Clarendon Press 1963); Humphrey Palmer, *The Logic of Gospel Criticism*, (Macmillan 1968); cf. pp. 82ff. infra. Cf. also E. L. Mascall, *The Secularisation of Christianity* (Darton 1965), ch. 5.
11. *The Semantics of Biblical Language* (OUP 1961); *Biblical Words for Time* (SCM 1962).
12. OUP 1969.
13. Darton 1972.
14. Collins 1971.
15. Now Lord Ramsey of Canterbury.
16. Longmans 1936.
17. Cf. my review of Küng's book in *The Tablet* (31 July 1971), 739f.
18. Sands 1970. French original, Paris, Aubier-Montaigne, 1968.
19. Op. cit., 98.
20. Ibid., 98f.
21. Cf. Xavier Rynne, *Letters from Vatican City* (Faber 1963), 79.
22. 'This, our Common Crisis', *Faith*, IV (1972), 5ff.
23. *Summa Theologiae*, I, i.
24. *Sacra Doctrina: Reason and Revelation in Aquinas* (Oxford, Blackwell, 1970), 7f.
25. *Holy Writ or Holy Church* (Burns Oates 1959), 20.
26. Ibid., 22.
27. Op. cit., 69f.
28. *Summa Theologiae*, Blackfriars edn. Eyre and Spottiswoode, I, 1964), App. 11, 134.
29. W. O. Chadwick, *From Bossuet to Newman; The Idea of Doctrinal Development* (Cambridge, CUP, 1957), 164ff. Cf. K. Rahner, *Theological Investigations* (Darton, IV, 1966), 3ff.
30. Chadwick, op. cit., 39f., 203f.

31. Op. cit., 48. All Fr Gilby's appendices to this volume are most useful.
32. E. Gilson, *The Christian Philosophy of St Thomas Aquinas* (Gollancz 1957), 11.
33. Ibid., 14.
34. Ibid., 12.
35. Burns Oates 1967.
36. Op. cit., 75.
37. *Theological Investigations* (Darton, V, 1966), 209ff.
38. *Le Fils Eternel* (Paris, Cerf, 1974), 510.
39. *Jesus God and Man* (SCM 1968), 325ff.
40. Op. cit., 117.
41. Ibid., 186f.
42. Collins 1963.
43. Darton (1965), 245ff.
44. 'The Worth of Arguments', in *Women Priests? Yes – Now!*, ed. Harold Wilson, (Denholm House Press, Nutfield, Surrey, 1975), 21.
45. Ibid., 23.
46. Ibid., 23f.
47. 'A Partner for Cinderella' in *What about the New Testament?*, ed. Morna Hooker and Colin Hickling (SCM 1975), 143ff.
48. Cambridge, CUP, 1967.
49. SCM 1974.
50. Op. cit., 7.
51. Ibid., 17.
52. Ibid., 104.
53. Ibid., 38.
54. Ibid., 52.
55. Ibid., 54.
56. Ibid., 115.
57. Ibid., 118.
58. Ibid., 122.
59. '"The Re-making of Christian Doctrine"', in *Theology*, LXXVII (1974), 619ff. Cf. also 'The Remaking of the Remaking' by the Roman Catholic philosopher Dr Hugo Meynell in *Theology*, LXXVIII (1975), 338ff., and Dr Wiles's reply to both these critiques, 'The Remaking Defended', ibid., 394ff.
60. Art. cit., 623.
61. *Mart. Pol.*, 9.
62. 'The Theology of the Humanity of Christ', in *Christ, Faith and History*, 53ff.
63. *Theological Investigations* (Darton, XI, 1974), 3ff. Cf. also Fr Bernard Lonergan's discussion, under the heading 'Pluralism and the Unity of Faith' in *Method in Theology*, 326ff.
64. Op. cit., 3.
65. Ibid., 5.
66. Ibid.
67. Ibid., 6f.
68. Cf. E. L. Mascall, *Via Media* (Longmans 1956), 157ff; *The Openness of Being* (Darton 1971), app. iii, 217ff.
69. Op. cit., 17.
70. Ibid., 18.

71. *On Heresy* (*Quaestiones Disputatae* 11) (Burns Oates 1964), 48.
72. Ibid., 62f.
73. Ibid., 63.
74. Ibid., 67.
75. Ibid., 39f.
76. (Dacre 1950), 1.
77. Reported by Peter Hebblethwaite in the *Month*, CCXXX (1970), 131ff., 163ff.
78. OUP 1969.
79. Cf., e.g., his discussions of Apollinarianism and of Athanasius in his *Theology in Reconciliation* (Chapman 1975), chs. 4, 5.
80. Op. cit., 286.
81. Cf. pp. 35ff. supra.
82. OUP 1969.
83. OUP 1971.
84. *God and Rationality*, 40f.
85. Ibid., 68.
86. *Theological Science*, xvii f.
87. Darton 1972.
88. Longmans 1957.
89. *Method in Theology*, 5f.
90. (Darton 1971), chs. 4, 5.
91. *Method in Theology*, 24f.
92. Ibid., 103.
93. Ibid.
94. Ibid., 104, 105.
95. Ibid., 107.
96. Ibid.
97. Ibid., 9.
98. *Philosophy of God, and Theology* (Darton 1973), 48.
99. *Method in Theology*, 330.
100. Ibid., 332f.
101. Ibid., 368.
102. Cf. pp. 155ff. infra.
103. *Philosophy of God* . . . , 10. Cf. *Method* . . . , 123.
104. *Philosophy of God* . . . , 57.
105. I have discussed some of these doubts in rather more detail in the first chapter of my *Nature and Supernature* (Darton 1976).
106. 'Lonergan's Method: its Nature and Uses', in *Scottish Journal of Theology*, XXVII (1974), 162ff.
107. 'Some Reflections on the Origins of the Doctrine of the Trinity', in *Working Papers in Doctrine* (SCM 1976), 1ff.
108. L. Hodgson, *The Doctrine of the Trinity* (Nesbit 1943), 25.
109. Op. cit., 11.
110. Ibid.
111. Ibid., 17.
112. Ibid., 106.
113. Ibid.
114. Cf. G. H. Tavard, *Holy Writ or Holy Church* (Burns Oates 1959).

115. Cf. my *Corpus Christi*, 2nd edn. (Longmans 1965), chs. 5, 6.
116. Cf. J. J. Hughes, *Stewards of the Lord* (Sheed & Ward 1970), 90ff.
117. H. de Lubac, *Surnaturel* (Paris, Aubier, 1946).
118. Cf. G. Sweeney, 'The Primacy: The Small Print of Vatican I', in *Clergy Review*, LIX (1974), 96ff.
119. *Working Papers . . .* , 106.
120. *The Dynamic Element in the Church* (Burns Oates 1964), 76.
121. *Working Papers . . .* , 106.
122. Op. cit., 153f. The foregoing paragraph is adapted from my *Theology and the Future* (Darton 1968), 35f.

CHAPTER 2

1. Cambridge, CUP, 1972.
2. *Soundings: Essays concerning Christian Understanding*, ed. A. R. Vidler. Cambridge, CUP, 1962.
3. Op. cit., 165.
4. Ibid.
5. Ibid.
6. Ibid., 165f.
7. J. Knox, *The Church and the Reality of Christ* (Collins 1963), 185.
8. *The Humanity and Divinity of Christ* (Cambridge, CUP, 1967), 113, his italics.
9. *The Secularisation of Christianity* (Darton 1965), 246.
10. *Kerygma and Myth: A Theological Debate*, ed. H. W. Bartsch (SPCK 1953), I, 220.
11. 'The Theology of the Humanity of Christ', in *Christ, Faith and History*, 56.
12. Op. cit., 5.
13. Ibid.
14. 'The Enterprise of Emancipating Christian Belief from History', in *Vindications: Essays on the Historical Basis of Christianity*, ed. Anthony Hanson, (SCM 1966), 64f.
15. H. P. Owen, *Revelation and Existence* (Cardiff, Univ. of Wales, 1957); Walter Schmithals, *An Introduction to the Theology of Rudolf Bultmann* (SCM 1968); André Malet, *The Thought of Rudolf Bultmann* (Shannon, Irish U.P., 1969).
16. *The Historian and the Believer: The Morality of Historical Knowledge and Christian Belief* (SCM 1967), 140f.
17. Id. ibid., 145 (my italics). Cf. also *Rudolf Bultmann in Catholic Thought*, ed. T. F. O'Meara and D. M. Weisser (New York, Herder, 1968), *passim*.
18. *The Secularisation of Christianity*, ch. 5.
19. Oxford, Clarendon, 1963.
20. Op. cit., 187ff., 189ff. In my book I have given more extensive quotations.
21. Ed. W. Hooper (Bles 1967).
22. Op. cit., 153f.
23. SPCK 1928.
24. Op. cit., 241.
25. It appears from an article in *Theology*, LXXI (1968), 267ff, by Dr T. F. Glasson, that Lock was in error in attributing these comparisons to J. Drummond. This does not affect the argument; the comparisons are familiar enough.
26. Op. cit., 154ff. Cf. the following testimony of the well-known translator of the New Testament, Dr J. B. Phillips:

I have read, in Greek and Latin, scores of myths but I did not find the slightest flavour of myth here [sc. in the Gospels]. There is no hysteria, no careful working for effect and no attempt at collusion. These are not embroidered tales: the material is cut to the bone. One sensed again and again that understatement which we have been taught to think is more 'British' than Oriental. There is an almost childlike candour and simplicity, and the total effect is tremendous. No man could ever have invented such a character as Jesus. No man could have set down such artless and vulnerable accounts as these unless some real Event lay behind them.

Thus the only small point which I will concede to the de-mythologisers is that several times I get the impression that the first three evangelists, naturally enough, did not quite realise what a world-shaking happening they were describing. But how could they? . . . Obviously they could not have anything approaching our historical perspective, but against this we must set the fact that they were living very much nearer to the actual point of time when Jesus was alive [*Ring of Truth: A Translator's Testimony* (Hodder 1967), 58].

Dr Phillips records a similar impression received by another distinguished translator of the Gospels, Dr E. V. Rieu (ibid., 55f.).

27. Op. cit., 157.
28. Ibid., 157f.
29. Ibid., 161.
30. Ibid., 162.
31. Ibid., 164.
32. SCM 1967.
33. Outlined in my *Secularisation . . .* , 225f.
34. *The Gospels and the Jesus of History* (Fontana 1970); French original *Les Evangiles et l'histoire de Jésus* (Paris, Seuil, 1963).
35. *The New Theology and Modern Theologians* (Sheed & Ward 1967), 133.
36. *The Logic of Gospel Criticism* (Macmillan 1968), 185.
37. 'The Meaning of Christmas', in *Theology*, LXXIII (1970), 159.
38. *Theology*, LXXIII (1970), 272f.
39. Ibid., 273.
40. Art. cit., 160 (my italics).
41. Op. cit., 223ff.
42. Cf. W. Pannenberg, *Jesus – God and Man* (SCM 1968), *passim*.
43. C. F. Evans, *The Beginning of the Gospel* (SPCK 1968), 12. The same strange judgement is expressed by J. A. Baker: 'To suppose that Jesus himself related this intensely personal experience to his disciples . . . is *utterly out of keeping with everything else that we know about him*' (*The Foolishness of God* (Darton 1970), 226, my italics). That this attitude is not typical of Canon Baker is clear from the passage quoted on p. 100 infra.
44. John 12.16.
45. *A Historical Introduction to the New Testament* (Collins 1963), 302.
46. Macmillan.
47. Review in *Theology*, LXXII (1969), 322.
48. Of which, we sometimes forget, written language is the most familiar, if not the most accurate example.

49. I.e., B. C. (now Bishop) Butler.
50. Art. cit., 323.
51. Op. cit., 142.
52. Black 1957. Cf. my *Secularisation of Christianity*, 218.
53. Op. cit., 136.
54. Review in *Religious Studies*, VI (1970), 196.
55. *Memory and Manuscript* (Lund, Gleerup, 1961), 10.
56. *Downside Review*, XC (1972), 76.
57. *Theological Reflections of a Christian Philosopher* (The Hague, Nijhoff, 1970), 15.
58. *What is Redaction Criticism?* (SPCK 1970), viii.
59. Ibid., 25.
60. Cf. D. J. Harrington, 'Ernst Käsemann on the Church in the New Testament: I', in *Heythrop Journal*, XII (1971), 249.
61. *What is Redaction Criticism?*, 71.
62. *The New Testament in Current Study* (SCM 1963), 40f. Cf.: 'The primary criterion of tradition history . . . is that sayings which conflict with the post-Easter faith of the church are *prima facie* authentic' (ibid., 50). What assumptions does such a sentence as this conceal about (1) the Gospels, (2) the resurrection, and (3) the primitive Church?
63. Ibid., 41.
64. Op. cit., 72f.
65. 1 Cor. 15.6.
66. Op. cit., 66f.
67. Review of Perrin, *Theology*, LXXIII (1970), 565.
68. Ibid., 564f.
69. Ibid., 565.
70. *Theology*, LXXV (1972), 570ff.
71. Op. cit., 70.
72. Art. cit., 573.
73. Ibid., 574f.
74. Ibid., 575.
75. Ibid.
76. Ibid., 576.
77. Ibid.
78. Ibid.
79. Ibid., 577.
80. Ibid.
81. Ibid., 578.
82. Ibid., 580.
83. Ibid.
84. Ibid., 580f.
85. Ibid., 581.
86. Ibid.
87. Cf. p. 67 supra.
88. Review of C. F. Evans, *Is "Holy Scripture" Christian?* (SCM 1971), in *Theology*, LXXIV (1971), 420.
89. SCM 1967.
90. SCM 1967.

91. *Christ, Faith and History*, 168.
92. Ibid., 172.
93. Ibid., 175.
94. Ibid., 176.
95. Ibid., 178.
96. SPCK 1960.
97. Ibid., 185f.
98. Ibid., 186.
99. Ibid., 187.
100. Ibid., 189.
101. *Kerygma and Myth*, I, 220.
102. Op. cit., 189.
103. Heb. 11.1.
104. 2 John 7.
105. 'The Golden Handshake?', *Christian*, Easter 1973, 29.
106. Hodder 1967. Cf. note 26 supra.
107. Op. cit., 7.
108. C. F. Evans, in *Industrial Christian Fellowship Quarterly* (Spring 1973), 15f. (italics mine).
109. We are apparently even threatened with a further stage, 'composition-criticism'. Cf. Perrin, op. cit., 65ff.
110. Chicago Univ. Press, 2nd edn 1970.
111. Athlone Press 1976.
112. Op. cit., 5f.
113. Ibid., 8.
114. Ibid., 13f.
115. Ibid., 14.
116. Cf. pp. 38ff. supra.
117. Op. cit., 18.
118. Ibid.
119. Ibid., 18f.
120. Ibid., 19.
121. Ibid.
122. Ibid., 20.
123. Ibid.
124. Ibid., 20.
125. Ibid.
126. Cf. pp. 3f. supra.
127. Op. cit., 21.
128. Ibid., 21f.
129. Ibid., 9, italics in original.
130. SCM 1976.
131. Op. cit., 8f.
132. Ibid., 93.
133. Ibid., 13.
134. Ibid., 352.
135. Ibid., 135.
136. Ibid., 186f. The '[sic]' in this passage is Robinson's addition, not mine.

137. Ibid., 340.
138. Ibid., 340f.
139. Ibid., 342.
140. Ibid., 344.
141. Ibid., 345.
142. Ibid., 347.
143. Ibid., 350.
144. Ibid., 352.
145. Ibid., 354.
146. Ibid.
147. Ibid., 355.
148. Ibid.
149. Ibid.
150. Cf. p. 70 supra.

CHAPTER 3
1. Cambridge, CUP, 1967.
2. Op. cit., 106, 113 (italics in original).
3. 'Does Christology rest on a mistake?', in *Christ, Faith and History*, ed. S. W. Sykes and J. P. Clayton (Cambridge, CUP, 1972), 3ff.
4. 'A Deliberate Mistake?', ibid., 13ff. Wiles has reprinted his paper, without mention of Baelz's criticisms, in his *Working Papers in Doctrine* (SCM 1976), 122ff.
5. *God in Patristic Thought* (SPCK and edn 1952), title of ch. 13.
6. Nisbet 1959.
7. SCM 1970.
8. *Prospect for Theology*, ed. F. G. Healey (Nisbet 1966), 139ff.
9. Op. cit., 148f.
10. Ibid., 149.
11. Ibid., 150.
12. Ibid., 155.
13. Ibid., 159.
14. *Christ, Faith and History*, 279ff.
15. Ibid., 297.
16. Op. cit., 165f.
17. Ibid., 166.
18. Sheldon 1974.
19. Op. cit., 141.
20. *God and the Universe of Faiths* (Macmillan 1973), ix.
21. *Truth and Dialogue*, 154f.
22. Ibid., 151.
23. *The Humanity and Divinity of Christ*, 95.
24. Ibid., 97.
25. Cambridge, CUP, 1955.
26. Op. cit., 98.
27. Ibid.
28. Ibid.
29. Ibid., 99.
30. *The Formation of Christian Dogma* (Black 1957), *passim*.

31. SCM 1973.

32. SCM 1963.

33. E. L. Mascall, *The Secularisation of Christianity* (Darton 1965), ch. 3.

34. *Heythrop Journal*, XIV (1973), 425ff.

35. *Downside Review*, XCI (1973), 232ff.

36. *Theology*, LXXVI (1973), 486f.

37. Ibid., 486.

38. Art. cit., 232.

39. Op. cit., 37, ix.

40. Ibid., 145 (italics in original).

41. Ibid., 144.

42. Ibid., 116f.

43. Ibid., 147f.

44. Cf. ibid., 151.

45. Ibid., 144 (italics in original).

46. Ibid., 145. Cf. Pannenberg, *Jesus, God and Man* (SCM 1968), 143. It is remarkable how Pannenberg, who is normally most scholarly and discriminating, becomes biased and inaccurate as soon as the Mother of Jesus is involved. Thus he takes Mariology and Mariolatry as synonymous (ibid., 141ff.).

47. Helen Oppenheimer, *Incarnation and Immanence* (Hodder 1973), 214.

48. *The Human Face . . .* , 179 (italics in original).

49. Op. cit., 67.

50. Op. cit., 50f.

51. River Forest, Illinois, Aquinas Library.

52. Op. cit., 154.

53. Ibid., 155.

54. Ibid., 155f.

55. Cf. p. 38ff. supra.

56. *The Human Face of God*, 88ff. et al. Cf. 'Need Jesus have been perfect?', in *Christ, Faith and History*, 39ff.

57. 'One Jesus, many Christs?', in *Christ, Faith and History*, 142.

58. *The Secularisation of Christianity*, 240ff.

59. Ibid., 244.

60. *Summa Theologiae*, Blackfriars edn, XLIX, 84f, Liam Walsh, OP.

61. *Theological Investigations* V (Darton 1966), 203; cf. 209f.

62. *Theological Investigations*, IV (1966), 113 (italics in original).

63. Ibid.

64. 'A Changing God', *Downside Review*, LXXXIV (1966), 247ff. On the general question of divine impassibility I cannot refrain from mentioning Fr Jean Galot's brilliant work *Dieu souffre-t-il?* (Lethielleux 1976).

65. III (Burns Oates 1969), 192ff. Reprinted in *Encyclopaedia of Theology*, ed. K. Rahner (Burns Oates 1975), 751ff.

66. *Theological Investigations*, V (1966), 176.

67. Ibid., 177f.

68. *Theological Investigations*, I (1961), 192 (German original 1954).

69. S. Theol. III, iii, 5.

70. *The Trinity* (Burns Oates 1970), 85f.

71. *Theological Investigations*, V (1966), 209f.

72. Op. cit., 325ff.

73. Cf. A. A. Galloway, *Wolfhart Pannenberg* (Allen & Unwin 1973), ch. 8.

74. *Le Fils éternel* (Paris, Cerf, 1974), 510.

75. 'Interview with Karl Rahner', *The Month*, CCXXXV (1974), 637ff.

76. 'Christology in Historical Perspective', *Heythrop Journal*, XV (1974), 66, 69.

77. SCM 1963.

78. Burns Oates 1967.

79. *The Christ* (Sheed & Ward 1972), 87.

80. Paris, Seuil, 1974.

81. Op. cit., 80f.

82. Ibid., 18.

83. R. V. Sellers, *The Council of Chalcedon* (SPCK 1953), is a welcome exception. Another, quite recently, is Jaroslav Pelikan, in the admirable second volume of his five-volume work *The Christian Tradition* (Chicago, University of Chicago Press, 1974). John Meyendorff's work, referred to later, first appeared in French.

84. Op. cit., 272.

85. Cf. also his remarks on doctrinal development, op. cit., 520f.

86. Rahner, *The Trinity*, 82ff.

87. Op. cit., 299.

88. Ibid., 483.

89. Ibid., 484.

90. Ibid., 485.

91. Ibid., 489.

92. Ibid., 490.

93. Ibid., 491, 492, 494.

94. Ibid., 501.

95. Ibid.

96. Cf. Tresmontant's discussion of this point on pp. 520f. of his book.

97. Ibid., 677.

98. Ibid., 678.

99. Paris, Cerf.

100. Op. cit., 185.

101. Ibid., 187f.

102. Ibid., 239.

103. Ibid., 254.

104. Methuen 1903 and later edns.

105. Black 1958.

106. Cambridge, CUP, 1967.

107. Hodder 1966.

108. This judgement is confirmed by the recent book of John Meyendorff, *Christ in Eastern Christian Thought* (Washington, D.C., Corpus Books, 1969), ch. 4.

109. Ibid., 406. It may be noted that, between the publication of the two editions of G. L. Prestige's *God in Patristic Thought* (Heinemann 1936); (SPCK 1952), the writings ascribed to Leontius of Byzantium became reascribed to two Leontii, of Byzantium and Jerusalem respectively. Bouyer remarks that for Leontius of Jerusalem the *hypostasis* of Jesus was the divine Word, while for Leontius of Byzantium it was a new *hypostasis* constituted by the essential union of the two natures (op. cit., 404). Cf. Meyendorff, op. cit. n. 108 supra, 53ff.

110. Cf. *St Vladimir's Theological Quarterly*, XI (1967), 150ff; XIV (1970), 222ff.
111. *Acta Apostolicae Sedis*, LXIII (1971), 814.
112. Op. cit., 400.
113. Ibid., 418.
114. Ibid., 419.
115. Ibid., 421.
116. Cf. pp. 152ff. infra.
117. Op. cit., 477.
118. Ibid., 476 (italics in original).
119. Ibid., 486.
120. Ibid., 502.
121. Cf. John Meyendorff, *A Study of Gregory Palamas* (Faith Press 1964).
122. Ibid., 510; cf. p. 137 supra.
123. Ibid., 510f.
124. Ibid., 511f.
125. Gembloux, Duculot; and Paris, Lethielleux.
126. Op. cit., 7.
127. Ibid.
128. *Early Christian Doctrines* (Black 1958), 274f.
129. *La Personne du Christ*, 30.
130. Ibid., 37f.
131. Ibid., 39.
132. Ibid., 39f.
133. Ibid., 40f.
134. Ibid., 42.
135. Ibid., 42f.
136. Ibid., 49.
137. Ibid., 51.
138. English readers may like to be reminded that, in French, *conscience* means 'consciousness' and *connaissance* means 'knowledge'. *Conscience de soi* is thus 'self-consciousness'.
139. Ibid., 53.
140. Ibid., 60.
141. Ibid., 64.
142. Ibid., 73.
143. Ibid., 75.
144. *A Second Collection* (Darton 1974), 259.
145. Ibid., 25.
146. *La Personne du Christ*, 75f.
147. Ibid., 77.
148. Ibid., 78.
149. Ibid., 82.
150. Ibid., 94f.
151. Ibid., 104.
152. Ibid., 119.
153. Gembloux, Duculot; and Paris, Lethielleux, 1971.
154. Op. cit., 55.
155. Ibid., 82f.

156. Ibid., 83.
157. Ibid., 82.
158. *Worship in the New Testament* (Butterworth 1961), 76.
159. Op. cit., 86f.
160. Ibid., 87.
161. Ibid., 90f.
162. I use the word 'ego' to translate the French *moi*, used as a noun substantive.
163. Paris, Beauchesne.
164. Cf. H. Denzinger/A. Schönmetzer, *Enchiridion Symbolorum* . . . (Friburg, Herder, 1965), n. 3905.
165. Op. cit., 112f., 113, 115f.
166. Ibid., 122f.
167. Ibid., 125.
168. Ibid., 126.
169. Ibid., 127.
170. Ibid., 151f. It should be noted that the word 'kenosis' as used by Galot has little in common with its use in the so-called 'kenotic Christologies'.
171. Ibid., 158.
172. Ibid., 168f.
173. Ibid., 175.
174. Ibid., 177. I am not entirely happy with the use of the word 'distance' here, which can be misleading in view of the concrete creative conservation of all creatures by God. 'Disproportion', on the other hand, is appropriate.
175. *The Humanity and Divinity of Christ*, 67. Cf. p. 66 supra.
176. Op. cit., 178f.
177. Ibid., 179f.
178. Ibid., 180.
179. Ibid., 182.
180. Cf. p. 150 supra.
181. Op. cit., 183f.
182. Ibid., 190.
183. Ibid.
184. Ibid., 191.
185. Gembloux, Duculot; and Paris, Lethielleux, 1971.
186. Op. cit., 31f.
187. Ibid., 32f.
188. *The Christ* (Sheed & Ward 1972), 87.
189. E. T. *A New Catechism* (Burns Oates 1967). Criticisms made by a Commission of Cardinals were met in a supplement published later (E.T., *The Supplement to A New Catechism* (Burns Oates 1969)).
190. Cf. p. 46 supra.
191. Op. cit., 39.
192. Ibid., 40.
193. Ibid., 42.
194. 'The Origins of Christian Realism', in *A Second Collection*, 252f.
195. (Darton 1971), ch. 2.
196. Op. cit., 44ff. It is true that the Chalcedonian definition does not say explicitly that the 'one prosopon and one hypostasis' into which the two natures 'run together'

(*syntrechouses*) is the divine Word, but this is clearly implied in its endorsement of the Nicene and Constantinopolitan creeds, with their assertion that the One Lord Jesus is *homoousios* with the Father.

197. Ibid., 46f.
198. Ibid., 48.
199. Ibid.
200. Ibid., 62.
201. Ibid., 62ff.
202. Ibid., 63.
203. (Chapman 1975), 160ff.
204. Cf. his *The Absolute and the Atonement* (Allen & Unwin 1971), 152ff. Trethowan has returned to this question quite recently in an article entitled 'Christology Again' (*Downside Review*, XCV, 1977), 1ff.
205. Op. cit., 74.
206. Ibid., 76.
207. Ibid., 83.
208. Ibid., 84f.
209. Op. cit., 172.
210. For this insight into the weakness of kenoticism I am indebted to my friend and former pupil Dr Thomas Weinandy, OFM Cap.
211. (Longmans 1956), 94ff.
212. *P.G.* lxxvii, 196, cit. R. V. Sellers, *The Council of Chalcedon* (SPCK 1953), 247.
213. *Fathers and Heretics* (SPCK 1940), 238, 331, 369f. Cf. my *Via Media*, 98f.
214. Galot himself has made this point very emphatically in his second volume, but chiefly with reference to the psychological aspects of Jesus' human nature. Cf. pp. 164ff. supra.
215. *S.c.G.*, IV, xxvii.
216. Op. cit., 90.
217. Ibid., 91f.
218. Paris, Lethielleux 1976.
219. Op. cit., 170.
220. Ibid., 172.
221. Ibid., 166. Dr Thomas Weinandy, in an unpublished thesis on the immutability of God in relation to Christology, has made a somewhat similar distinction to Galot's between two types of 'mixed relations'. One of his chief contentions is that, when God is the subject of becoming, *becoming* does not involve *change*.
222. Cf. my *He Who Is* (Darton 2nd edn 1966), ch. 8; *Existence and Analogy* (Longmans 1949), ch. 6.
223. *Vers une nouvelle christologie*, 95.
224. Ibid., 97f.
225. Ibid., 96.
226. From a slightly different angle Dr Weinandy has made a very similar criticism of this particular point in Galot's Christology, while expressing great admiration for it as a whole.
227. Cf. p. 149 supra.
228. Op. cit., 102.
229. Ibid., 104f.
230. Ibid., 107.

231. Ibid., 109. Cf. *La conscience de Jésus*, 176f.

232. *Honest to God* (SCM 1963), ch. 4. Robinson derived the description from Dietrich Bonhoeffer.

233. Op. cit., 110.

234. Greg. Naz., *Ep.* ci.

235. Op. cit., 111.

236. Ibid., 111f.

237. Ibid., 113.

238. Ibid., 115f.

239. Ibid., 116.

240. *Theological Investigations* (Darton, XII, 1974), 161ff.

241. Darton 1964.

242. Cf. p. 68 supra.

243. Cf. p. 137 supra.

244. L. Dewart, *The Future of Belief* (Burns Oates 1967); *The Foundations of Belief* (Burns Oates 1969); discussed in my *The Openness of Being*, (Darton 1971), ch. 8.

245. *Method in Theology* (Darton 1972), *passim*; *Philosophy of God and Theology* (Darton 1973), ch. 1.

246. *Nature and Supernature* (Darton 1976), ch. 1.

247. 'The Dehellenisation of Dogma', in *A Second Collection* (Darton 1974), 32.

248. Ibid., 28f.

249. Ibid., 25. I presume that 'precritical' refers to the Kantian critique, not to Biblical criticism.

250. Ibid., 26f.

251. P. 172 supra.

252. *Sic*, but I suspect that Lonergan wrote 'person and natures'.

253. *A Second Collection*, 259.

254. Ibid., 201f.

255. 'Christ as Subject: A Reply', in *Collection* (Darton 1967), 192f.

256. I should like at this point to mention the powerful defence of Cyril of Alexandria and Chalcedon in ch. 4 of Dr T. F. Torrance's quite recent book *Theology in Reconciliation* (Chapman 1975). It provides a welcome counter-blow to the common British assessment of both the Father and the Council.

257. D. Bonhoeffer, *Christology* (Collins, Fontana, 1971), 109.

258. Ibid., 105.

259. Ibid., 106.

260. (Collins, Fontana 1967), 11ff.

261. H. A. Williams, *Poverty, Chastity and Obedience: The True Virtues* (Beazley 1975), 104f.

262. Cf. pp. 132f. supra.

263. *S. Theol.* III, xxxiii.

264. *The Mother of God*, 158.

265. *On the Grace and Humanity of Jesus* (Burns Oates 1969), *passim*.

266. *Summa Theologiae* (Blackfriars edn) LII, xv.

267. Washington, D.C., Corpus Books.

268. Paris, Cerf.

269. *The Christian Tradition, A History of the Development of Doctrine, II: The Spirit of Eastern Christendom (600–1700)*. Chicago Univ. Press 1974.

270. Cf. pp. 146f. supra.
271. *Problèmes actuels de Christologie*, ed. H. Bouëssé and J.-J. Latour (Paris, Desclée 1965), 30 (my trans.), cit. Meyendorff, *Le Christ* . . . , 291. The passage appears also in K. Rahner, *Theological Investigations*, IV (Darton 1966), 117. In the English version of Meyendorff (p. 165) there is substituted, strangely, a less relevant and extremely involved passage from Rahner, *Theol. Inv.*, I (1961), 181f.
272. Meyendorff, op. cit., 165f.
273. K. Rahner, *The Trinity* (Burns Oates 1970), ch. 3. Cf. *S. Theol.* III, iii, 5.
274. *S. Theol.* III, iii, 8. Cf. *C. Gent.* IV, xlii.
275. Cf. p. 152 supra.
276. Cf. Ceslaus Velecky, OP, *Summa Theologiae* (Blackfriars edn, VI, 1965), 30n.
277. Cf. n. 221 supra. Perhaps this consideration might be extended analogically to the case of God 'becoming' the creator, which Rahner includes under his concept of God being mutable *in alio* though not *in se*; but this cannot be further discussed here. Cf. my *Openness of Being*, ch. 10.
278. Chapman 1975.
279. Op. cit., 270.
280. Edited by John Hick (SCM 1977). References are to that book, except where indicated.
281. p. ix.
282. pp. x–xi.
283. p. 165.
284. SCM 1974; cf. pp. 38ff. supra.
285. p. 4.
286. p. 178.
287. p. 37.
288. p. 140.
289. pp. 65ff.
290. p. 118.
291. pp. 54f.
292. p. 59.

CHAPTER 4

1. *The Kingdom of Christ* (SCM, reprint 1958) I, 286, 283.
2. *Theological Investigations*, II (Darton 1963), 135ff.
3. *Christ the Sacrament of Encounter with God* (Sheed & Ward 1963), 191ff.
4. 2nd edn (Longmans 1960), 349.
5. *De Ecclesia*, §11; *De Sacra Liturgia*, §§7, 47ff., 69 *et al.*
6. *Structures of the Church* (Burns Oates 1965), 166.
7. In K. Rahner and J. Ratzinger, *The Episcopate and the Primacy* (Nelson 1962), 75.
8. 2nd edn (Longmans 1965), ch. 1.
9. Cf. *The Apostolic Tradition of Hippolytus of Rome*, ed. G. Dix (2nd edn H. Chadwick, SPCK 1968), 4f.
10. Cf. pp. 152ff. supra.
11. *Categoriae*, ch. 4.
12. *De Trinitate*, V, v.
13. Cf. e.g. St Thomas Aquinas, *S. Theol.* I, xxix, 4; St Bonaventure, *Breviloquium*, I, iv, 2.

14. Cf. his book *Coresponsibility in the Church* (Burns Oates 1968).
15. Cf. Michael Dummett, 'How corrupt is the Church?', *New Blackfriars*, XLVI (1965), 623.
16. This model seems to have strongly influenced the constitution of the Anglican Church in the U.S.A., to give one instance.
17. Heb. 3.1.
18. *De Unitate Ecclesiae*, 4.
19. J. Meyendorff *et al.*, *The Primacy of Peter* (Faith Press 1963), 28.
20. *Unitas*, XVII (1965), 87f.
21. *The Church and the Ministry*, rev. edn (SPCK 1936), 154.
22. It can be argued that the authority personally inherent in the Pope as Peter's successor is very small indeed and that most of the authority which he quite legitimately exercises comes to him by implicit delegation from the Church. Cf. Garrett Sweeney, 'The Primacy: The Small Print of Vatican I', *Clergy Review*, LIX (1974), 96ff. This is not the precise point referred to in the text, but cognate with it.
23. 2nd edn (Longmans 1956), 64ff. 227ff.
24. *De Ecclesia*, §21.
25. Ibid., §22.
26. Ibid., §23.
27. Ibid., §28.
28. *De Ecclesia*, §10.
29. Ibid., §§32, 37.
30. *Ep. ad presb. et diac.*, 5, 4, cit. H. Küng, *Structures of the Church*, 68.
31. Prayer at the laying-on of hands at the ordination of a priest in the Ordinal of the Church of England.
32. Which term is used will depend on the precise definition that is adopted of the word 'sacrament'.
33. *The Dynamic Element in the Church* (Burns Oates 1964), 76.
34. I do not, of course, overlook that, as a matter of pure logic, if *A* has the relation -R-to *B* (*A*-R-*B*), then having-the-relation-R-to-*B* (-R-*B*) may be considered as a property or 'logical quality' of *A*. This is, however, very different from a real quality. And what is important for our present purposes is that, even if real relations imply logical qualities, real qualities do not in general imply relations. Relation is thus a wider category than quality.
35. The recently adopted Roman Catholic practice to extend the term 'ordination' to include the consecration of a bishop is, I think, regrettable, if only because the phrase 'episcopal ordination' now has to do duty both for consecration *to* the episcopate and for ordination performed *by* a bishop.
36. *The Church Today and Tomorrow* (SPCK 1965), 11ff. It is said that signs of a welcome reversal of this attitude were visible at the fifth assembly of the World Council of Churches at Nairobi in November 1975.
37. *A.A.S.*, XXXVIII (1946), 14ff.
38. *Structures of the Church*, 215.
39. Cf. p. 214 supra.
40. 'Be you ready, with all faithful diligence, to banish and drive away all erroneous and strange doctrine contrary to God's word; and both privately and openly to call upon and encourage others to the same?' (*Consecration of Bishops*, attached to *The Book of Common Prayer* (1661)). Cf. the revised Roman rite: 'Are you prepared to

safeguard the body of doctrine handed down by the apostles and keep pure and undefiled what has been taught everywhere and at all times?'

41. Church Union 1965.
42. Op. cit., 3f.
43. *Theology*, LXVIII (1965), 89ff.
44. Ibid., 202ff.
45. Ibid., 245ff.
46. Op. cit., 7.
47. Ibid., 9.
48. Op. cit. (SPCK 1973), §16.
49. Cf., e.g., G. Dix, *The Shape of the Liturgy* (Dacre 1944), chs. 4–9; L. Bouyer, *Eucharist* (Notre Dame, Indiana, Univ. Press 1968), chs. 3–6; E. L. Mascall, *Corpus Christi* 2nd edn (Longmans 1965), ch. 6.
50. Dr E. W. Trueman Dicken has remarked to me that in a Jewish *berakah* God is, strictly speaking, not so much *thanked* as *praised*; this is, I think, important, though it does not affect the argument of the text. The two notions, though closely connected, are distinct; there is a difference between thanking God for giving us something and praising him for his glory which is manifested in the gift. But how often the *Gloria Patri* is said in church as an act of *thanksgiving*!
51. Cf. G. Dix, *The Shape* . . . , 128ff.
52. Cf. G. Egner (pseudonym), *New Blackfriars*, LIII (1972), 354ff., 399ff., LIV (1973), 171ff. Discussion by E. L. Mascall and H. McCabe, LIII (1972), 539ff., 546ff.
53. Cf. my essay 'Recent Thought on the Theology of the Eucharist' in *A Critique of Eucharistic Agreement* (SPCK 1975), 63ff.
54. *Mysterium Fidei, Acta Apostolicae Sedis*, LVII (1965).

INDEX OF NAMES

The more important entries are in bold type